Honor and the Political Economy of Marriage

CW00952996

Thank [you] the book support! with love Jo [signature]

The Politics of Marriage and Gender: Global Issues in Local Contexts

Series Editor: Péter Berta

The Politics of Marriage and Gender: Global Issues in Local Context series from Rutgers University Press fills a gap in research by examining the politics of marriage and related practices, ideologies, and interpretations, and addresses the key question of how the politics of marriage has affected social, cultural, and political processes, relations, and boundaries. The series looks at the complex relationships between the politics of marriage and gender, ethnic, national, religious, racial, and class identities, and analyzes how these relationships contribute to the development and management of social and political differences, inequalities, and conflicts.

Joanne Payton, *Honor and the Political Economy of Marriage: Violence against Women in the Kurdistan Region of Iraq*

Honor and the Political Economy of Marriage

Violence against Women in the Kurdistan Region of Iraq

JOANNE PAYTON

Foreword by Deeyah Khan

RUTGERS UNIVERSITY PRESS

NEW BRUNSWICK, CAMDEN, AND NEWARK, NEW JERSEY, AND LONDON

Library of Congress Cataloging-in-Publication Data

Names: Payton, Joanne, 1972– author.
Title: Honor and the political economy of marriage : violence against
women in Kurdistan region of Iraq / Joanne Payton.
Description: New Brunswick : Rutgers University Press, [2019] |
Series: The Politics of marriage and gender: global issues in local contexts |
Includes bibliographical references and index.
Identifiers: LCCN 2019006592 | ISBN 9781978801714 (paperback) | ISBN 9781978801721
(hardcover) | ISBN 9781978801752 (pdf) | ISBN 9781978801738 (epub)
Subjects: LCSH: Marriage—Economic aspects—Iraq—Kurdist?an. |
Kinship—Iraq—Kurdist?an. | Honor killings—Iraq—Kurdist?an. |
Family violence—Iraq—Kurdist?an. | Women, Kurdish—Violence against—
Iraq—Kurdist?an. | Women, Kurdish—Iraq—Kurdist?an—Social conditions.
Classification: LCC HQ666.3.Z9 K877 2019 | DDC 306.8109567/2—dc23
LC record available at https://catalog.loc.gov/vwebv/search?searchCode=
LCCN&searchArg=2019006592&searchType=1&permalink=y

A British Cataloging-in-Publication record for this book is
available from the British Library.

♾ The paper used in this publication meets the requirements of the American
National Standard for Information Sciences—Permanence of Paper for
Printed Library Materials, ANSI Z39.48-1992.

www.rutgersuniversitypress.org

Manufactured in the United States of America

CONTENTS

SERIES FOREWORD

The politics of marriage (and divorce) is an often-used strategic tool in various social, cultural, economic, and political identity projects as well as in symbolic conflicts between ethnic, national, or religious communities. Despite having multiple strategic applicabilities, pervasiveness in everyday life, and huge significance in performing and managing identities, the politics of marriage is surprisingly underrepresented in both the international book publishing market and the social sciences.

The Politics of Marriage and Gender: Global Issues in Local Contexts is a series from Rutgers University Press examining the politics of marriage as a phenomenon embedded into and intensely interacting with much broader social, cultural, economic, and political processes and practices such as globalization; transnationalization; international migration; human trafficking; vertical social mobility; the creation of symbolic boundaries between ethnic populations, nations, religious denominations, or classes; family formation; or struggles for women's and children's rights. The series primarily aims to analyze practices, ideologies, and interpretations related to the politics of marriage, and to outline the dynamics and diversity of relatedness—interplay and interdependence, for instance—between the politics of marriage and the broader processes and practices mentioned above. In other words, most books in the series devote special attention to how the politics of marriage and these processes and practices mutually shape and explain each other.

The series concentrates on, among other things, the complex relationships between the politics of marriage and gender, ethnic, national, religious, racial, and class identities globally, and examines how these relationships contribute to the development and management of social, cultural, and political differences, inequalities, and conflicts.

The series seeks to publish single-authored books and edited volumes that develop a gap-filling and thought-provoking critical perspective, that are well-balanced between a high degree of theoretical sophistication and empirical richness, and that cross or rethink disciplinary, methodological, or theoretical boundaries. The thematic scope of the series is intentionally left broad to encourage creative submissions that fit within the perspectives outlined above.

Among the potential topics closely connected with the problem sensitivity of the series are "honor"-based violence; arranged (forced, child, etc.) marriage; transnational marriage markets, migration, and brokerage; intersections of marriage and religion/class/race; the politics of agency and power within marriage; reconfiguration of family: same-sex marriage/union; the politics of love, intimacy, and desire; marriage and multicultural families; the politics (religious, legal, etc.) of divorce; the causes, forms, and consequences of polygamy in contemporary societies; sport marriage; refusing marriage; and so forth.

Joanne Payton's study is a perfect fit within the scope of the series. In *Honor and the Political Economy of Marriage,* Payton examines the changing relationship between the meanings of "honor" and the patterns of violence against women in Iraqi Kurdistan. Explaining honor-based violence from an analytical perspective based primarily on the anthropology of kinship and marriage rather than that of religion, Payton demonstrates, in an innovative and convincing way, why the concept of "patriarchal violence" (frequently associated with Islam itself) should be treated critically, and how the topic of honor-based violence is often used strategically in Islamophobic discourses in the West. Payton's book also sheds light on the consequences of the widespread use of culturalization in conceptualizing and explaining honor-based violence as well as in justifying and legitimizing it—highlighting the intense need for and usefulness of a less culturalizing and less religion-focused analytical approach.

Péter Berta
University College London
School of Slavonic and East European Studies

FOREWORD

DEEYAH KHAN

Back in 2012, after turning my back on a career as a musician, I decided to shoot a documentary film. I had no training. I had no experience. All I had was a camera and a story to tell.

My own, personal story had started with being forced out of my musical career, due to pressure from Islamist extremists who believed that women shouldn't sing, least of all sing Western pop songs on television. The sudden change in a life-course that I, and my father, had laid out for me since my early childhood was devastating. I felt unmoored, lost. During this period I painfully developed a new sense of purpose through reading all the letters and emails I had received from my fans: through hearing their stories. Many of them came from young people from backgrounds like my own South Asian, Muslim background. They described the pressure from their family and community to conform to restrictive standards of respectability, whether through accepting forced marriage, wearing *hijab* against their wishes, or giving up on careers or studies that they aspired toward. Many of these stories came from women and girls, feeling the limitations of family "honor."

In the end, the story I chose to tell wasn't my own, nor was it any of the stories I had heard from my young fans. Instead I found a story that encapsulated them all: the story of Banaz Mahmod. Banaz was a young Kurdish woman who had grown up in London and who was pushed into marriage at a young age in order to suit the demands of her family. The marriage failed, due to the horrendous abuses of Banaz's husband. Banaz moved on to a new relationship, falling head-over-heels in love with a young man who meant everything to her, but who did not have her family's approval. She refused to give him up, despite extreme family pressure. Her choice was intolerable to her family. They held a council meeting where they determined that her life should be ended in order to appease family honor. And so, for "honor," Banaz was raped, strangled, and buried in a suitcase by a group of men who had been hired by her uncle. This was an act that ended Banaz's life and ruined several others: those of her broken family, her bereft lover who ultimately committed suicide, her father and uncle imprisoned for life, and a devastated community.

To me, Banaz became an emblem of all the suffocation that comes from living in a repressive community that polices its young, and particularly its women: of all the frustration of being unable to live and to love freely, of having every public act judged by a court of community opinion that wields the power of life and death. It was also an emblem of the failure of the wider British society to react effectively to violence within minority communities. Banaz's murder was not just the responsibility of her community: it was also a failure of the state to comprehend and intervene in violence against women, which was considered to be part of "their culture." Banaz repeatedly sought help to escape her family, from police and other services; she was repeatedly rejected.

It was in investigating Banaz's story that I met Joanne Payton, the author of this book, through the Iranian and Kurdish Women's Rights Organisation (IKWRO). IKWRO is a UK-based charity that supports Middle Eastern, North African, and Afghan women who are victims of male violence, particularly focusing on honor-based violence and forced marriage. Her insights were central to the understanding of honor presented in the documentary *Banaz: A Love Story*, which went on to win an International Emmy; a testament to the powerful nature of Banaz's story. Jo had thoroughly immersed herself in the topic; at the time she was working on her PhD. She had attended every day of the trial of Banaz's killers, and she had broad experience with cases of honor-based violence drawn from her work with IKWRO. She was investigating how risk profiles differed between cases of honor-based violence and other forms of violence against women.

She explained honor violence to me in a way that seemed clearer than anything I had heard previously, in a way that circumvented tired, and often prejudiced, conversations that always seemed to revolve around culture or religion. I already knew that crimes like the murder of Banaz occurred in various religious groups, in various different cultures. As a South Asian woman I knew that Hindu and Sikh women are not spared from the demands of representing family honor; as a Muslim and a feminist I knew that the minority faiths of the Middle East and North Africa were just as implicated in these crimes as the Muslim majority were. I knew that honor crimes stretched across boundaries of nation and culture and faith.

Instead of using these categories, Jo talked to me about the way marriage organizes relationships in families and communities, and about how women are expected to conform to the standards of marriageability in order to maintain these relationships between families, relationships that glue communities together. Honor was not about the individual, but the collective: the family, tribe, or clan. It was entwined into the knit of our identities as individuals, and as members of families and communities. Jo described honor as underpinning family systems organized by marriage; where links between families, formed by marriages, were a central method of social organization. For women, honor was conformity to the community's standards for marriage. From powerful political dynasties to family-run businesses and farms, family honor—and the repression of women in its name—is strongest where connections forged through marriage organize relationships of power and status. Women who fail to live up to their community's standards of marriageability jeopardize the linkages that marriage forms between and within families. In this book, Jo outlines the phenomenon of honor, then moves from a detailed examination of how forms of traditional marriage are based in complex interactions of honor and status to an analysis of original survey data, showing honor reinventing itself within a modernizing society.

Honor-based violence is not a dying tradition. Women and girls are at risk of becoming victims every day. Despite being widely discussed, often in crude and prejudiced ways, the dynamics that underlie honor crimes are still poorly understood. There are still failings in protection due to misunderstandings of what an honor crime looks like, and how it needs to be dealt with. Crimes against women are still excused on the basis of honor in many communities and states. It has been over ten years since Banaz was murdered, and the lessons have still not been fully learned. We need to understand the structures that underlie these crimes if we are to work toward a society in which women and girls like Banaz, and so many thousands of other victims of honor crimes and oppression, can live and love freely.

NOTE ON ORTHOGRAPHY

The Sorani dialect of Kurdish spoken in Iraq is normally rendered in Arabic-style script but is here rendered in Roman type. As script-based languages have a phonetic rather than conventional orthography, transliterations into English take varying forms—for example, *jin be jine*, a form of marriage discussed in this book, can also be found spelled as *zhymbyzhn* (in Dzięgel 1982, p. 251). The orthography within this work strives to be internally consistent but should not be considered definitive.

Honor and the Political Economy
of Marriage

1

Honor

Honour killing is a tragedy in which fathers and brothers kill their most
beloved, their daughters and sisters, . . . Here, affection and brutality
coexist in conflict and unity.

—Shahrzad Mojab (2002, 61)

Femicide

Coomaraswamy (2005, xi), writing as the United Nations (UN) special rapporteur
on violence against women, describes honor-based violence (HBV) as follows:

> Honour is generally seen as residing in the bodies of women. Frameworks
> of "honor" and its corollary, shame, operate to control, direct and regu-
> late women's sexuality and freedom of movement by male members of a
> family. Women who fall in love, engage in non-marital relationships, seek
> a divorce or choose their own husbands are seen to transgress the bound-
> aries of "appropriate" (that is, socially sanctioned) behavior. Regulation
> of such behavior may in some cases involve horrific direct violence—
> including "honour killing," perhaps the most brutal control of female
> sexuality—as well as indirect subtle control exercised through threats of
> force or the withdrawal of family benefits and security.

Writing in his personal journal, Captain Rupert Hay, a contemporary of T. E.
Lawrence, recorded several murders of women in Kurdish areas while he was
serving under the British Mandate for Iraq (1914–1932):

> With regard to a woman's honour the law is most strict. A woman of any
> social standing who misconducts herself, or who is suspected on reason-
> able grounds of misconducting herself, must surely die; and the husband,
> brother, or whoever is responsible for her, who fails to put her out of the
> way, is considered to have lost his honour; and a Kurd's nāmūs or honour
> is one of his most precious possessions. Many women must have been
> murdered in this way while I was at Arbil, but very few cases came to my
> ears, and then usually a long time after the event. I know of one fair lady
> who was tied up in a sack and thrown into the river. Even when I did get

wind of such affairs it was out of the question to take any action, seeing that the entire tribal opinion supported the murderer, and it was impossible to obtain evidence. With regard to the man who is the cause of a woman's downfall the law is not so severe. In some cases he, too, is murdered, but more usually he escapes by paying the price of the woman's blood. (Hay 1920/2008, 56)

Historically, there are references to similar violence in Kurdish regions as early as the 1850s. "They even kill their own wives, daughters, mothers and sisters. And to [punish] such bad deeds women also kill; for instance, mothers also strangle their daughters in the night or poison and kill them and mothers-in-law do it to their daughters-in-law and sisters to sisters. No chief [agha[1]] and no village elder [rî şpî[2]] will ask why you have killed [this woman]"[3] (Mela Mehmud Bayezidi (1858–1859) cited in Mojab 2004a, 112).

The Kurds originate from the Taurus and Zagros mountains. Conquest and domination have been an overriding theme of Kurdish history, from the seventh century Arab conquest to attacks by the Seljuks, Safavids, and Mongols. After the fall of the Ottoman Empire, the Treaty of Sèvres (1920) promised Kurdish independence, a promise that was shattered in the subsequent Treaty of Lausanne (1922) wherein Kurdish regions were divided between the new nation-states of Iraq, Iran, Turkey, and Syria. In each of these states, Kurds faced discrimination as minorities. This took its crudest form in the Kurdistan Region of Iraq (KRI): an attempted genocide, enacted by Saddam Hussein's Ba'ath party to further the violent suppression of emergent nationalist activism. Since the establishment of the no-fly zones in 1991, the Kurdish region was controlled by the two most significant political parties—the *Partîya Demokrata Kurdistan* (Kurdistan Democratic Party [KDP]) and the *Yeketî Nîştîmanî Kurdistan* (Patriotic Union of Kurdistan [PUK]). Their relationship has been both peaceful and bloody by turns: a violent civil war known as the *birakuži* (fratricide) in the 1990s was followed by a power-sharing pact in 1998. A third party, Gorran (meaning "movement for change") was founded in 2009 and has become the largest opposition party, channeling popular frustration at the endemic corruption within Kurdish politics. Following the Gulf War of 2003, U.S.-led troops seized Iraq, meeting little resistance. Saddam Hussein's Ba'ath Party was dissolved, and the army and security forces disbanded, leading to massive unemployment. This dissolution had followed upon years of punishing economic sanctions that had particularly impacted upon Kurdish areas. The Kurdish regions took advantage of the chaos to claim territories such as Kirkuk, which had previously been aggressively "Arabized" under Hussein. Thus the Kurdistan region achieved a degree of federal independence within a federalized Iraq, a comparatively peaceful state with a native oil economy. The region comprises the three governorates of Arbil, Duhok, and Sulaymaniyah, and parts of the disputed areas in northern Iraq. It has a growing population of over four million and covers over 40,000 square kilometers (over 15,400 square miles). Meredith Tax describes the KRI as closely linked to Turkey, and despite appearing progressive within the Middle Eastern context, she identifies that it is internally dogged by corruption and tribalism (2016, 38).

The postwar chaos elsewhere in Iraq catalyzed Islamist extremism, leading to the formation of the so-called Islamic State (Da'esh). Kurdistan was again embroiled in conflict when ISIS seized territory, including Mosul, and carried out a massacre of the Yezidi religious minority in Sinjar. The KRI is currently housing over 1,500,000 refugees and internally displaced people (IDPs) in the region. Over 6,000 Yezidi women were captured and trafficked into slavery by Da'esh members. They were treated with unspeakable brutality on the basis of their minority religion (Otten 2017); the explicitly sexual nature of the abuse they underwent was justified by references to Islamic history and law. Simultaneously, mainstream Western media portrayed "bad-ass" female Kurdish resistance fighters in "sensational and neo-Orientalist" presentations (Begikhani et al. 2018, 18) while the left focused on the revolutionary potential of the "left-wing, non-state democratic formation developing in the liberated cantons of Syria" springing from Kurdish resistance to Islamization—a resistance in which women were strongly represented (Tax 2016, 34). The contrast of victimized Yazidi women and militarized female fighters created a bifurcated imaginary of Kurdish women. Whether as heroes or as victims, Kurdish women stand as signifiers of their ideological and ethnic groups, defending their territories, or suffering when their borders are breached. This bifurcation—women presented either as victims of war or taking up male roles due to the absence of men is a recurring representation of Kurdish women (Begikhani et al. 2018).

Militarized Kurdish women are often depicted as liberated from the patriarchy through the paraphernalia of fatigues and rifles; however, as Tax notes (2016, 142) they were also expected to follow a strict rule of celibacy. This ensures that women's honor is safeguarded and reduces family resistance to women joining the militias, reducing clashes between the conservative values of rural Kurdistan and the revolutionary ideology of the militants.

For Yazidi women, sexually victimized by Da'esh, the feeling of being dishonored adds an additional level of trauma and increases feelings of exclusion (Kizilhan and Noll-Hussong, 2017), despite the Yazidi leadership's proclamation that sexually victimized women continue to be full members of the Yazidi community regardless (Kreyenbroek and Omarkhali, 2016).

The concepts of honor and violence against women remain linked for Kurdish women.[4] Within the KRI, honor-based violence such as that described by Hay and Bayezidi across history remains endemic and well attested (Alinia 2013; Begikhani 1998; Begikhani 2005; Begikhani et al. 2010; Danish Immigration

Service 2010; Mojab 2002, b; Taysi 2009; UNAMI 2009), where there is a general consensus that these crimes have been increasing since the 1990s (Mojab 2004b). A representative of the women's rights organization WADI (a German nongovernmental organization with a focus on self-help programs that works in the KRI) stated in 2016 that the "official number of honor killing cases is 50–60 per year," adding that this was likely a significant underestimate as many crimes remained unrecognized and/or unrecorded by police or medical practitioners (Home Office 2017, 19). Many more women and girls live their lives circumscribed by the threat of violence in the name of honor.

This book addresses the issue of honor-based violence against women within the KRI from a materialist perspective, taking a mixed-methods approach that combines a theorized account of local structures of marriage and the family discerned from various ethnographic and cross-disciplinary sources, along with a quantitative analysis of original survey data.

This chapter introduces and defines the topic, then outlines the theoretical basis of the analysis.

In the Bodies of Women

Definitional attributes that distinguish HBV from other forms of violence against women are *agnation* (the perpetrators are members of the same patriline as the victim), *collectivity* (the active or tacit collaboration of members of a patriline and the wider community in perpetration), and the deployment of a discourse of *honor* to justify violence (Payton 2014). Crimes are often predicated upon a supposed shaming act committed by the victim, which casts the patriline as a whole into disrepute within the community. Shame is considered to be expiated through violence. According to a Pew study (2013, 190), only 22% of Iraqi citizens believed that honor crimes were never justified against women; only 33% believed they were never justified against men. Iraq showed the highest support for HBV across the whole survey. In Iraq, Pew found that 44% of respondents believed that the honor killings of women were "often acceptable," whereas 5% or fewer participants in Azerbaijan, Bosnia-Herzegovina, Indonesia, Kazakhstan, Kosovo, and Uzbekistan agreed with this proposition. From the entire Middle East and North Africa (MENA) region, only in two countries—Morocco and Tunisia—did a majority agree that women should never be killed on the basis of honor (2013, 90).

While the UN's Country Team for Iraq identifies that family violence against women and girls in the KRI is extremely high, some indicators suggest that it is higher still in South/Central Iraq (Iraq Women Integrated Social and Health Survey 2011). This implies that the prominence of the issue in the Kurdish region is not necessarily an indication of greater incidence, but of greater attention. This is due at least in part to the efforts of the dynamic indigenous feminist movement, which has identified this issue as central to the oppression of women in the region.

Since the 1990s, through Das's study (1995) of the murders of Bangladeshi women who had been raped during the war with Pakistan, Jordanian women's activism against discriminatory laws in the late 1990s (Husseini 2009), the publicity surrounding the murder of Samia Sarwar in 1999, Asma Jahangir's (1999) decision to include honor crimes within her brief as special rapporteur on extrajudicial killings to the UN, various reports by the United Nations, reports by Amnesty International and Human Rights Watch, and the murder of campaigner Fadime Şahindal in Sweden in 2002, honor crimes have emerged as an issue of contemporary feminist concern in the twenty-first century.

Not Exceeding Three Years

Crimes described as being motivated by honor have had a mitigating legal status in many Arab countries (Zuhur 2005), including Iraq. While legally, the Kurdistan Regional Government (KRG) removed the statute of Iraqi law that allowed for reduced sentencing for crimes of honor in 2003 (Begikhani 2005), this was not extended into practice for some time (Mohammed 2009), and a culture of impunity has been reported (Greiff 2010). Al-Ali and Pratt (2008, 144) noted that Kurdish women's rights activists remain frustrated by the failure of this federal legal code to be brought into practice, where there is a preference for using family and tribal mediation, particularly when political and economic interests are at stake. As, technically, Iraqi law is sovereign over the semiautonomous Kurdish region, the KRG's reforms have no sound legal basis for enforcement (al-Ali and Pratt 2011). Furthermore, research by the Kurdish Human Rights Project in 2008 (Yıldız et al. 2008, 39–40) found that the older Iraqi law unquestionably remained in use, despite the 2003 reform, implying that where this applies, the maximum jail sentence in a case of honor killing may just be a few years—which may be commutable if the defendant has no criminal history.[5]

Kurdish media also report convicted killers being freed in general amnesties, along with failures to pursue and prosecute offenders (Bahaddin 2010a; Iraqi Civil Solidarity Initiative 2013). It may also be difficult to prosecute honor crimes even if there is willingness to do so: in Urfa (in the Kurdish region of Turkey), over a third of cases of honor killings resulted in acquittal due to an inability to penetrate family solidarities in order to gain sufficient evidence for a conviction (Belge 2011, 103). Due to family complicity, murders can be readily presented as suicides or accidental deaths. This is accompanied by a tendency for victim-blaming rhetoric at high levels. Tavqa Rasheed, speaking as the KRG's director of the Ministry for Human Rights in a 2007 interview (Mason 2010, 14), gave three reasons for the high levels of honor killings and female suicide in the KRI—mobile phone technology, modern television programs, and women's "lack of social awareness."

Nevertheless, Kurdish women in Iraq certainly have greater faith in the police's ability to address domestic violence than women in the South/Central region (Iraq Women Integrated Social and Health Survey 2012, 49–50). The Kurdish polity have made commitments to reducing violence against women that often exceed those of their neighbors (Natali 2010, 91–92), and certainly some perpetrators (often those of low social status) are sentenced commensurately with the offence of murder, regardless of their claims of an honorable motivation— much to their chagrin (Alinia 2013,53–83). This shows an increasing, if uneven, determination to tackle issues of violence against women within the KRI.

'His Rights Have Been Violated'

Taysi's (2009) and Sır's (2005) examinations of attitudes toward honor among predominantly Kurdish populations in Iraq and Turkey, respectively, show varying levels of support for HBV. Sır investigated the attitudes of 423 respondents in predominantly Kurdish villages in Turkey (2005). In a vignette describing an unhappily married woman's adultery, over 37% of Sır's respondents agreed that the woman should be killed, and many other suggestions also proposed violent responses. "His rights have been violated," stated a police officer in the KRI, in justification of HBV(Taysi 2009, 35). Only 16% did not believe she should be punished (232). Taysi's interview-based research in the Sulaymaniyah region of the KRI found that 30% of respondents felt violence against dishonorable behavior was justified on at least some occasions (34) and that 90% understood the word "honor" to relate to the control of women's sexuality.

Honor killings have attracted the most attention of all forms of honor-based violence, yet these are just the most extreme forms of a continuum of violence that can be enacted, including forced marriage, beatings, imprisonment, forced hymenoplasty and abortion, and public humiliation (Hassanpour 2001). Victims are normally, but not exclusively, women (Danish Immigration Service 2010). Significantly, women are almost always killed by their own families, whereas men tend to be killed by the families of women they are accused of dishonoring. The killing of a man by non-kin may tend to institute family feuding, leading to reprisal killings from his own relatives, whereas the contained nature of the family means that a woman can be killed without any such ramifications. There may be little sympathy for a girl or woman who has endangered the lives of her male agnates through providing a provocation that could result in interfamilial feuding.

It could be considered then, that a decision to kill a woman rather than a man operates like the dueling culture of early modern Europe: it provides a way of maintaining honor without leading to prolonged and damaging blood feuds (King 2008b, 328). On the other hand, tribal leaders attempting to reach an agreement have required families to kill their own sons in preference to instituting a feud (Begikhani 2005; Danish Immigration Service 2010, 7), particularly where a family lacks the necessary political influence to withstand communal pressure.

In more practical terms, a family may kill a co-resident female first due to proximity, giving her "accomplice" advance warning to flee, initiate negotiations, raise supporters to mount a counterattack, or raise blood money to ransom his life. Males suspected of homosexuality, however, may be targeted for honor killings and violence by their own families and vigilantes (Copestake 2006). That the discussion of HBV against males is limited within this work is not meant to dismiss or ignore male victims: it is a recognition that most of these crimes tend to pivot on the presumed dishonoring of a girl or woman as a primary motivation for violence.

Honor crimes are by no means perpetrated solely by men, as women may both participate in violence and play an active role in policing women's behavior (Awwad 2001; Glazer and Abu Ras 1994; Nelson 2003; Sen 2005), although according to Sır's research, male relatives are predominantly considered to bear executive responsibility for safeguarding family honor; a husband appears to hold less responsibility for the behavior of his wife than her agnatic kinsmen.[6]

A study of 180 perpetrators of honor killings in Turkey observed that the perpetrators may be lauded by their families and community (Gezer 2008). The favorable treatment of honor killers by the forces of social control ranges from reduced sentences and sympathetic treatment in custody, to lackluster investigation of honor crimes.

This legitimation of honor crimes at several levels seems to position the honor killer as an *altruist*—one who is prepared to make their children burnt offerings upon the altar of normative morality. The decision to kill is not necessarily taken lightly. Onal's sensitive interviews with sentenced honor killers in Turkey (2008) found deep wells of regret expressed by some perpetrators, along with evidence of extreme social pressure upon them. She describes the case of Ilyas, a Thracian man living in the squatter settlements of Turkey, who endured months of public abuse from his Kurdish neighbors, including broken windows and children spitting at him and pelting him with stones in the street, until he "reclaimed his 'honor'"—through killing his sister (134–139).

Such communal pressure has also been indicated in British murder cases, where the behavior of the fathers of Banaz Mahmod[7] and Heshu Yones (Bedell 2004) suggested the existence of harassment within the Kurdish communities in which they lived engineered to compel them to "correct" the "deviant" behaviors of their daughters. In the Yones case, as Mojab (2004b, 16) notes, the harassment of Abdallah Yones, Heshu's father, was reconfigured into shows of support from his harassers after he killed her. Abu-Rabia (2011, 38) observes that the perpetration of an honor killing may be best considered "an organized social act by the family, not a matter of personal preference."

A dishonored family thus could be described as being in a condition of stigma, as described by Goffman (1963), having a spoiled, discredited identity, which separates them from the community as a whole until they restore their status. "Neighbors won't say hello, they won't trade with members of the group and they won't marry their other daughters until the deed has been done," according to Turkish author Mehmet Faraç (interviewed by Pope 2012, 201). In the Kurdistan region of Iraq, an imprisoned perpetrator of a crime he described as an honor killing identified community exclusion as a major motivation behind his murder: "[S]he took my honor . . . Now I prefer to die here than live outside and be ridiculed. Now I can hold my head up. I did not dare to go to a funeral or to go out in public because people were ridiculing me" (in Alinia 2013, 66).

Withdrawal of such reciprocal relations is a salient sanction. Those who do not redeem their honor may therefore become excluded from the social and economic life of the community. The sense of erasing humiliation that characterizes Katz's (1988, 18–19) description of the "righteous slaughter" is meshed with the collective basis of Tilly's (2003, 81–102) "violent rituals," which "reflect and reinforce existing systems of inequality" (p. 87).

Honor killings are performative acts, carried out for the benefit of a wider collective: an act of purification through sacrifice, which leads to reintegration into the community. According to Ghazzal, Syrian honor killers, for instance, mark the performative nature of honor killings through taking pains to describe the act in specific terms in front of the judge—making an analogy to the sacrifice of an Eid lamb—to situate the crime as honor-based without explicitly using the language of honor, and thus make a tacit claim for juridical sympathy (Ghazzal 2011).[8]

Hence, honor-based violence can be described as a metanorm (Horne 2004), in being a normative response to norm violation. In the case of honor crimes, then, it appears that the socialization of the family to kill an "errant" member is *nondeviant*; it is the *victim* who is seen as deviant, within a politics that is situated in the custodianship of women's bodies, centered upon their sexual and reproductive capacities. Violence as a means of re-establishing social control is a phenomenon well described by Black (1983), who identifies that many violent aggressors perceive and justify their actions in this light. This motivation is particularly significant in discussing collective violence, where collectives enforce and enact community norms.

The Panoptic Community

In the neighborhood,[9] the social boundary shrinks to houses, courtyards, or blocks at most for women. . . . People passing through the neighborhood and downtown can be neighbors, co-villagers or neighboring

villagers of her husband's family. Any one of them can observe her wherever she goes and warn or humiliate her husband and his family for her
"misconduct" which risks their honor. She can go out without fearing disciplinary gossip and rebuke only when she has a legitimate companion
and her husband's permission. Yet the husband's permission is not
always easy to obtain because most husbands are sensitive to gossip
which can endanger their honor.

–Him and Hoşgör 2011, 338

Gossip, as a means of generating, enforcing, and policing social norms, has been
identified as a foundational aspect of human distinctiveness (Dunbar 1998). It
is an important source of social control in all communities. According to
Brenneman (2007), "Kurds constantly worry about falling victim to gossip,
whether or not the subject of gossip is true" (117). As honor is defined in practice
by the collective, reputation is a point of vulnerability for individuals, families,
and other collectives. To allege sexual misconduct on the part of a man's wife,
daughter, or niece is a method of indirectly attacking a rival. Discussion of a person's female relatives may be circumlocutory in order to avoid implications that
might be considered to disparage the reputation of a family's womenfolk.

This vulnerability to gossip is connected to a regime of constant surveillance by family and community. The complex interdependencies of communal
life equip it to function as a panopticon. Sır's examination found that over 12%
of respondents stated that the primary duty of the community was "to keep a
watch on women living on one's street and in one's neighborhood."[10] Wolf (2010),
in a short documentary on honor crimes in southeastern Turkey, shows elderly
men apparently occupied playing card games outside their homes; closer view-
ing shows that these men are simultaneously monitoring women's excursions
outside the domestic realm with close attention. Fischer-Tahir (2009) observes
that women of the urban middle classes in Sulaymaniyah in the KRI are aware
of being under surveillance by their families and neighbors, meaning that they
feel they cannot, for instance, use a taxi service to leave or return to their own
neighborhood, lest they be criticized for sharing a car with an unrelated man.
Thus the community assumes the role of defining female deviance, and of policing it through a regime of constant surveillance (Glazer and Abu Ras 1994;
Awwad 2001).

VanEck (2003) characterizes honor as being normative and contingent
rather than prescriptive, describing honor as existing in a state of constant definition and redefinition within collectives that claim a stake in the control of
women. In these collectives, the most significant stakeholders in a woman's
honor are her agnates and potential affines. A woman's violation of honor may
pass without any repercussions, so long as knowledge of the "shaming act" can

be confined within the household or lineage. According to VanEck, families frequently *do* make efforts to contain any knowledge of a transgression from the community at large, in order to avoid any escalation to violence (43).[11]

The "Eleventh Commandment" may hold primacy over all the other directives of honor culture. An advocate working with survivors of HBV in the KRI told Alinia (2013, 97) that "[f]amilies do not like their problems to become public knowledge and, therefore, a precondition for the possibility of reconciliation [i.e. of a 'dishonorable' girl or woman with her family] is that the community does not know about the case." Reconciliation is considered less viable, then, where knowledge of shame cannot be contained. Honor operates above the level of the household, despite being central to its identity and status. Honor and shame are defined at the level of the community—even to the extent of allowing vigilante honor crimes, as the following apologue from Kurdish myth exemplifies: "A shepherd, while grazing his sheep one day, came across a boy and girl doing something *sherim* (shameful). . . . [T]he shepherd immediately took his long dagger and killed them both with one stab. The villagers considered him as a man concerned with the honor of the village, and even the parents of the boy and girl were more ashamed of their children than angry at the shepherd" (Brenneman 2007, 59–60).

Universality and Particularity

As Ertürk (2009) identifies, a challenge for those working in the field of violence against women is in accounting both for its *universality* and for its *particularity*: in this instance, of negotiating the universality of the murder of women by male family members with the particularity of honor as a justification (cf. Mojab 2004b). Violence against women, and against children, is a universal phenomenon. It has been argued that it is invidious to provide a distinct terminology to any particular form of violence within this category. This is particularly the case where honor violence is overwhelmingly associated with Muslims, and this occurs within a toxic contemporary discourse drenched with xenophobia (Spruyt and Elchardus 2012). Thus the existence of HBV is used to denigrate populations in which it occurs, whether as evidence for the presumed superiority of Western social norms or, for instance, within Turkish discourses that deploy HBV as a reason to denigrate the Kurdish minority population (Pervizat 2006; Koğacioğlu 2011).

Justifying violence in the name of honor abuts a similarly long-standing practice of justifying violence against women in the name of passion. These categories are not only similar in terms of framing women's offenses against male control as provocation, but intersecting, since a defense of passion may provide the basis for mitigatory sentencing for honor crimes in Arab states with a heritage of Napoleonic law (Zuhur 2005), wherein killers motivated by honor may represent their crimes as being committed as unpremeditated *crimes passionnel*.[12]

The legal defense of provocation as it relates to murder in Europe and the Anglophone world is also frequently used in gendered terms to position male violence as a disciplinary response to "deviant" female behavior—"nagging and shagging"—that challenges hegemonic constructions of masculinity and male control of women (Veleanu 2012). These justifications continue be used to exonerate violence against and the murder of female intimate partners, even where provocation is removed as a legitimate defense (Fitz-Gibbon 2009). Whether crimes are related to honor or to passion, the reversal of focus from the perpetrator's violence to the provocation of the victim is similar.

As honor-based violence is a current, severe, and ongoing phenomenon, a great deal of current literature prioritizes exposure and description rather than explanation, with the pressing aim of critiquing and improving policy and practice (Gill 2009; Bano 2010; Begikhani et al. 2010), and of critiquing the discriminatory nature of legal codes that may permit honor killers reduced sentences (Faqir 2001; Abu Hassan and Welchman 2005; Hoyek et al. 2005; Warraich 2005; Warrick 2005). Another trend in current scholarship regarding HBV within diasporic communities is to examine the effects of the growing awareness of honor crimes in Europe and the Anglophone world, often through inaccurate and stigmatizing media reportage, and the effects this has on attitudes toward minority communities within a climate of anti-Muslimism (Bredström 2003; Pratt Ewing 2008; Korteweg and Yurdakul 2009; Gill and Brah 2014).

A detailed and systematic literature review (Kulczycki and Windle 2011) finds that most studies of honor killings in the MENA (Middle East and North Africa) region are flawed by poor generalizability, few have original data, and those that do suffer from inevitable methodological difficulties, such as poorly verified data. This is largely due to the secrecy surrounding the topic, poor record keeping, and the uncertainties of informants' accounts (1445). Kulczycki and Windle also raise the areas that have been scrutinized: characteristics of perpetrators and victims, the legal status of honor crimes, and public opinion and sociostructural determinants.

In the main, explanations of the phenomenon itself are either absent or tacit and unexplored, where the writers' most urgent aims are to provide better services and to identify mechanisms for crime reduction.

Many attempts to provide *explanations* of the honor complex itself, and its relationship to violence, terminate in one or another of a pair of grand abstractions: attributions to culture (Hirsi Ali 2007; Chesler 2010), or patriarchy (Sev'er and Yurdakul 2001; Gill 2006; Reddy 2008). Both approaches inevitably confront Ertürk's dilemma of universality and particularity. A cultural definition of such crimes cannot be generalized beyond the specific ethno-religio-cultural identities of their perpetrators and victims and is particularistic; a patriarchal explanation suggests that they can be generalized more broadly to all male-dominant societies (which is to say, all societies) and are therefore universal.

The collective punishment of women's sexual "deviance" in order to police collective norms, is, or has been, a widespread feature of many human societies, such as public head-shaving of French women considered to have collaborated with the Nazis at the end of WWII. However, HBV with a collective and familial basis, where violence is seen as a duty that is specifically owed to the wider community by the family of the presumed offender is less apparent.

Arguments based in culture frequently overassociate HBV with Islam. Chesler's (2010) study, for instance, which is widely cited by right-wing sources for its linkage of honor crimes with Islam, suffers from serious methodological and conceptual flaws (Deccan 2016). Such conceptualizations run the risk of ignoring the prevalence of such crimes outside the Muslim world, such as in contemporary India, which is no less prominent for honor killings than neighboring Pakistan. There are also large Muslim communities within Southeast Asia where honor crimes have not currently been identified, and there is less evidence of the agnatic supervision of women's sexual behavior (Dube 1997, 49–70). Honor crimes are also committed by religious minorities within Muslim communities, including the Yezidi of the Kurdistan region.

Most significantly, cultural arguments tend to lack historicity: situating HBV as a Muslim or Middle Eastern/South Asian phenomenon ignores the broader patterns of distribution across Eurasia, both current and historical. Recent history suggests that similar honor-based acts of violence have occurred in European regions currently or within living memory (Peristiany 1966; Tillion 1966/2007), including Italy, Greece (Campbell 1964; Safilios-Rothschild 1969), Spain (Pérez-Molina 2001; Shiba 2003), and the Balkans (Denich 1974), including the former Yugoslavia (Puhar 1997). In Albania, honor crimes are predominantly associated with Catholic communities (Mangalakova 2003; Mustafa and Young 2008). Other Central Asian countries, particularly those with Turkic and Indo-Iranian linguistic heritages, also show strong continuities with honor culture: in Chechnya, the dictator President Kadyrov expressed support for the principle of killing for honor (Markosian 2012), and literature from Uzbekistan (Minnesota Advocates for Human Rights 2000), Azerbaijan (International Rescue Committee 2004), and Tajikistan (Haarr 2010), indicate instances of agnatic HBV. Historically, China could also arguably be related to honor culture, since there was an expectation that dishonored females commit suicide (Hsieh and Spence 1981; Elvin 1984; Tien 1997; Theiss 2004).

Outside Eurasia, agnatic honor appears as a Spanish colonial importation to Latin America (Gutiérrez 1985; Lipsett-Rivera and Johnson 1998), although this has vastly declined in significance over time (Caulfield 2000; González-López 2004; Mayblin 2011). This wide dispersal prohibits a purely ethnocultural explanation through the sheer overwhelming fact of the enormous religious, ethnic, and linguistic diversity of peoples practicing HBV. Subsuming various faith groups—Christians, Sikhs, Muslims, Yezidi, Hindus, and so forth—and various language groups—Indo-Iranian, Turkic, Romance, and Arabic—into the same cultural category is to extend the definition of "culture" as a semiotic collective well beyond the breaking point.

The problem posed by Ertürk—that of accounting for the universality of violence against women while acknowledging particularities within its forms and structures—remains unanswered by cultural explanations.

Death by Culture

The rise of identity politics since the 1980s (Moghissi 1999), has led to a trend to identify delimited social phenomena closely with the identities of the groups in which they occur. This tends to build upon a conceptualization of cultures as discrete and static units, failing to capture either the heterogeneity within any group, their changes over time, or the porosity between collectives; a prominent failing in an age of globalization. The concept of culture, as Moghadam argues, "is ambiguous in the assumption that 'cultures' are shared rather than multiple, often associated with 'traditional' societies which are considered inert; masking more than it reveals and making claims on people (especially women) rather than for them" (1994, 7).

Perpetrators of crimes that have been categorized as cultural may claim that the crime was "part of their culture" and thereby appeal for reduced punishments (Torry 2001; Song 2007; Ballard 2011). This may be depicted as a form of tolerance; an indulgence of difference, neglecting the corollary that the cultural defense is in itself a cultural intervention, whereby minority cultures are imagined as "stable, timeless, ancient, lacking in internal conflict, premodern" (Pollit 1999, 29)—and their values placed beyond scrutiny. When Abdallah Yones pled guilty to killing his daughter Heshu, the tariff for his sentence was reduced on the basis of his Kurdish culture and the provocations of his "dishonorable" daughter. This maneuver positioned Abdallah Yones as authentically Kurdish; correspondingly Heshu Yones was rendered peripheral to her own ethnicity. Diasporic masculinities are thereby reified as the representation of their communities. The vibrancy of Kurdish feminism and the hybridized worldviews of younger generations are among the positions located as external to an elemental, male-defined Kurdishness (Alinia 2013). Respect for the presumed values of othered cultures easily devolves into a disrespect for the rights of women subordinated within those groupings (Mojab 2004b, 27). The efforts of Kurdish feminists and other dissidents against the patriarchal order are thus disparaged through being framed as being exterior to their own culture— despite the fact that Kurdish women have been independently organizing for their rights for almost a century (Mojab, 2004b, 31). As Koğacıoğlu (2004) points out, framing the problem of HBV as one of culture or tradition is a mechanism that exculpates the state and other institutions from potential complicity in its continuance.

As mentioned earlier, within diasporic contexts, Islam is often identified as the *differencia specifica* between the (supposedly) HBV-free West and the (supposedly) honor-obsessed Muslim world, despite recent histories of violence against women identifiable in relation to honor in many European and other territories and a lack of consistent approval for HBV across Muslim-majority nations.

Narayan (1997, 41–81), in a generative discussion of dowry murders in India, describes similar readings as insinuating the idea of "death by culture," for their susceptibility to position othered peoples as arational subjects of culture— "traditional creature[s] of habit and violence," in Abu-Lughod's terms (1997, 110). Narayan constructs an explanation of bride-burning that focuses on the economic exploitation of the powerlessness and isolation of young brides within normative marriage expectations of exogamous patrilocality and the dowry tradition, none of which can be considered exclusively Indian practices, but as patriarchal structures that impact upon women.

Narayan locates violence within domestic economies and kinship structure, exposing motivations that are instrumental, rooted in political and economic exploitation and the affordances by which loose garments and domestic gas stoves allow a perpetrator to disguise a deliberate murder as a kitchen "accident." The easy availability of firearms and gendered inequalities inflect violence against women in the United States, she notes, and yet discussions of American expressions of violence against women are qualitatively different in addressing these aspects of American culture. Describing HBV as cultural tends avoid the question of how it serves the material interests and goals of the perpetrators.

This leads to the second great abstraction: *patriarchy*. While patriarchy is intrinsic to honor there is a need to examine the dynamics of universality and particularity on this axis—to consider what configuration of patriarchy can be considered in connection with honor crimes.

I am here indebted to many feminist writers who have written on the subject of honor and violence against women. For the formulation of my own position, the following writers have proven particularly generative: Khan (2006, ix–xxiii) provides a compelling rationale for advancing understandings of HBV using a materialist methodology. While she identifies the continued undervaluation of women's labor in regions with a reputation for HBV, this cannot be considered explanatory since HBV occurs far more widely. As Sev'er and Yurdakul (2001, 978–979) identify, increased entrance into the workforce has not relieved women of any of the burdens of representing family honor. It may indeed have made honor all the more precarious, since women now face the sexual ordeals and opportunities of the workplace.

Sev'er and Yurdakul have argued that an approach based in radical feminist ideas around male power may be usefully applied to honor. King (2008b), drawing from a detailed and sympathetic ethnographic study of the KRI, very usefully describes women's honor as operating as a barrier around "patrilinear sovereignty," suggesting that norms and metanorms around female sexual behavior may have a linkage to particular orientations of kinship, adding an extra dimension to the radical position raised by Sev'er and Yurdakul. Alinia's (2013) intersectional position, combining the gendered aspects of these crimes with a wider political focus on broader power structures and group identities, provides a valuable synthesis of the problem at hand within Kurdish regions. Lastly, Begikhani's (1998, 2005, 2010, 2016) continuing research in this area has provided a wealth of theory and data to explore.

While these generative and illuminating attempts do not provide an acultural explanation as to why HBV is predominantly identified within Eurasia but not universally across Eurasia, these will form the starting assumptions of this work, which uses a combination of these insights: taking a materialist approach, focusing on the hierarchical relations of sex, gender and kinship at the level of the household, and in interactions between households, and then later attempting to position this within the external power structures. This line of analysis is inevitably partial; its basis in structures of kinship tends to place the focus on the domestic and other small-scale expressions of gendered inequality, which inevitably lead to lessened emphasis on the wider political setting and a variety of intersecting issues. The emphasis on kinship is not intended to supervene alternate explanations but to work toward generalizing potential commonalities around HBV.

Etymologically, patriarchy is itself a kinship relationship, situating dominance in the figure of the father/*pater*, after the Roman *paterfamilias* who possesses *patria potestas*: the power of life or death over all his dependents, including his wife, children, and slaves. Second-wave feminism extended the term "patriarchy" to apply far more widely to systems of male dominance, regardless of the nature of male power within those systems. According to Joseph (2000b, 16), Middle Eastern patriarchy cannot be disarticulated from kinship structures.

Charrad (2000, 71) asserts that if a *differencia specifica* between women's roles is to be sought, it should be investigated through an analysis based in *kinship* rather than religion or culture. Joseph further argues that Western feminism has long concentrated on the conjugal bond as a producer of gendered inequalities, to the neglect of the extended family (2000a, 117). The extended, multigenerational family form further complicates sex-based inequalities with other intersections of privilege based in seniority and other factors. For Sacks (1982, 111) this lacuna around the study of the extended family results from the pervasive influence of the capitalist ideation of the nuclearized domestic realm, within a scholarship that neglects the nature of extended kinship relations in favor of analyzing the functionality (or otherwise) of the conjugal breadwinner/homemaker dyad, which is falsely presumed to be normative and universal.

The *cultural materialist strategy* developed by Harris (2001) seemed particularly relevant to the exploration of aspects of human life that *inhabit* culture at a deep level, but where it is not tenable to posit a cultural point of origin. Harris's materialism places humanity's endeavors to achieve basic biological survival as foundational to the development of social structures and models of thought. This book attempts to develop an explanation of honor and honor killings that addresses the central problematic identified by Ertürk (2009)—that of universality and particularity—to consider the reasons why a society would choose to adopt such a costly and restrictive system; to explain why the labor demands of constant surveillance of female kinfolk and the human costs of murder and violence required in the name of family honor have been reproduced over centuries of history and within several discrete territories.

The key insight of the cultural materialist strategy is derived from Marx's (1859, 43) proposition that "[t]he mode of production in material life determines the general character of the social, political and spiritual processes of life." The cultural materialist position argues that aspects of human behavior which have been related to culture have etiologies based in the strategies developed by individuals and collectives in order to achieve subsistence within their environment. Infrastructure (such as ecology, technology, and the mode of production) may supervene societal structures (such as kinship and power hierarchies), given that similar infrastructures appear to generate societal structures within similar constraints, in order to address similar challenges.

In order to do this, I take the dynamics of universality/particularity not just as foundational to defining the problem but also to developing the epistemology in contextualizing the primary research within a comparative, transdisciplinary, and historicized framework. This aims to ensure that my description of how honor operates within the KRI is neither exceptionalized and overreliant upon ideas of cultural difference nor incongruous with understandings applicable across wider territories and periods. Thus I will tend to evade important and unique political contexts and intersecting issues within the Kurdish milieu, which are better explored through the knowledge and analysis of the pioneering work of feminists who work directly in the region. While the direct survey research was conducted using respondents within the Kurdistan Region of Iraq, I have often used data and observation from other Kurdish regions, with a full acknowledgment that while these may be illuminating, they do not necessarily reflect practices in Iraq, as Kurdish cultures, including marital practices, often vary widely from region to region.

The next chapter will commence this exegesis by addressing the ecological aspects of the KRI with reference to the environment, the development of the mode of subsistence, and its kinship patterns.

2

The Problems of Earthly Existence

[S]exuality is lived primarily as a relation of antagonism between groups, within groups, and at the level of the subject. Relations between communities are basically antagonistic involving power struggles over land, pasture and labor power. These antagonisms mean that other communities are cast as immoral and weak and that relations between them (including marriage alliances) are fraught with danger and deep-seated hostility.

–Sirman (2004, 41)

Cross-culturally, many societies are sexually liberal, or may be repressive but without licensing violent mechanisms of control (Schlegel 1995). As Meillassoux (1981) suggests, there is less impetus for the control of filiation within hunter-gatherer societies due to a lack of proprietary interest in the land. Even where cultures *are* violently punitive of women's sexual autonomy, this is not always expressed through the requirement to agnatic violence characteristic of honor.

This chapter considers ecology and its relationship to kinship patterns and social practices.

Men and Mountains

Kandiyoti (1988) and Caldwell (1982) describe a "patriarchal belt" across Eurasia, a geographical region that comprises many of the areas associated with honor culture. Other regions with cultural connections to this type of violence—Southern Europe, the Caucasus, and Central Asia—are contiguous with this region, extending in a northerly direction, possibly terminating in southern France (Goody 1983, 17). Such a distribution does not accord with any historical empire, state, or other collective.

As Tax (2016, 23) stresses, "The 'patriarchal belt' is a geographical designation, not a religious one, for the region also contains Christians, Jews, Zoroastrians, Parsees, Sikhs, Hindus and many smaller religious groups, while Muslims themselves have a great range of doctrinal variations and cultural practices." Kandiyoti (1988) associates her "belt" with the concept of "classical patriarchy," in tune with Rubin's (1975) narrow, anthropological definition. For Rubin, this is closely related to the lifestyles of pastoral nomads, structured by patrilinearity—a formation that has deep continuities with the foundational structures and ideologies of the earliest Eurasian civilizations: effectively the Urkultur (common culture) of agrarian life within the continent.

The patriarchal belt formation encompasses part of the Alpides, a particularly mountainous region, formed by the collision of the Indian, Eurasian, Arabian, and African tectonic plates in the late Mesozoic period. It encompasses the Kurdish homeland of the Zagros and Taurus mountain ranges. Diamond (2007) suggests that the premodern transmission of technology, animals, and knowledge occurs more readily along lines of latitude because similar climatic and ecological conditions are more suitable for the spread of people, livestock, and agriculture, who spread culture across the world on horizontal axes. Thus the belt formation may suggest an ecosociological explanation, where similar modes of adaptation to the environment were shared across lines of latitude: a historical odyssey in which patterns of power and authority within the family were transmitted along with plow technology, livestock, seed crops, and the myriad other innovations and adaptations of the Neolithic revolution. The transmission of agrarian technologies, as evidenced by genetic, linguistic, and archaeological evidence (Cavalli-Sforza 1996; Renfrew 1996; Zilhão 1993), suggests a primary wave reaching Southern Europe around 4800–4400 BCE, which then spread to the rest of the continent in 4000–3500 BCE. The Neolithic revolution occurred in the Near and Middle East. This formed the epicenter for the diffusion of wheat, barley, sheep, goats, and probably cattle and pigs to Europe, Egypt, and South Asia (Cavalli-Sforza 1996, 51). Cereal production commenced in the Middle Euphrates River Valley, reaching the foothills of the Zagros Mountains in the seventh millennium. Around the same period, goat and sheep herding was developed in the lower regions of the Zagros–Taurus Mountains (Harris 1996, 554), in craggy terrain that only the most nimble beasts could navigate.

Pastoralism has the longest established history in a region extending from the Mediterranean to the Indus and can also be found in the Caucasus and northern Eurasia (International Encyclopedia of the Social Sciences 1968)—coinciding with the patriarchal belt described by Kandiyoti and Caldwell. Archaeology, genetics, linguistics, and anthropology tend to suggest large prehistoric, macrocultural blocs, often transmitted along mountain ranges, with broad but nonidentical patterns of intersection between linguistic groupings, genetic similarities, and, importantly, kinship patterns (Burton et al. 1996; Jones 2003a). Within these groupings, the largest geographical area—the "Middle Old

World"—occupies the majority of central Eurasia, but excludes the peripheries of the continent. For Jones (2003a), northern Eurasia and the circumpolar regions originated in distinct political economies based on foraging and horticulture with bilateral kinship structures, developed during a period of postglacial settlement; the Middle Old World, on the other hand, was historically dominated by pastoralism coexisting with intensive agriculture, patrilinearity as the basis of political power, and rule by pastoral nomadic tribes (Jones 2003a, 507, table 2). With very few exceptions,[1] pastoralist societies are patrilinear, clannish, and male dominated, with sharp gendered divisions of labor (Food and Agriculture Organization 2001, 36).

Kinship structures are frequently paradigmatic of social and political organization. Jones's delineation of the cross-cultural dimensions of kinship assumes two vectors: matricentricity/patricentricity and unilinearity/bilaterality. These have profound ramifications for the organization of the family: "Traits characterizing patricentric societies include bride-price, sororal polygyny, patrilocal residence, exogamous or clan communities and transhumance or nomadism, while matricentric traits include matrilocal residence, segmented communities, nonextended families and the absence of marriage exchange. . . . Traits characterizing unilineal societies include clan communities, unilineal kin groups, nonsororal polygyny and cousin marriage while bilateral (nonunilineal) traits include bilateral descent groups, ego-centered kindreds, bi-local or neolocal residence" (Jones 2003a, 503).

The Middle Old World is particularly likely to have patricentric structurations of the family, which are overwhelmingly patrilinear in form. This has impacts on the organization of the family and domestic life. For instance, Dyson and Moore (1983) attribute the greater autonomy, more balanced sex ratios, and lower fertility found in the southern states of India to their matrilineal kinship structures, in comparison to the firmly patrilineal north (which encompasses the regions that are most notorious for honor-based violence [HBV]).

Dube (1997) poses a key question based on her comparative studies within South Asia, where she finds the agnatic control of women's sexuality is pronounced in Southwest Asia, but comparatively weak in Southeast Asia: "Can it be a coincidence that women in bilateral and matrilineal Muslim communities do not observe seclusion[2] whereas for women in patrilineal and patrivirilocal kinship organization it has become a mark of identity?" (1997, 67).

King (2008b) answers Dube's question by arguing for a very direct relationship between HBV and patrilinearity in the Kurdistan Region of Iraq (KRI), asserting that patrilinear structures place a heightened symbolic value upon chastity and virginity, seen as a barrier against agnatic outsiders, placing female reproductive capacities under the control of agnatic groups. HBV then, might be associated with unilineal, patricentric (patrilocal/patrifocal) structures of kinship occurring within the central landmass of Eurasia. Its lesser prominence in other regions may potentially be attributed to the predominance of bilateral and matrilineal kinship structures.

Attempts to schematize kinship relations have stumbled between Lévi-Strauss's so-called universal structures to looser, social constructivist readings in which relationships are defined in emic terms. Jallinoja (2011) makes a graceful synthesis of these contestations, locating a common ground between Lévi-Strauss, Bourdieu, Schneider, and Carsten, in distinguishing between "official" kin (using Carsten's term) and "practical" kin (using Bourdieu's). This recognizes the discrepancies between the ways in which persons represent their relationships. To provide a simple example, an English-speaking uncle and nephew of similar age may present themselves as cousins, feeling that a fictive attribution is a better expression of their actual, lived relationship.

Official and practical relations necessarily coexist. Official kinship has a great deal of cross-cultural variance: in English, a father's brother and a mother's brother are both designated by the term "uncle" due to the bilateral system of kinship, in which individuals claim their heritage from both their paternal and their maternal lineages on an equal basis. In Kurdish, a paternal/agnatic uncle is called *mam*,[3] whereas a maternal/affinal uncle is called *khal*. The existence of distinct terminologies indicates a social need to make kinship distinctions. These reflect social structures: the attribution of a specific kinship term denotes "how that person stands in relation to the means of production and therefore to other people in the same and different relationships to these means," (Sacks 1982, 110).

The agnatic/affinal differentiation is particularly significant in the arrangement of economic and labor relationships in traditional agricultural corporatism with diffusive inheritance patterns. Within these arrangements, a man is expected to co-labor and share the resources of the patrimony with his brothers. Kinship-based collectives have historically performed most of the social, economic, and political functions of rural communities across the world, including providing mutual support and conducting the various tasks of pastoral life, from digging wells to regulating access to grazing lands.

Where the patriline is the primary lineage in terms of patrimonial inheritance and labor, matrilateral relations are peripheral in contrast. They may, for this reason, be less afflicted by conflict related to disputes over inheritance and have a more affective tone. However, official relationships may be somewhat flexible where, for instance, a tribe[4] with an exclusive identification that wishes to arrange a valuable marriage alliance outside the collective may find a method of mythologizing the relations between them to smooth over the ambiguities between the systems of official kinship and the realpolitik of practical kinship.

The Kinship License

The family is an association if you like, a corporation or a clan. It is something more than the sum of the individuals, with their human and fallible
complexities, that compose it; to ensure its safety, it has a supreme and
primordial right to the devotion of all its members.

–Barret Wendell, *La france d'aujourd'hui*, 1910 (in Nye 1993, 98)

This section argues that a fixation on women's honor is a system of accountability, and further, that it has been generated due to the ways in which marriage is
used to organize social relations within patricentric agrarian-pastoralist societies. Cooperation beyond kinship groupings is a particular point of interest in
marriage, which has the power to either extend or consolidate a kinship group.

Wolf's (1982) ecosociological history describes how kinship can be viewed
as a distinct *mode of production*, particularly predominant among those people
on the peripheries of "tributary" empires. This would aptly describe the mountainous and inaccessible terrain of the Kurdish regions, which has historically
been the location where successive Middle Eastern civilizations and empires
have petered out (Houston 2008, 10). The historic defensibility of the Zagros
Mountains and the terrain's suitability for guerrilla warfare have often led to
the Kurds being considered uncontrollable by various imperial powers, from the
Achaemenid Empire of 550–330 BCE (Wiesehöfer 2009), to the British Mandate
and beyond (Fieldhouse 2006, 108).

Following Engels (1884/2010), Wolf addresses kinship, property claims, and
the status of women as linked phenomena. He describes the kinship-ordered
mode of production as "a way of committing social labor to the transformation
of nature through appeals to filiation and marriage, and to consanguinity and
affinity" (1982, 91). There is a crucial need for collectives to negotiate access to
resources such as farmland, pastures, and water. This is particularly the case in
the absence of clear and impartial juridical property rights. Access to these
resources is thus allocated via a *kinship license* (Wolf 1982, 91). According to Meillassoux (1981), while the frangible but intense bonds of sexual partnership were
sufficient for adhesion within foraging societies, intensive agriculture places a
higher stake on kinship claims to resources. These resources are then allocated
by the more formalized structures of lineage, which involve a greater number of
interests.

According to McDowall (1996, 8), "In the mountains, land was traditionally
controlled by the tribe, and the *agha* was responsible for the equitable allocation of pastoral rights." Prior to the division of Kurdish territories into the new
nation-states of the Middle East after the Treaty of Lausanne, transhumant pastoralism was the predominant economic mode. "Under the Ottoman Empire,"

writes Tax (2016) most Kurds were "peasants or pastoral herders who moved around from place to place. Land was concentrated in the hands of *aghas* . . . who collected taxes for the sultan, and were often predatory" (45). By the end of WWI, she adds, "a small class of rich absentee landlords and middle class Kurds had moved into the cities, especially in Iraq, but most Kurds were still peasants who grew subsistence crops: wheat, barley, and lentils; tomatoes, onions, cucumbers, melons" (59). As late as 1976, Kurdish farmers were still using wooden plows, and reaping with sickles and scythes, paying their landlords with tithes, ruled by sheikhs and *aghas*, subjected to a quasi-feudal control by their landlords (59). Sedentary agriculturalism increased afterward (Head 1974), followed by the development of industry, and later the exploitation of native oil wealth leading to a rapidly modernizing economy.

Where resources are mediated by kinship, marriage becomes a collective transfer event, allocating rights and responsibilities to both parties and to their kin. Therefore it may become a subject of collective strategizing by kin groups. "The idiom of filiation and marriage is used to construct transgenerational pedigrees, real or fictitious" (Wolf 1982, 91). This "idiom" provides compelling symbolic narratives of ownership to mythologize and justify control over land and water. This is particularly relevant if resources are contested or inadequate.

In Iraq, legal systems of landownership did not exist until the colonial period. King and Stone (2010) found an intense preoccupation with lineage in their studies of Kurdish families. These featured a strong patrilinear bias, which tended to erase or subsume female histories into phallocentric narratives of descent. The geography of mountainous regions has been described as creating moral microclimates with a tendency toward conservatism, featuring intense, if agonistic and unstable, local loyalties, underpinned by an ethos of individualism and self-reliance (Izady 1992, 187).

This is typical of pastoral life, where pastoralists face the difficulties of negotiating and maintaining informal control over pastureland (Campbell 1964; Schneider 1971). In transhumant arrangements, pastoralists are sporadically absent from their pastures and unable to protect them from exploitation by outsiders. Moreover, their livelihood is based on sheep and goats, which can be driven away by a rival. Hence, pastoralism is an insecure means of subsistence with a great potential for conflict. It is also a mode of life that obliges pastoralists not wishing to subsist entirely on milk, meat, and butter into contact with other groupings to obtain cereals, vegetables, legumes, and manufactured goods. These must be acquired through trade with, exploitation of, or raiding of settled communities (Lindner 1983, 11). Successful individuals in pastoral societies need to express the personal characteristics that address these vulnerabilities, which include self-reliance and the ability to display aggression (Goldschmidt 1971; Moritz 2008).

The formulation of tribal links often mystifies kinship in order to increase potential allies in the face of conflict. However, these relations are mutable and constantly contested: "Loyalties of one group to another are not immutable, and can be severed and different ones negotiated, in response to tribal or economic situations. When an ambitious chief tries to extend his territory or the number of loyal groups under his control, there will almost certainly be a counter-move and shift of alliances as others endeavor to contain his ambition. This counter-move may be inspired by central government, or by neighboring tribal groups who do not wish the 'equilibrium' to be disturbed" (McDowall 1996, 9).

Van Bruinessen (1978) states that nomadic and transhumant tribes histori-cally used their military power to negotiate with farming communities, which could range from the provision of protection from other tribes in exchange for tribute, to the extraction of protection money to escape attack—relations based on asymmetric interdependency and might. It is typical of pastoralists in gen-eral to subordinate farming communities (Cavalli-Sforza 1996, 56).

From the time of Ibn Khaldūn (1377), much of the Middle East's early history features waves of conquest by successive nomadic pastoralist groups, using their greater mobility to plunder and subordinate other civilizations. Van Bruinessen's ethnology of the Kurds (1978) found that every respondent who was questioned regarding the functions of kinship structures—tribe, clan, village, lineage—gave the same response: that kinship relations were necessary for participating in intertribal wars, disputes, and blood feuds provoked by claims over territory or over women. Further, both participating in feuds and mediating other people's quarrels were methods of claiming status and authority within the community (Tax 2016, 60).

If relations between tribal nomads and settled farmers were characterized by exploitation, then intertribal relations could be characterized by intense hos-tilities: in the Mediterranean region, Schneider finds that a pattern of coexist-ing/competing pastoralism and agriculture led to the development of an internal social code, where groups were "competing for the same resources[5] in a way which fragmented the social organization of each community and blurred the boundary between them. In the absence of a state, pastoral communities and agricultural communities in their midst, developed their own means of social control—the codes of honor and shame—which were adapted to the intense con-flict that external pressures had created within them and between them" (1971, 3).

According to Wolf (1982), the impact of socioecological pressures on the family is for each patriline to treat marriage as a method for forming political alliances and for negotiating territorial claims: "[T]hey organize the exchange of persons between pedigrees through their definition of ties of affinity; marriage, instead of being a relationship between a bride and a groom and their immedi-ate relatives only, becomes a tie of political alliance between groups. . . . On the level of filiation and marriage, kinship sets up individuated linkages among shareholders in social labor" (Wolf 1982, 92).

Thus the kin-ordered mode maintains power through control over parentage and the reproductive powers of women. According to Wolf, this grants "rights over the social labor embodied in females, offspring, and affines: the second defines not only descent, but also collaterality—the genealogical range of movable allies" (93), such as the "vengeance group," who can be called on to support the family in feuds and small-scale wars as well as the day-to-day labor of collective life. The license for sharing in a patrilineal resource entails a reciprocal requirement to participate in patrilinear labor.

There are therefore constant tensions between patrilinear exclusivity—the need to retain control of resources within the kinship group—and inclusivity, through the need to gain allies, supporters, collaborators, and laborers to defend—and expand—those resources. Such an ordering of society has two consequences: first, instability and antagonism between patrilines; and second, the delimitation of women's sexual autonomy due to the positioning of women's honor as a form of symbolic capital.

Instability and Antagonism

As stated by Prince Sharaf al-Dîn Bitlîsî, the first historian of the Kurdish peoples, (1597/2005, 18, verse 42), "Within the Kurdish nation, none follows nor concurs with the other, nor is there solidarity among them." A patrilinear kinship-ordered society may be particularly vulnerable to fission and internal and external conflicts: between original settlers and interlopers, between junior and senior lines, and between prospering and declining patrilines. This pattern has been described as *segmentary agnation*. The fissile nature may be exacerbated by resource shortage, and "contradictions between individual–household–corporate subgroup centrality in production and corporate ownership of productive means" (Sacks 1982, 117). The Middle Eastern proverb "Me against my brother, my brothers and me against my cousins, then my cousins and me against strangers," (Urban 2016, 4) illustrates the strengths and the internal contestations of patrilinearity and segmentary agnation.

Patrilines are in constant contestation with rivals to maintain their position in order to escape subordination or absorption by a stronger patriline, and to maintain continuities through producing male heirs. For Ibn Khaldūn, successful patrilines express *asabiyaa*—deep kinship solidarities that provide cohesion and display collective strength. In the Pashtun context, for instance, any explicit vulnerability may imperil the future of the family: "Households which demonstrate weakness, by failing to control either women's behavior or their independence in the arrangement and completion of a marriage, lose honor and credibility and find themselves on a downward spiral and extremely vulnerable. They are likely to become economically and politically dependent on a stronger (and more honorable) household, and may suffer outright exploitation and oppression" (Tapper 1981, 393).

Power accrues to individuals who can foster strategic marriages and place other persons and families in positions of obligation. Yet any one man's attempt to gain supremacy is ultimately constrained by the limitations of his own fertility and that of his wife (or wives). It is based on how many sons he can claim to his own lineage, and how many daughters he can deploy to gain or reinforce allegiance from others. Even where polygyny is practiced, there are natural limitations to this method of advancement.[6]

The combination of potential antagonism with practical interdependence means that the necessary evil of extrafamilial interactions is conducted with an extreme sensitivity to any exterior encroachments upon male/familial status. Schneider outlines the operations of such an agonistic environment within hybrid pastoralist/agrarian zones:

> As a political phenomenon, honor can attach to any human group from the nuclear family to the nation state. The problem of honor becomes salient when the group is threatened with competition from equivalent groups. It is especially salient when small, particularistic groups, such as families, clans or gangs are the principal units of power, sovereign, or nearly so over the territories they control. Concern for honor also grows when contested resources are subject to redivision along changing lines, when there is no stable relationship between units of power and precisely defined patrimonies, i.e., when the determination of boundary lines is subject to continual human intervention. Finally, concern for honor arises when the definition of the group is problematic; when social boundaries are difficult to maintain, and internal loyalties are questionable. (1971, 2)

The most significant aspect of this form of honor is that it requires an assertive, even choleric, response to status challenges. Honor serves as a carapace that protects and conceals vulnerability, through displaying readiness to use violence against any slights to their status. The reputation of being formidable foes discourages challenges to their position and property. This can be achieved through cultivating a sensitivity to slights; "greatly to find quarrel in a straw / When honor's at the stake."[7]

From Evans-Pritchard's studies of the Nuer in the 1940s onward, honor has been understood within anthropology as a means of developing social order. However, as Bates (2010, 30) and Collins (2008, 191–237) identify, social orders based on honor may be fragile, unforgiving, and violent. This is particularly evident where external agencies of social control are lacking or unreliable, or where the actors are marginalized and unlikely to have their concerns treated seriously (Black 1983, 41). For Collins (2008), honor has the potential to create a stratification by violence: "the community is palpably divided into an elite of tough guys and tough groups (whether they are called gangs, families, clans, aristocrats, etc.) and those who are subject to them" (231).

Honor may allow individuals and groups to deploy displays of dominance by a violent elite as part of the cultivation of an asymmetric power-dynamic in which slights are given freely, but not suffered, by those with the greatest capacity to make violent reprisals. The deterrent effect of threatened violent reprisal is not equally available to weaker members of society and smaller groups lacking in male bodies and the capacity for aggression. As Bates (2010) observes, "Interactions thus take place in a volatile ambience of honor and impudence [in which] young hotheads move to the fore; and a culture of machismo permeates the society" (30).

This can include the humiliation and exploitation of female members as proxy attacks on less powerful groupings, which may often be sexualized in nature. As Collier (1988) suggests, within classless societies, a major source of inequalities is the ability to claim "rights" over women's bodies.

Three basic aspects of honor can be seen to interlock here:

1. Violence as a normative response to status challenges
2. Interactional group norms around reciprocity and reputation
3. A collective stake in the control over women's bodies

I now consider the nature of agnatic rights over women's bodies in greater detail.

The Supreme Gift

By restricting the interaction of men and women and by assigning men the dominant role . . . it becomes possible for both men and women to view the female as an object, a part of the capital goods of the patrilineage to be kept for itself or exchanged.

−Rassam (1980, 173)

The foundational insight of Lévi-Strauss's notion of the "exchange of women" (1949/1969) is that marriage alliances have the function of creating social connections. Women are the "supreme gift," transitioned from one family to another through marital arrangements in order to forge alliances. The "exchange of women," for Lévi-Strauss, was the basis of human civilization. "The fact that I can obtain a wife is, in the final analysis, the consequence of the fact that a brother or father has given her up," he claims (61).

The claimed universality of Lévi-Strauss's application of the exchange of women has been challenged (Harris 2001, 165–216), along with his androcentricism in effecting an almost complete erasure of female agency (Weiner 1992).

However, the kernel of his theory was productively re-examined by Rubin (1975). She recognizes that the exchange of women (or, more accurately, interfamilial transferences of rights over women and girls) is by no means universal. In fact, she observes that there may be communities where a more appropriate description of marital relations might be the *exchange of men*. There are also many societies with an entirely different orientation to marriage, including some where it may be considered to be entirely absent (Hua 2008).

However, Rubin does identify the exchange of women as a significant organizational principle within many societies. Women have historically and cross-culturally lacked the ability to make marital decisions on their own behalves (Broude and Greene 1983), indicating that external influences are significant in the formation of marital relations.

Rubin says, "If women are the gifts, then it is men who are the exchange partners. And it is the partners, not the presents, upon whom reciprocal exchange confers its quasi-mythical power of social linkage. The relations of such a system are such that women are in no position to realize the benefits of their own circulation" (1975, 174).

She redefines Lévi-Strauss's "exchange of women" as "shorthand for expressing that the social relations of a kinship system specify that men have certain rights over their female kin, and that women do not have the same rights either to themselves or to their male kin. In this sense, the exchange of women is a profound perception of a system in which women do not have full rights to themselves" (177).

If, by exchanging women, men and families are brought into alliance, then women are the *conduits* by which that alliance is created. As conduits, women's roles as wives are an extension and reaffirmation of kinship relations.

Women may be far more active participants in the negotiation of marital exchanges than Rubin's formulation allows. Arguably, within patrilinear societies, it is not merely *men as men* who hold rights over their female kin but a wider kin network, including both parents, and other members of the kin group. These rights may be derived from a person's membership of the same patriline, rather than being derived from their sex role. Junior males do not escape from parental pressure; some may themselves be forced into marriage unwillingly in order to meet familial requirements.

Nevertheless, as a way for expressing the inequities of those forms of marriage arrangement in relation to Wolf's kinship-oriented mode of production, Rubin's feminist reclamation of Lévi-Straussian theory appears to be apt for the discussion of patricentric, patrilinear societies where marriage normatively represents a woman's transition from a parental to a patrilocal marital household.

Naziha al-Dulaymi, of the League for the Defense of Women's Rights in Iraq, wrote a scathing attack on Iraqi marriage practices in the 1950s.

She claimed that women of "the peasant class" were treated as a means of production by their fathers and later their husbands. At an early age, they start working for their fathers, who hope to profit further from their daughter's *muhur*[8] as soon as they reach puberty. . . . They are traded for livestock or other women, their prices influenced by market conditions. Child marriages, more prevalent in years of drought and grave economic need, have seen fathers offering their daughters at very young ages for paltry sums, or even without a *muhur* so as to be absolved of the burden of supporting them. . . . Moreover they could be offered as compensation for murder, theft, humiliation and as debt payment. (in Efrati 2005, 581–582)

Ertem and Kocturk (2008), conducting focus groups with Kurdish-speaking women in Turkey, found similar patterns of marriage transactions, along with a pattern of endogamous cousin marriage so far considered normal in the Middle East that it is likely that al-Dulaymi did not identify it as worthy of particular comment.

Ertem and Kocturk's respondents appeared very aware of the political and economic factors of the various forms of marriage while remaining respectful of the presumed legitimacy of parental power. According to Hassanpour (2001), the patterns referred to by al-Dulaymi and Ertem and Kocturk continued to occur within both rural and urban regions of Kurdish regions in Iraq into the twenty-first century.

Rubin's notion of the role of women in marriage as *conduits*, expressing relationships between men and families, takes a central position in the conceptualization of honor. Women quite literally *embody* marriage alliances within patrilinear societies: their transmission from one household to another, their provision of domestic labor, and their ability to reproduce their recipient patriline is the enactment of the kinship alliance that the respective families have forged through marriage. A woman's compliance to the demands of her affines and to reproduce her husband's patriline—he ability to embody normative wifehood—forms the substance of the inter-/intrafamilial link. This may be jeopardized by the wife's failure to live up to the accepted standards, both overt and tacit, of the interfamilial marriage contract.

As "partible aspects of patrilinear identity" (Strathern 1990, 229), women serve as representatives of their own family's commitment to the norms of the collective to their affines and the community at large. Should a woman or girl fail to satisfy the expectations of the transaction involved in her transference from her natal household to that of her affines/husband, and their/his ability to command her labor, sexual functions, and reproductive capacity, then she may endanger the alliance her marriage made between the families.

The breaking of a marriage alliance means the jettisoning of social capital and the potential for alliances to dissolve into resentment and potential conflict,

TABLE 2.1

Summarized content analysis of group discussions conducted by Ertem and Kocturk (2008)

	Opinion		
	Most frequent (>75%)	*Common (25–75%)*	*Less frequent (<25%)*
Arranged marriage	▪ In this region marriage decisions are made by the family.	▪ Parents do not have to inform a girl about marital arrangements or ask for her opinion.	▪ Nowadays, girls decide, because they are more intelligent.
Cradle betrothal	▪ This is rare nowadays.	▪ This is good because families know each other and the bride is well received by her in-laws.	
Cousin marriage	▪ A girl is the right of the (paternal) uncle's son. If he doesn't want her, the girl's family can accept proposals from other family men or outsiders.	▪ It is easier to take a bride from relatives. Relative brides easily understand the family rules and adapt. ▪ It is more economical. Fathers know the economic situation of their relatives and do not demand a high bride-price. ▪ Marriage between cousins is better. He cannot divorce the bride if she is a relative.	▪ Girls who are homely in appearance and lazy at housework are given away to outsiders. Good girls remain inside, bad girls go out.
Direct exchange	▪ This is an option for poor people.		▪ This is a reason for early marriage.
Choice marriage/ elopement		▪ If a girl falls in love and elopes with a boy against the wishes of her parents, this will damage her family honor	▪ Nowadays girls refuse marriage before meeting their suitors. They want to make their own decisions. ▪ It is necessary to be in love. Marriage is impossible if there is no love. ▪ Youngsters should meet and get acquainted before getting married.

which then call into question unstable "kinship licenses" providing access to resources and kinship-based labor. In one case identified by Alinia (2013, 71) in the KRI, for instance, it appeared that the men involved considered the relationship between them enacted by marriage to have a long-term obligation, even extending beyond the lives of the partners. A wife-killer described the attitude of his father-in-law: "Her father is a very good man. He said that it is your right to do as you did. He even said that he would bring me a new wife."

Women bear the responsibility of maintaining this relationship through conforming to the normative ideals of wifehood. The families' rights over the women they exchange, in Rubin's sense, map onto their responsibilities to socialize them so that they meet the societal standards of marriageability operating within the collective. These standards underwrite the delicate political and economic connectivities that marriage creates.

The norms of honor are socially constructed through the interactions between the individual and the group (Awwad 2001), all of whom are current or potential stakeholders, participants, and competitors in the political economy of marriage alliances.

Women's Honor as Symbolic Capital

For Bourdieu (2001), women's reputations are an aspect of *symbolic capital*[9]— which he identified within systems based on the exchange of women in Kabylia. This symbolic capital is a prerequisite of their circulation and the social capital that accrues to their patrilines through their marriages:

> [W]omen are assets which must be protected from offence and suspicion and which, when invested in exchanges can produce alliances, in other words social capital, and prestigious allies, in other words symbolic capital . . . [T]he value of these alliances, and therefore the symbolic profit they can yield, partly depends on the symbolic value of the women available for exchange, that is their reputation and especially their chastity— constituted as a fetishized measure of masculine reputation, and therefore of the symbolic capital of the whole lineage—the honor of the brothers and fathers, which induces a vigilance as attentive, and even paranoid, as that of the husbands, is a form of enlightened self-interest. (45)

Women's honor, then, is the symbolic capital of a woman's reputation, expressed in terms of conformity to normative modes of female sexual behavior, which conditions her acceptance into the category of "marriageable" women, occurring where marriages are intended to bring her family social capital and connectivity—both in Wolf's sense of the ability to mobilize social labor, and in Bourdieu's sense of interpersonal connections.

The English word "honor" (a common gloss for symbolic capital) is necessarily an imprecise placeholder for a variety of terms used in Kurdish. Normative

TABLE 2.2

Comparison of *şeref* and *namûs*

Şeref	Namûs
Collective: *şeref* belongs to the patriline	Individual: *namûs* is embodied within the person
Masculine/public	Feminine/private
Active: assertive responses to status challenges, generosity, social networking capacity, dominance	Passive: conformity to communal norms, acquiescence to requests, subordination to family
Infinite: *şeref* can be restored through vengeance, blood feuds, and honor killings	Finite: *namûs* cannot be regained once lost

femininity is merely one aspect; honor also regulates masculinity and interpersonal relations in general. Honor requires that both males and females be generous, courageous, honest, loyal to their in-groups, respectful of norms of hospitality, and actively concerned for the reputation of their collective. Thereafter, the qualities associated with honor and dishonor begin to break down into gendered forms (Pitt-Rivers 1965). For Tapper (1991, 15), the first, nongendered sense is seen as a transcendental morality; the second is competitive and secular (cf. Wolf 2001, 173).

In the Kurdish language, many terms relate to matters of reputation, honor, shame, and pride (Hassanpour 2001), including *bext*, meaning a reputation for fair dealing, and *qedir*, meaning reputation or prestige (Sweetman 1994, 94). Of most significance to honor as a system of male/familial control of women, and a justification for violence, are the interlocking concepts of *şeref*, which is also used in Arabic, and *namûs*, which has a Persian derivation. The two terms are mutually constitutive (Baron 2006; Bourdieu 1965, 2001).

While *şeref* and *namûs* are coded on a gendered axis, this should not be taken to mean that only men have *şeref* and only women have *namûs*, as aspects of the reputation of either group can be described with either term. Yet a male's violations of *namûs* are not catastrophic to his status within the family in the way that a woman's would be. As Kandiyoti (1988) observes, masculinity is an *achieved* status, which is dynamic; whereas femininity is an *ascribed* status, which is commensurately passive. Men have a greater ability to restore lost status through active means, which are less available for women, whose value is often conceptualized in terms of restraint and delimitation. As Begikhani and Faraj (2016) note: "Honor is not physically located nor defined for men; it is placed outside their bodily domain and they are perceived as guardians of women's honor through their control over their bodies and sexuality" (133).

The categories are interdependent: the *şeref* of the patriline is founded upon the *namûs* of the women associated with the patriline; a woman who has become *bênamûs* (i.e., dishonored in the eyes of the community) cannot restore her status herself. If her agnates do not respond assertively to her behavior, it undermines their self-presentation and self-conceptualization as an honorable *şerefî* family within the community.

Men's honor is thus dependent on the behavior of women. A language of contamination may be used: dishonor is described as *rûreş*—a black face, whereas *rûyê xwe sipî kirin*—making one's face white—is a phrase used to denote the restoration of honor (Sweetman 1994, 94).

King (2008b) identifies *namûs* as a symbolic boundary in the KRI, which is used to exclude agnatic outsiders within a patrilinear society. While this is a strong component, Fischer-Tahir's (2009) summarization of 150 respondents' opinions in Sulaymaniyah found further emic associations of *namûs*, with telling gendered distinctions.

In contrast to the complex, measured, and ambivalent associations around *namûs* within Fischer-Tahir's educated middle class population in the liberal city of Sulaymaniyah, Alinia (2013, 64) notes that convicted murderers in the KRI who claimed an honorable motivation were very invested in *şeref* and *namûs* as terms but were unable to describe their meanings. Alinia describes this as "internalized discourse"—deep-founded, unconscious beliefs, and values, taken as apparent universals. They appear to be self-evident for these perpetrators: ineffable but foundational. "For us *sharaf* is the greatest thing. For us, I mean, the most important and greatest thing is *sharaf.* It is like that. It is above everything else," stated one perpetrator (2013, 63).

As heterodoxy within the concepts of *şeref* and *namûs* becomes more evident, particularly differing across rural/urban and class lines, the decreasing acceptance of such crimes within the KRI means that these perpetrators are finding themselves increasingly out of tune with the changing values of their society. Alinia observed that three of the four perpetrators she interviewed expressed a keen sense of injustice over being punished for the murders they had committed. One said, "I think it is unfair. If I had killed innocent people, I mean if I had killed two persons without any reason or if I had attacked people and robbed them, it would be justified to punish me and even kill me. But unfortunately now I have been sitting here for two years for my sharaf and my namus" (63).

But while there has been a shift in the acceptability of violence as a form of reputation management, the expectations of women's conduct remain slower to change. According to Taysi (2009, 21) Seventy-nine percent of respondents in the

TABLE 2.3

Meanings of *namûs* (Fischer-Tahir 2009)

	Male respondents	*Female respondents*
Related to	jin, afret, mê (woman) perde (hymen) mal, xêzan (house, family) nîştîman (homeland)	perde (hymen) pak-u xawênî (chastity)
Acts	parastin (protection) tole (revenge)	şerim (shame) xoperestin (self-protection) aramî (calmness, patience) cil-u berg (clothing)
Function	pêwist (necessary) ṛez (respect)	pêwist (necessary)
Interpretation	pîrozî (sacredness) pakî (purity)	pîrozî (sacredness) ciwanî (beauty)
Criticism	bê mane (unreasonable)	deselatdar (authoritative) zordar (tyrant)
Context	keltûr (culture) dab u-nerît (tradition) rewşt/exlaq (moral, ethics) be agayî (unconsciousness)	

KRI identified the following behaviors as dishonorable when engaged in by women:

1. Marital infidelity
2. Premarital (illegal) sexual relationships
3. Romantic relationships (i.e., nonsexual, but affective, relationships with a male, whether the woman is married or unmarried)
4. Disobeying parents
5. Sexual misbehavior[10]
6. Other behavior deemed inappropriate, including violations of normative dress codes

These factors relate to marriage as a locus for the constraint of female sexuality, particularly when one bears in mind that the majority of honor crimes related to Taysi's fourth point, disobeying parents, may be directly related to resistance toward an arranged marriage. These findings echo those of Sır (2005) in Turkey. In Sen's (2005) theorization, honorable behavior for a woman connotes "Modest sexual behavior, fidelity in marriage, no pre- or extramarital relationships with men, no unchaperoned rendezvous with men outside the family, meeting motherly obligations to children, meeting wifely obligations to husband, meeting daughter's obligations to parents, meeting daughter-in-law obligations to parents-in-law and so on" (47).

Women who request divorce, and divorcées who claim child custody, are also frequently considered to have offended honor, even though these are transgressions against the gender/kinship order rather than sexual offenses.

A synthesis of Sen's, Sır's, and Taysi's accounts indicates that women's honor seems to rest on three conditions:

1. Acceptance of a parental marriage arrangement
2. Protection and maintenance of marriageability by conforming to communal social norms related to gender relations and sexuality before marriage
3. Meeting the standards of normative wifehood after marriage by remaining subordinate to affines and through fidelity and persistence in the relationship even if this is to the woman's detriment

A woman's honor then, appears to be a valuation of her utility within the political economic systems of marriage, built on her compliance with marriages that are considered beneficial by the collective, and her conformity to normative roles of femininity within her milieu. This suggests that households and patrilines within the kinship mode of production have mutually, catallactically,[11] developed a requirement for women to display *namûs* as a precondition for participation in the marriage market; a market that is deeply integrated into the socioeconomic life of the community.

Namûs also represents a point of vulnerability. Ginat (1981), suggests that "political and economic reasons underlie any accusation [of immorality] made at the value level" (153). Women, as weak points in an agonistic network of interrelations, can provide a means for a proxy attack on the family: alleging sexual impropriety upon the part of a female can bring a family into disrepute and internal dissent.[12]

It is important then, that a woman's honor be such as to preemptively rebut any disparagement of her character since allegations raised against her do not need to be evidenced. The central "crime" against honor is often less the specific violation of a moral code than of bringing a family's honor into disrepute through provoking gossip. Many of the victims of honor killings on the coroner's examining tables of the KRI were found to have intact hymens (Begikhani 1998). It is incumbent upon a woman or girl to behave in such a manner that her honor is not just maintained but is utterly beyond challenge, because it reflects not only upon herself but upon her entire lineage.

The next chapter situates honor within the structures of the patriarchal household and family.

3

The Patriarchal Order

The patriarchal privileging of males and seniors combined with patrilineality enhances the power of male elders within the kingroup, particularly their power over women of the lineage. A father's brothers can
have authority over their nieces and nephews, and male cousins can
have authority over their female counterparts. The intersection of patriarchy and patrilineality increases the range of men with authority over
women–an authority nested in kinship terms.

–Joseph and Slyomovic (2001, 3)

The restrictions on sexual freedom came . . . as a dictate to the young that
they not obey their hearts' desires lest confidences be broken, assets
divided, and boundaries of the group weakened.

–Kressel (1992, 167–168)

This chapter considers how the structure of kinship organizes gendered, domestic, and family relations.

Triandis's (1995) delineation of individualism and collectivism poses
these qualities as opposing ends of a continuum. He identifies honor crimes as
a feature of collectivist societies, where an individual's detachment from the
family is minimal, and where people identify themselves as parts of their collectives and are expected to subordinate their personal goals to those of the
group. Children in collectivist communities tend to be socialized to value interdependence, continuity, and familial obligations (Kağitçibaşi 1989) rather than
independence. Within unilineal descent patterns the moral conformity of a collectivist society reaches exaggerated proportions, since even the potential synthesis of norms through marriage connections is stratified to favor the norms of
the recipient family. The implication this raises is that, within collectives, certain
groups have a greater power to direct and define the goals of the family. Patrilineal descent patterns will prioritize value systems that are favorable to patri-
centricity, shown through being more traditional in their values than neolocal
units (Aykan and Wolf 2000).

When children are encouraged to sacrifice their personal goals for the good of the collective or are not allowed the psychic space to explore their own desires, they become vulnerable to becoming instrumentalized by their parents and other kin. It is of course not the case that all marriage arrangements are self-serving on the part of the parents, who may well have the very best of intentions for their children (see, for instance, Shaw and Charsley 2006). However, we cannot blithely treat parental marriage arrangement as a purely altruistic act. There are varying desires of parents and children in relation to marriage. For instance, Buunk et al. (2008) find that diasporic Kurdish parents and children have very different priorities in marital choice: young Kurds express a preference for partners who are personable, whereas their parents are more concerned with maintaining group identities (57, table 3). Pressures on young people to accept arranged marriages may be intense (Abu-Lughod 1990). There is no "bright boundary" between forced and arranged marriages (Gangoli et al. 2006); notions of consent and duress that form the basis of attempted distinctions are slippery in practice.

An Intimate Politics

Youth are expected to defer to age; females are expected to defer to males. These are the asymmetries of a system with dual axes of power: age and sex. Within patrilocal systems, this means that the subjects of marital translocations—girls and young women—who have the greatest stake in their own future also have the least ability to influence or benefit from decisions made on their behalves. These benefits accrue to the patrilineal group: a group from which they are destined to be excluded due to the requirement for relocation upon their marriage. Their family gains social and political capital and access to collateral relatives through the extension of family ties. In patrilocal/patrifocal households, mothers-in-law gain a domestic under-laborer; husbands gain an admittance to adulthood and the pleasures of licit sex and parentage; unmarried brothers may see their own prospects for marriage improve, either through the payment of bride-price or the prospect of receiving a bride in exchange, or simply through raising the status of the family.

Brides, on the other hand, leave their natal home to face an unfamiliar and potentially hostile environment, in which they are at the bottom of the domestic pecking order. The Kurdish proverb *bûme bûk; bûme pepûk* (Alakom 2002, 51) expresses the trauma of marital translocation bluntly: "I became a bride; I became miserable."

The extended family may seek to inhibit pair-bonding between the couple, which could threaten the family through encouraging nuclearization (Charrad 2001, 51–61). This may underlie social prohibitions around displays of affection. Uxorious husbands are described as *alî*, which suggests emasculation in Kurdish (Hassanpour 2001), and subjected to teasing (Yalçın-Heckman 1991, 142).

Morsy (1990) provides a revealing history of women's progression through the life cycle. While a young bride is subjected to great stresses, including frequent threats of divorce during early marriage, subordinacy to her affines, the trauma of estrangement from her natal family, elder women accrue domestic power with increasing age and numbers of children. Being usually significantly younger than their husbands due to the requirements for a compliant and virginal bride, they are able to command the household once their husband reaches senescence, through their close relationships with their sons, and through having a position of dominance over their daughters-in-law. Thus the characteristic of women's subordination has a temporal quality; the status of a young bride is distinct from that of a mother, especially a mother of sons.

Women as Stakeholders

The motivation for males, as political actors in the public sphere, to conform to the norms of honor has been explicated in terms of building profitable alliances. This raises the question of why women may support this system, since it limits women's autonomy in multiple ways, such as prohibiting political participation, education, employment, and extramural leisure, among many other activities they may wish to participate in.

First, marital arrangements that are beneficial to the collective benefit female members of that collective as well; mothers, sisters, and aunts benefit indirectly from a prestigious or instrumental alliance. They are stakeholders within the system too. Secondly, it is common among subordinated peoples for a normative system that favors their oppressors to have become internalized through socialization. Thirdly, since the symbolic capital of *namûs* is based on distinctions between the categories of honorable and dishonorable, women can gain status and self-esteem by including themselves in the former category and demonstrating their own status by stigmatizing other women.

The Matriarch and the Patriline

Where patrilocal and patrifocal structures predominate and where sex-based segregation operates, elder females may frequently become dominant in the private realm. A senior woman's power may be delimited outside her domain, but within the domestic realm, she holds authority over all residents' children, junior co-wives, daughters-in-law, and other relatives—except the nominal patriarch. On the other hand, outside the private sphere, men's interactions are inflected by their consciousness of their own insecure status vis-à-vis their fellow men, which forms a ground for anxiety and potential contestation.

One of the first lessons a bride has to learn upon entering the patrilineal extended family, according to Wolf (1974), is that her husband cannot be counted on to support her in disputes with her mother-in-law—that she has no effective allies within the household. In this instance she has only one hope: to bear a

TABLE 3.1

Axes of power by age and sex within the patrilinear extended family

	Male	*Female*
Senior	• Executive dominance over household • Executive role in marital arrangement for children • Reliant on family connections for survival (brothers/cousins, etc.) within a competitive agora	• Practical dominance in the private sphere of the household, but subject to husband's executive power • Selective role in marital arrangement for children • Reliant on male support for survival (husband/son/brother)
Junior	• Subordinate to parents; dominant over sisters/wife • Little ability to influence marital arrangement • Reliant on parents/agnates; not yet considered adult	• Subordinate to all other household members • Least ability to influence marriage arrangement • Liminal status between agnatic and affinal families

son, which will cement her into the affinal patriline. This not only leads to an improvement of her position in the family but also provides her with a male supporter, able, in due course, to participate in public life on her behalf, and whose affection she can be surer of commanding over the long term than that of her husband.

Women's ability to wield power comes through the development of a "uterine family" (Lamphere 1974) that is nested within the patriline. In order to protect her interests, she binds her son closely to her as her representative in the public sphere and her source of security in old age. White (1999) finds that mothers-in-law seek to monopolize a daughter-in-law's labor for the benefit of the affinal network and may restrict her abilities to tend to her own mother and father, using strategies from restricting her movements to encouraging spousal violence against her.[1] Thus a woman's strategy for self-advancement within a patrilineal system is one that is supportive of patrilinear structures.

Patrilines are primarily affected by lateral conflicts—competition between brothers and rivalries between neighboring families and tribes—whereas the uterine family is beset with vertical conflicts of generation and status, confrontations between mothers and daughters-in-law in which mothers assert their dominance over an incoming bride, assuring their primacy in their relationship with their son and maintaining their command over the domestic realm. This can lead to violence and abuse (Nazneen 1998). Fischer-Tahir (2009), for instance, observes that Kurdish mothers-in-law have full license to criticize their son's wives, but that wives cannot counterattack (61).

Kurdish mothers have historically played a predominant role in the selection of wives for their sons (Hansen 1961). In societies that practice sexual segregation, males rarely have contact with unrelated females. Thus it may fall to the mother to identify potential partners for her son. If the mother-in-law and daughter are to be coworkers in the same kitchen, then the mother is likely to spend significantly more time in her presence than the husband will, so the success of their relationship may be more significant to the family functioning than that of the marital dyad. Through this close contact, it is also the mother-in-law who is in a position to judge the bride's behavior; this includes the ability to raise allegations against her honor.

For these reasons, it is not necessarily in the interests of elder women to subvert the patriarchal order: it would put them in the position of having made great investments in building their personal power bases within the household through the established patriarchal bargain, which brings status in return for longitudinal conformity (Kandiyoti 1988). Further, through dissenting to the doctrine of honor, they risk relinquishing the ability to bring an interloper—and a challenger for the affections of their son—into check.

The Awkward Age

Cross-culturally, girls in their middle to late teens are disproportionately subjected to checks on their sexual behavior compared to boys.[2] These can upset family marriage plans (Schlegel 1995) and lead to early pregnancy. Kurdish victims of honor killings may be of any age but are predominantly between the ages of 13 and 20 (Begikhani 1998). This presents a similar profile to other countries where statistics on honor killings have been available for analysis, with young married women being the most likely victims (Hoyek et al. 2005; KA-MER 2005; Kressel et al. 1981; Nasrullah et al. 2009; Shalhoub-Kevorkian 2004). It should be noted, however, that the impetus for a family to kill for honor may not dissipate over time. "We have heard of women with grandchildren who have been murdered because they eloped to get married in their youth" (Düzkan and Kocali 2000, 385).

Alinia's (2013) research interviews with survivors of honor-based violence, which were conducted across twelve women's shelters in the Kurdistan Region of Iraq (KRI), revealed a startling fact: of unmarried survivors, *all* had refused arranged marriage (111); of married survivors, *all* had been married without much in the way of explicit consent (116). In the KRI in 2004, 6.8% of girls were married before the legal age of 15, and 26% before the age of 18 (UNICEF 2004); almost all were married by 25 (WHO/Iraq 2006/7). For over 65% of married women and girls aged 15–19, their husband was over 5 years older than they were; for around 28%, this age difference exceeded 10 years (UNICEF 2004).

In some circumstances, girls may be considered eligible for marriage from menarche. Where this implies leaving their natal patriline, menarche marks the point at which a girl's peripheral status becomes manifest. At this point surveillance of her behavior increases. This is an age where it becomes possible that girls may be removed from school to protect their honor. Brenneman (2007, 81) remarks on the loneliness of his own daughter due to the disappearance of her playmates from the streets and schools from the rural Kurdish village where they lived. From age 10 to 12, he says, these girls were restricted to the domestic realm to be protected from potential dishonor in anticipation of marriage.

A young bride also remains marginal to her husband's patriline until she reproduces it through bearing a male child. For women in patrilineal societies, the period between menarche (at around 13 years) and the birth of a first son could be described as a state of liminality; peripheral to the male-defined core of her own family, and not yet fully integrated into that of her affines (cf. Turner 1964; Wolf 1972, 149). This is also a period where the intense preoccupation with young women's bodies is most keenly expressed, focusing specifically on the physical manifestation of virginity.

Come Down from That Tree

Houzan Mahmoud, activist with the Organisation for Women's Freedom in Iraq, told me an incident where, as a young girl, she caused a scandal among her peers by climbing a tree. "Come down from that tree," they called up to her, "or you'll lose your virginity."[3]

According to Cooper (2001, 102) attitudes in Ancient Mesopotamia bore no resemblance to the complex of honor and shame identified by writers such as Péristiany in the 1960s: there was no fixation on the breaking of the hymen, a membrane that does not appear to be part of early Mesopotamian understandings of virginity. The "hymenization" of virginity, as the demarcation between the classes of women, a prerequisite for marriage, and the responsibility of the agnatic collective, appears to originate from the Hebraic worldview. Deuteronomy 22:13–20 insists on bloodied sheets as proof of virginity; the Babylonian Talmud notes several cases of men raising complaints about a lack of blood when engaged in first marital coitus (Kelly 2000, 19–20). This fixation on the hymen is also found in Islam and in Kurdish culture. As Fischer-Tahir finds, the hymenization of women's sexuality is found in everyday usage in the Kurdish language: "To find out whether a certain man is married or not, a person might ask 'Has he taken a wife (*jin-î hênawe*)?' A man who 'takes' something is active. . . . To discover if a woman is already married, a person might ask 'Has she married (*şû-î kirduwe*)?' But both men and women tend to ask 'Is [she][4] a virgin or a woman? (*kiç-e yan jin-e*)?'" (2009, 50).

If women's honor, in the sense of *namûs*, is considered a form of symbolic capital that is essential to marital arrangements, then this raises the question of why there should be such wide and cross-cultural consistency across Eurasia in the connection of women's symbolic capital with sexual restraint: why honor in women represents chastity, virginity, and restraint rather than sexual prowess, wit, athleticism, or any other of the many personal characteristics a woman might exhibit.

Sexually active women are not less industrious, less healthy, or less fertile than others. There can hardly be a better indicator of fertility than having already birthed a healthy child. Yet the linking of a woman's symbolic capital with chastity is deeply rooted in Eurasian culture, from the Bible, to the clinics profiting from performing hymenoplasties in the present day.

The hymen, unforgettably described by Nawal El Saadawi as "that very thin membrane called honor" (1977/1980, 38), holds a crucial relevance to women's eligibility for marriage. It remains a point of anxiety for young women across the Middle East. Virginity is also presumed to be in the state's domain in this region, where virginity tests are conducted by officials (Parla 2001), and even used as a means of political repression (Taher 2012).

The state of the hymen then, is a public rather than a private matter. In conducting psychosocial research into Kurdish women living in Norway, Ahlberg (2007) found virginity was an extreme concern to all her clients. Her respondent Aisha remarks that women who do not bleed on marriage have their head shaved and are returned to their family on the back of a donkey[5] (87). Fatima records the shame of failing to bleed sufficiently on her own wedding day. She was discarded by her proposed husband, who cried, "You are no virgin! I have been deceived; I believed I was getting a proper wife." Shamed, she was forced to leave the village with her family (Ahlberg 2007, 122). Fatima's description of the ritual of defloration is similar to that recorded by Hansen (1961) who says that the young husband is expected to consummate the marriage abruptly and then "leave the field to the waiting woman, who roughly dries the bride's genital opening in order to obtain as clear a trace on the sheet as possible."

Fatima (Ahlberg 2007, 122) adds that this ritual, as she observed it, was by no means private, as at all the weddings she had attended, guests crammed the wedding meal down in order to crowd around every available window and door crack and observe the first act of coition between husband and wife. Rather than a nightdress, there were linen strips (*çarşeb*) safety-pinned to the bed. As soon as the act was completed, observers burst into the room and ran through the village treating the strips as trophies. These strips were then retained by the bride, who maintained them as proof of her virginity. These may be particularly valuable during the liminal period of early marriage. Otten (2017, 110) similarly notes that this practice was also followed by Yezidi families making hasty "marriages" to avoid having Da'esh jihadists take their daughters' virginity.

Broude and Greene (1983) observe that, cross-culturally, the more likely it is that marriage is nonconsensual, the less likely it is that newlyweds are granted privacy for their first sexual act; and that the more sexually repressive a society is, the more likely that consummation is ceremonialized. Within a culture in which public displays of affection between couples are normally proscribed, this ritual appears to be a rather nerve-wracking experience for both newlyweds. The bride may be sensible of the risk—now completely beyond her control—of being shamed if she does not produce sufficient blood; the groom must attempt congress, possibly for the first time in his life, with a tense and potentially terrified woman who may be a virtual stranger to him, with the task of maintaining an erection of sufficient rigidity to pierce her hymen—and all of this before an audience.

This suggests there is more in play here than the purity of the bride; the groom is also being subjected to a test of potency in his ability to perform sexually under adverse conditions (cf. Abu-Zahra 1970, 1086; Lindisfarne 1994). Hassanpour (2001, 239) notes that the Kurdish noun *piyawetî* (manliness) connotes "the ability to fuck . . . with the given example [in a Kurdish-language dictionary] . . . 'he that has become a man over the bride . . . he has removed her hymen.'"

"Within a patriarchal system," says Moruzzi (2013), "men are as firmly tied into a binary identity as women are: The equivalent to women's entrapment in the duality of the mother/whore opposition is men's confinement to the roles of protector and patriarch or victimizer and criminal. . . . Within the family, a woman is a mother or a possible mother-to-be; outside the family, a woman is a possible whore. Within the family, a man is a protector or a possible patriarch; outside the family, a man is a possible libertine or a thug" (see Moruzzi 2013, under "Gender and the State").

The ritual on the male side, binding them into new roles as family men, has more in common with the hazing of a U.S. college fraternity or military unit than an erotic encounter; phallic masculinity is displayed to gain admittance to the homosocial community of adult married men. Virginity does not just demarcate the boundaries between girl and woman; taking it makes a boy into a man (Donnan and Magowan 2010, 140). The ritual described earlier should by no means be considered contemporary practice—most urban Kurds will commence married life in privacy. The state of the hymen, however, may well remain a point of interest to their families, and some may still demand sanguine proofs.[6] A judgment pronounced in Duhok, in the KRI, on October 9, 1999, stated, "The father killed his daughter after she told him that she could not marry in Dihok because she was no longer a virgin. . . . It is confirmed to the Court by the post-mortem that the girl's hymen was broken while she was not married and this indicates that the girl was badly behaved and honorable motivation is reached in this case" (in Begikhani 2005, 215).

"Honorable" motivation meant that despite witnesses to the murder, the father and uncle received a one-year suspended sentence (Begikhani 2005, 215). In the case of Du'a Khalil, a Kurdish teenager from the minority Yezidi religion, who was publicly stoned to death in Bashiqa, northern Iraq, in 2007, the political ramifications of the state of her hymen were such that her body was disinterred in order to conduct postmortem gynecological examinations. Her (intact) hymen occasioned more interest than the pulverized skull and fractured spine, which were the actual causes of her death (Lattimer 2007).

There are, as Stone (2006, 241) identifies, few solid reasons to account for the value of virginity; there is neither intrinsic nor functional value to the hymenal membrane. Accounts of the high status of virginity seem to proceed from the curious notion that men have an innate sexual desire for virgins, which desire is most fully expressed where males have greater power over marital choice. However, virgin preference on the part of males is by no means universal and may not even be cross-culturally predominant (Schlegel 1995, 141).

While there is a common argument based in evolutionary psychology that virgins are desirable as brides because they cannot be already pregnant, thereby hoodwinking a man into supporting a child that does not bear his genetic code, virginity is by no means the only method of ascertaining the status of any woman's uterus. It is not even reliable, given the wide range of methods of faking a hymenal bleeding available since antiquity, such as the ninth century Persian recommendation of a pessary fashioned from dove's intestines and animal blood (Blank 2007, 91). The prophet Muhammad, writing within a pagan milieu where marriage, divorce, and remarriage were very frequent (Bianquis 1996), instituted the *iddat* waiting period into Muslim practice, in which a woman is obliged to wait for three menstrual courses between marriages in order to ensure that there is no uncertainty about paternity. There is no reason why such a method could not be applied to never-married women to ensure a husband's reproductive dominion over his wife's uterus.

Schlegel (1991) addressed the obsession with virginity in functional terms noting that virginity has high status where women either command dowries or expect inheritance. Her argument is that in agrarian societies, illegitimate children are unwelcome because they drain resources from the natal family without benefiting from the additional resources brought in by the father. Virginity is prized in order to prevent opportunistic or otherwise unsuitable men from seducing women in order to benefit from their dowries and property rights. In support of this theory, we could note that in European history, women's virginity has often been a predominant concern of the propertied classes. However, Schlegel's argument loses momentum outside that milieu. The argument that illegitimate children are undesirable due to increasing the burden of family resources without providing an additional source of male income seems rather less convincing in a society as vigorously pro-natal as traditional agricultural corporatism, where children are put to work from very young ages (Dzięgel 1982, 248). There is no reason why the illegitimate child of a daughter would make a less effective farmhand or shepherd than the legitimate offspring of a son. The need for economic support would not be prolonged in subsistence farming economies, where children begin to produce surpluses as young as six years of age (Harris 1997, 205).

Schlegel's assumption that a premium on virginity prevents an opportunist from seducing his way into his wife's riches appears to depend on a principle of "shotgun" marriage. This assumes that an unmarried impregnated woman inevitably marries the man who has fathered the child, thereby passing on control of her pre- and postmortem inheritances. Abortion, infanticide, or lone parenthood are thus ruled out as viable options, as is marriage to a more eligible man willing to accept the role of *pater* to the offspring of a premarital association. Any of these options would effectively confound the strategies of a man hoping to impregnate his way into a fortune. If these options were not available to the nonvirgin woman, this suggests that the causal chain Schlegel proposes must be reversed: it is only *because* there is a high premium on a virgin bride that the seducer's strategy can be effective, because it is based on a belief that an unmarried, nonvirginal woman has no other prospects.

Moreover, in Islamic marriages, there is no assumed commonalty of property through marriage, as there is in the European assumption of *coverture*, nor are there substantial dowries or "portions" payable to the groom from the bride's family. While a Muslim husband may attempt to persuade his wife to contribute to the household, he has no legal ability to force her to do so; and while he does potentially inherit from her estate, the amounts of inheritance from women are comparatively smaller. Since women often outlive men, particularly in societies riven by conflict, and since wives are typically younger than their husbands, particularly in strongly patriarchal societies, they are more likely to be beneficiaries of their husband's estate than testators of their own.

While the potential of women's inheritance rights can be problematic to patrilineal corporatism, within the Middle East these are often contained through preferential patrilateral cousin marriage (see chap. 4), which is a parsimonious strategy for retaining property within a kinship group, or through persuading women to waive their inheritance rights in exchange for guarantees of fraternal protection in the event of marital breakdown.

It seems more likely, as King and Stone (2010) and Altunek (2006) observe, that it is the overwhelming weight of patrilineal ideology that renders illegitimacy unthinkable—not to mention the difficulties of marrying off an illegitimate girl where honor is conceived not only as collective but as a heritable quality (Altunek 2006, 62). Ortner (1978) identifies a large region where virginity is considered men's concern, which includes the Mediterranean, Middle East, India, and China. She relates this to the rise of state ideologies of purity. While the dialectic of purity and contamination has symbolic resonances within many societies, this explanation tends to beg the question in eliding the hymen with purity. This is a peculiar notion, given that the supposed proof of physical virginity is a messy business. There is no necessity behind this association: in some societies the defloration of a new bride is performed by an intermediary to avoid "contamination" of the groom (Rubin 1975, 165 fn 1).

The discourse of purity and filth is commonly, and cross-culturally, deployed to make moral judgments (Nussbaum 1999). The linkage of hymenal blood with purity may speak more deeply to the emotional basis of conventional morality, which tends to carry cognitive connections with disgust (David and Olatunji 2011). Douglas's (1966) core position is that the language of contamination is deployed in *symbolic* terms, so it is worth considering whose interests are served by the symbolic linkage of a hymen with purity.

In the absence of trickery, a woman can appear as a virgin only once in her lifetime. In a community where she is known, falsifying virginity within a second marriage is an impossibility. If virgins are identified as the only acceptable category of marriageable women, then unhappy married women with no means of support but marriage may consider themselves unlikely to remarry well, and thus remain within their first marriage. Their options are to remain in an undesirable marriage, the uncertainties of a return to the natal family, or destitution. Thus making virginity a requirement for marriage serves to increase women's dependence on an individual man and reduces the chances that she will seek divorce.

Of the Abrahamic faiths, Islam has a comparatively liberal attitude toward divorce, to the point that Muslim marital bonds have been described as inherently fragile and unstable (Charrad 2001, 34). Christianity has, by contrast, been particularly resistant to divorce (Goody 1983, 41). Catholic women can testify to the lifelong claim a husband is presumed to have over the body of his wife, while patriarchal Protestant movements in the United States call for covenant marriages that eschew no-fault divorces as ungodly and damaging to children (Spaht 2002). Female-initiated divorce is particularly disruptive within patrilineal family structures, which seek to ensconce a woman and her children under the control of a man (and his family) for as long as it suits the man's (and the family's) purposes.

Islamic directives on divorce are asymmetric and do not favor women—men may divorce according to their whim through pronouncing a triple *talaq*, with few long-term obligations to support their former partner. Women must supplicate to religious authorities to be released from marriage, and ransom their freedom by repaying any monies or property they received as dower (*mehr*); some lose custody of their children in this process. Female-initiated divorce (*khul'*) remains possible for Muslim women, however, and may indeed have been very common in Middle Eastern history (Stowasser and Abul-Magd 2004), undermining male control in the family.

Bargaining theory addresses three points in relation to marriage: the first decision is when/whether to marry; the second, whom one marries; and the third is how the surplus value of marriage is distributed (Zelder 2002, 157). Within a system of marriage arrangement, the expectation is that the collective holds executive control over the first two points of bargaining. The dyad does, however, have to live together, arrange their lives as a couple, and develop patterns of the division of labor and resources. Economists see divorce as a "threat point" (Manser and Brown 1980; McElroy and Horney 1981) where either spouse will refuse an output share that makes him or her worse off than if the couple were to divorce. This mechanism works to maintain a limited degree of equilibrium within the marital division of resources and labor. Where women's ability to divorce is limited compared to that of men, power within the marital relationship accrues to men. Some men may threaten their female relatives with an easily accomplished divorce (for example, threatening daughters with the dispossession of their mothers in the event of noncompliance in marital arrangements), making divorce threat a means of power and control over women.

In order to maintain patrilineal control over the family and to solidify the bonds of obligation and alliance between families created by marriage, *women's* ability to deploy divorce threats must be contained, delimited, and penalized. So the premium on virginity and the exclusion from licit sexuality of unmarried nonvirgins combine to constrain female divorce threat; the high status of *women's* virginity—men's virginity being largely their own private affair (Mernissi 1982, 185)—may be linked to a strategic desire to limit women to one marriage over their lifetime, thus maintaining important connectivities between families.

Bois, writing in the late 1960s, suggests that divorce was infrequent among Kurds and was mostly initiated by males where a wife had failed to produce male children to reproduce the patriline, that women's remarriage after divorce was even more rare, and that the patriline always retained custody of any children, so that for a woman, divorce inevitably led to the loss of her custodial rights (1966, 44). Indeed, it continues to be rare: in 2009, of ever-married single women in Iraq, a mere 5.7% were divorcées: the rest were widows (United Nations 2009).

By comparison, within horticulturalist societies in New Guinea, Africa, and Amazonia, while first marriages are often arranged by parents, these are often short-lived, and divorce is treated unproblematically (Fisher 1992, 161–162). This suggests that where the kinship license is less central to domestic economies, marital permanence is also less significant. A premium on virginity then, may be an attempt to restrict women's ability to divorce in societies where this is an option legally and socially available to women, but in which it is disruptive to the social orderings of labor, resources, and reproduction.

A Broken Glass

Do not run. Do not jump. Do not ride a bicycle. Do not go in for sports at all. Otherwise you might injure the hymen and then "we'll lose our reputation." Do not speak in a loud voice, *'eyb-e*[7]! Do not sit with your legs apart, keep your eyes down, do not talk without permission, *'eyb-e*! Do not play with the neighbor's sons on the street . . . and so on.

–Fischer-Tahir 2009, 65

The hymen is of crucial significance to unmarried women, yet it is hardly a reliable indicator of a lack of sexual experience: hymens may be broken through nonsexual acts; they may be so tough or so flexible that penile penetration fails to rupture them; or they may, indeed, be nonexistent from birth (El Saadawi 1977/1980, 80). With these factors in mind, it is unsurprising that girls may be restricted from climbing trees, riding bicycles, and other physical pleasures of girlhood—superstition endows the hymen with a dangerous fragility precisely because of its importance. The protection of the hymen becomes metonymous for the restriction of the entire body, limiting the range of motion and expression available to a girl or woman.

The obsession with the physical hymen telescopes into an ethic of total control of virgins—"women must refrain from sexual activity . . . and from any act that might lead to sexual activity, and from any act that may lead to an act that might lead to sexual activity" and so on (Abu-Odeh 1996) to the extent that a woman or girl becomes an embodied extension of her own "thin membrane." In common idiom, a woman's loss of virginity and honor is described as like the breaking of glass, the staining of cloth, the striking of a match, the smashing of an egg, or the trampling of a flower into the mud—an irreversible act of destruction.

Underlying the conceptualization of *namûs* are perceptions of female sexuality: nonvirgin women are assumed to be lascivious and sexually indiscriminate, a belief that is exacerbated by the fact that women who are not married, cannot access the labor market, and do not have supportive families may be forced into forms of transactional sex for their own survival. The situation of divorced women in societies where virginity is considered an essential prerequisite to marriage is dire (Cohen and Savaya 1997). Divorcées may be considered unmarriageable due to their lack of virginity, thus treated as legitimate targets for sexual harassment, and even rape (Wehbi 2002, 296). It is unsurprising, perhaps, that a society which allows women a very limited capacity for discrimination in sexual affairs envisions them as being sexually indiscriminate.

According to Buunk and Solano (2012), there is a high correlation between parental marriage arrangement and "mate-guarding" behavior—their term for sexual jealousy—which may be expressed by both men and women. Goddard (1987, 190) describes this view of the omnivorously sexual woman as an expression of a deep ambivalence around sexuality based on the contradictions generated by the attempt to reconcile women's real existence as sexual agents within a system that depends on them acting as sexual subjects. This contradiction lies at the heart of the fragility of *namûs* and the valorization of virginity, which is, if anything, a requirement to eschew autonomy over one's own sexual and reproductive life.

The next chapter takes a microsociological approach to the interactions involved in certain forms of marriage, with particular attention to the operations of social capital.

4

Marriage

I don't want to marry a shepherd,
who always has mud on his trousers.
I don't want to marry a drover,
who has cracks in the soles of his feet.
I don't want to marry a scholar,
who is so proud of himself,
just for smearing ink with a pen.
I don't want to marry a rich man,
whose wealth shows a wound in his heart.
I don't want to marry a poor man,
that dare not look at my face.
Dear mother, kind mother,
I want to take the road[1] as I promised:
I want to marry the one that I love.

Kurdish folksong (Zaza 1962), my translation

Rites of Passage

This chapter covers various marriage strategies in more detail, progressing from those with the closest proximity to the family (endogamy, in the form of cousin marriage), to the balanced reciprocity of direct-exchange marriage (often occurring within small communities), to the monetized interactions of exogamy with bride-price, with a final discussion of the wild cards of abductions and elopements. These four forms of marriage are by no means distinctly Kurdish, nor to be understood as contemporary. They can also be found co-occurring within rural Italy in the 1950s (Pirro 2008), among the Roma in Bulgaria (Pamporov 2007), in Afghanistan (Kargar 2011), in Pakistan (Afzal et al. 1994; Jacoby and Mansuri 2007), and in Southern France (Segalen 1986, 16). This chapter draws comparisons with these forms as they arise in other territories to reflect on their dynamics where necessary. This distribution suggests that these forms may be logical formations operating within the political economics of marriage: that they are not distinctive traditions delimited to any one culture, but may be considered more in terms of maneuvers generated within the logics of the system—Bourdieu's concept of "regulated improvisations." These strategies may have developed within the framing of similar contexts, in similar ecological niches, and within similar familial structures.

I do not intend for the reader to take the forms of marriage described in this chapter as describing a predominant contemporary reality; although some of these modes are still practiced, they are declining in the face of modernity. Rather, I wish to identify these forms as ideal-typic models, modeled on Collier's (1988) treatment of three Amerindian marriage forms.[2] I am using these in order to consider how different forms of marriage relate to the structure of patrilineal societies featuring the exchange of women, and how these may motivate and inflect the societal preoccupation with *namûs*.

An ideal-typic approach necessarily risks giving the illusion of stasis and tends toward homogenizing diverse experiences. As Hansen (1961) notes, prior Western writers drew few distinctions between women's various differing situations in generalizing about Kurdish women. Accordingly, she takes care to attend to differences in educational level and urban/village backgrounds. Natali (2005, 31) points to the huge variety of socioeconomic and political statuses based on tribal/nontribal and Muslim/non-Muslim distinctions, as well as "warriors and tillers of the land, landowners, peasants and urban groups."

I commence with a discussion of a form of marriage that is considered distinctive to the Middle Eastern region: preferential patrilateral cousin marriage.

Eating Meat from One's Own Flock

Across the entire Middle East and North Africa zone and within diasporic Middle Eastern and North African communities there remain expressions of preference for cousin marriage, with patrilateral parallel cousin (PPC[3]) marriage being a particularly favored form. This section explores PPC marriage and posits potential explanations for its social utility.

A COUSIN'S RIGHT. Yalçın-Heckman's meticulous ethnography (1991) of members of the Kurdish Hamawand tribe, living in the Turkish village of Hakkari, indicates that of sixty-six marriages where the relationship between the couple was known, thirty-four were endogamous, and nineteen were real or classificatory PPC marriages. She notes that for Hakkari, PPC was considered the default (i.e., ordinary) marriage (1991, 236). In the city of Van, in the Kurdish region of Turkey, researchers commented that the high level of cousin endogamy (34.4%) was due to family pressure rather than choice (Akbayram et al. 2009). In Iraq, research into genetic illnesses found that 43.3% of the control group had consanguineous marriages, of which 35.6% were between first cousins (Al-Ani 2010).

In some cases, if a father wishes to marry his daughter to someone *other* than his brother's son, he must first seek permission from his brother(s) and nephew(s). PPC is far from being an absolute rule, therefore, but may remain a strong preference. A father might well give lip service to the importance of marrying his daughter to his brother's son, but this may not reflect practical reality for several reasons.

First, and most simply, PPC marriage may not be mathematically possible where there are disparities between the numbers of unmarried males and females within a patriline. Secondly, a growing awareness of the genetic risks involved has led to a decline in cousin marriages (Brenneman 2007, 73). Last, a father's choice may be weighted by individual preference rather than communal norms: for instance, if his brother's son is an idler, while his sister's is responsible and industrious, he may well pick the latter in the interests of his daughter and her future children's prosperity. He may, however, face opposition in this preference from his own brothers and nephews through their assumed right of "access": "When Haifa Khalil, from a village near Aleppo, refused to marry a cousin whom she found "disrespectful and childish," her parents tried to arrange a marriage to another, unrelated man. But they faced opposition from her uncle, who threatened them. He said she could marry any of his sons, but insisted they had priority over anyone else. Under pressure from tribal elders, Haifa finally agreed to the match. Now, she says, "I have no dreams or hopes in life. I feel that I am under sentence" (IWPR–Syria 2009).

Such "cousin-right" may be broadly supported by forces outside the family: in Diyana, in the Kurdistan Region of Iraq (KRI), a girl who refused to marry her cousin applied for the annulment of a marriage contract made while she was a baby. The village mullah informed the judge that the match had his approval and should be upheld, and the girl was threatened with violence until she complied with family wishes (Minwalla and Portman 2007, 17).

THE SCIENCE OF THE SHARES. Patterns of reciprocal cousin marriage have been strongly linked to female inheritance rights. Sanmartìn (1982, 664) finds, for instance, that in the Mediterranean region, while cousin marriage is very common where female inheritance is recognized, it is rare, and even considered deviant, where women do not inherit. Notably, PPC marriages are strongly and significantly more likely to be found if the area was part of the eighth-century Umayyad Caliphate, and they are far more likely to have been retained where the Islamic faith remains predominant (Korotayev 2000). Tillion's (1966/2007) ethnography of the Maghreb identifies the Islamic directive for female inheritance as a strong motivation for endogamy. Islamic laws on inheritance, known as 'ulm al-farā'idd, (the Science of the Shares), are diffusive, tending to spread wealth across many inheritors rather than concentrating it in the hands of a single individual. Islamic directives involve a great number of potential inheritors to any estate; moreover, testators can dispose of only a limited proportion of their estate at their own discretion. That discretionary proportion may not be bequeathed to an inheritor who already has a set share under Islamic principles (Esposito and DeLong-Bass 2007, 65).

A great deal of contemporary feminist attention to Muslim family law on inheritance confronts the injustice of a daughter's share being half that of a son. However, the very fact that females inherit at all can be disruptive to patriliny, through the potential to impede the smooth transmission of corporate holdings, most significantly land and flocks, down the patriline.[4]

Notably, the share accruing to the wife in the event of the husband's death is the smallest. This is the only transmission of money into the affinal patriline. Agnatic patrilineality is particularly favored within Islamic inheritance. The complex mathematics of inheritance rules may have been more practicable to the Arabian communities who were the first recipients of Islam and whose economy was based in mercantilism and cattle herding.

Mecca is, and was, extremely arid. Its prominence and livelihood arose from its role as a trading center, where each citizen—man, woman, and child—often had some trading interest in every camel train passing through the city (Wolf 1951). The disposal of the estate of a trader and herdsman is more readily *arithmetically* resolved through the division of units of camels and tradable goods, which can in turn be bred or traded for profit. However, for agricultural communities, the division of an estate rested far more firmly on the division of land or livestock, with the potential to threaten the basis of subsistence for the family as a whole. The estate of a farmer must be divided *geometrically*, in acres and feet, which would ultimately, through a few generations, render some partitions so small as to be unusable. Moreover, land is not, like tradable goods or livestock, a renewable resource. Plough technology, first utilized in Mesopotamia, requires land of sufficient dimensions to plough effectively. Agriculturalists are resistant to the division of their estates, which they prefer to hold as a corporate patriline; pastoralists have an interest in maintaining and defending their patrilineal claim to pastureland, and to prevent any divisions of their flock, particularly since sheep herding requires a flock of optimal size.[5] Inheritance directives, as Tillion observes, place Muslims who derive their subsistence from a corporate patrimony, whether agrarian, pastoral, or a combination of the two, into a theological quandary: do they follow the tenets of their religion? or do they safeguard the interests of the corporate family?

Muslim women retain, *in potentia*, a jural right to claim their portion. This potential disruption to the material basis of the family can be circumvented through ordaining endogamous marriage, suggests Tillion, which has the effect of binding a woman into the corporate family through marriage, and thereby assimilating her interests into those of the collective. It is as if, she observes, women gain control over property at the expense of losing control over their body (1966/2007, 42).

While anxieties around inheritance rights and the wish to maintain familial control over patrimony may account for cousin marriage becoming a widespread strategy, they do not fully account for the explicit preference for patrilaterality. Zoroastrians also were known to practice cousin marriage from early sources, and women also inherited (and inheritance was technically equal between brothers and sisters, rather than the half-share that Muslim women receive), but there was no lateral preference (Fischer 1973). So Tillion's explanation may provide a starting point, but it does not account for laterality, nor for the common cultural techniques for evading women's Islamic right to inheritance, nor for the prevalence of PPC marriage in groups that do not practice Islamic inheritance.

There are alternative mechanisms for evading the consequences of female inheritance: married women who are unable to work for themselves remain dependent on their brothers and fathers for shelter and support in the event of marital breakdown. Men may dissuade female relatives from asserting their right to inheritance through providing a guarantee of support in the event of marital estrangement.

FRATERNITIES. According to Charrad (2001), "The preferential right of a man to his [father's brother's daughter] actually entails a relationship between two men, the groom and the bride's fathers," Charrad identifies (59). Prescribing cousin marriage, specifically on the father's side, is a productive strategy, since it serves the purpose of solidifying relationships between brothers in economies that rely on collective, familial male labor (Holý 1989). The ability of endogamy to consolidate power and property has long been a facet of dynastic power.

The transferences of women from one grouping to another can be used to "stitch over" the potential fissures involved in the patterns of segmentary agnation that arise from patterns of diffused inheritance. In agricultural/pastoral economies, tensions between brothers who share juridical property rights may threaten the transmission of patrimony even more than women's inheritance. This is because they threaten the cooperative basis of male labor. Men may be discouraged from demanding exclusive use of their own portion of land, or from requiring the division of a flock, where such actions would cause uneasy relationships between themselves and their brothers and nephews/son-in-laws, and which would thereby disadvantage their own daughters and grandchildren. Cousin marriage effectively ties a father's interest in his own descendants to those of his brothers, particularly valuable if the death of a father in a classically patriarchal household leads to a *frérèche*—an acephalous household shared by brothers. These formations are particularly vulnerable to antagonism and fission.

Holý (1989) argues that PPC marriages' tendency to increase male solidarity is a particularly valuable strategy within an environment of tribal contestations. He notes that in Kurdish regions, tribal *ashireh* Kurds, who are more likely to have greater needs for solidarity in the face of tribal rivalries, have a higher level of PPC marriage than their nontribal, less belligerent, sedentary peers. This observation challenges the containment of female inheritance as a sole motivation for PPC marriage—*ashireh* Kurds, as members of a tribal grouping that may be nomadic or transhumant, locate their tribal solidarity within a notional patriline. Kurds engaged in sedentary farming have a more permanent relationship with their land, as the source of their livelihood, rather than with their comparatively low-status patrilines.[6]

As Yalçin-Heckman (1991) finds, Kurdish tribal identifications must be constantly reinscribed through the making and remaking of kinship linkages. Patrilateral cousin marriage maintains and reproduces both patrimony and patriliny simultaneously. Conjecturally, if a society were to regulate its marriage practices entirely through PPC marriage, all relationships would become agnatic and vertical, with no external horizontal relationships outside the patriclan that could mediate or discourage interclan hostilities. Thus a rigid pattern of PPC marriage would tend toward a continual regeneration and reinscription of the brittle, vertical structures of segmentary agnation. This, in turn, would tend to increase intertribal hostilities. Endogamous marriage preserves corporate property, but it also tends to increase segmentation, which in turn leads to hostility between families, tribes, and clans. These contestations increase the requirement for male solidarity formed through endogamous alliances.

Thus cousin marriage may appear as the consolidatory phase of a patriline—not least because any man who founds a new patriline is likely to do so because he is distanced from his own agnates. Kressel (1992) stated that among the Bedouin, cousin marriage does not occur until a patriline reaches the third or fourth generation, suggesting that in its early stages, a patriline is reliant on exogamous linkages to build social capital; but that subsequently a successful patriline becomes self-reliant in social and reproductive capacities. Kressel also finds that the networks of interfamilial reciprocity are delicately balanced, recounting an example where one individual within a family refused to accept a PPC marriage, which ultimately led to chaos, bloodshed, and long-lasting enmities across an entire extended family, a process he describes at length (Kressel 1992, 106–113). Thus normative cousin marriage, through knitting the interests of several individuals together through kinship and marriage, risks a tumultuous disruption in the event of any unraveling.

Khuri (1970), within a Freudian framing, suggests that the strategic merit of PPC marriage is that it tends to reproduce the family without changing its structure. Through avoiding the insertion of an interloper into the family, established kinship and domestic structures are maintained. PPC marriage introduces no new affines that could threaten the established familial order. PPC marriages are not just the "normal" form of marriage, they are also, in the words of a Kurdish informant, the "*safest*" marriage (cf. Fricke et al. 1986, 493).

Women are necessary for the reproduction of the patriline, but as interlopers within the virilocal household, they may hold a dangerous potential to threaten its continuity and cohesion. Their linkages with their natal families may raise suspicions. Related women, already inculcated with the family's values, sharing, to some degree, their goals and interests, pose a lesser threat to the collective. From the other direction, containing female relatives within the family lessens their ability to share family secrets or dishonor their family in front of unrelated persons. As potential loose threads, women are knitted back into the body of the family, so they cannot snag or pull, and thus unravel, the family reputation.

Containment is also the aim in marriages designed, and even coerced, to save honor; where a woman has become suspected of dishonorable behavior, it may be considered the duty of a cousin to step forward and provide a respectable, face-saving marriage. Zahra al-Azzo was 15 years old when she was kidnapped and raped. Her cousin married her in order to save her reputation. This was not considered adequate by the collective. Her family dispatched her brother to kill her, to the dismay of the widower, who had developed a genuine affection for the young woman.[7]

Cousin marriages are not only considered the safest form for the family's property, the family's cohesion, and the family's honor, they may also be relatively safer for the woman involved, as the degree of relatedness reduces the hazards of patrilocality for incoming brides. Cousin marriages may then have a lesser tendency toward intimate partner violence than exogamous marriages because the daughter-in-law/niece is not in the isolated position of a stranger-bride within patrilocal societies, who enters a household having few affective ties to the household (Ottenheimer 1986, 936). Lower rates of psychiatric morbidity are recorded in cousin marriages than in any other forms of marriage in Jordan, for instance (Daradkeh et al. 2006). This may reflect these dynamics. Fricke et al. (1986) find that women married to cousins tend to be older at the age of marriage than those married for bride-wealth. Fricke et al. hypothesize that this is due to the regime of agnatic surveillance: cousins, being part of that regime, do not need a child-bride to guarantee themselves of her virginity and pliability, as they can remain confident in their collective contribution to policing her behavior, and they have an intimate knowledge of the parental order under which she has been socialized.

Despite such advantages, such marriages may be difficult to exit in the case of violence or incompatibility. In all cases where marriages are arranged by a collective, divorce has wider effects on more persons than the marital dyad and their children. Where the couple is already related, however, this can lead to dangerous schisms between close relatives, which are deeply hazardous to group cohesion. Thus lower divorce rates in some forms of cousin marriage (Afzal et al. 1994), rather than indicating that such marriages are more satisfactory for the couples, may reflect that the social costs of divorce are higher.

A Moroccan proverb states that "He who marries the daughter of his father's brother is like him who celebrates his feasts with a sheep from his own flock" (Webster 1982, 180). Women married to cousins have the explicit purpose of consolidating and reproducing the patriline. There are strong expectations within every society for a person to identify potential sexual partners within a particular category, whether this be class, caste, or kin group, with social penalties for those who do not comply. To explicitly prefer another person outside the permitted categories for sexual expression can be conceptualized as an act of sexual deviance.

Barth found that murders of Kurdish women and girls who refused their cousins were "not infrequent" (1953, 28). And to some degree, such murders have persisted to a more recent period. In *A Voice from Kurdistan*[8] Rauf and Mohammedi record the following:

- On 23rd August 1994, Shadieh Hassan Rasool Tayraheh was shot dead by her cousin in the city of Erbil, because she refused to marry him.
- Chinar Abdulkhaliq was immolated by her cousin in Makhmoor district because she refused to marry him.
- In early June 1997, Chiman Ali Mineh Soor was stoned to death by the men of her tribe, in Ismaeel Abad, a village near the Shelair district. She refused to marry her cousin and was accused of having had a sexual relationship with a man.

Such violence indicates a sense of male and collective ownership of cousins. Such collective violence can also be seen in the most notorious case of a collective murder within recent Kurdish history, the stoning of Du'a Khalil Aswad in 2007. Du'a was a member of the minority Yezidi religion, under which women do not have inheritance rights; nevertheless, PPC marriage is practiced within this group (Allison 2001, 137). Du'a eloped with a young Muslim man and requested protection from his family. They were reluctant to shelter her due to the dangers of exacerbating long-running tensions between the Yezidi and Muslim communities. Islamist propaganda had long portrayed the Yezidi as infidels and devil-worshippers, leading in turn to reactive and defensive organization among Yezidi males, and a proliferation of intercommunity hostility. Without the support of her lover and his family, Du'a appealed to state and religious authorities for protection, but these handed her back to her killers.

The stoning was instigated by the paternal uncle, carried out by cousins, and observed by the male population of the village, who recorded and distributed the event on their mobile phones, leading to enormous media attention and local and international abhorrence. In this situation the assumed rights of cousins as prospective suitors overweighed the potency of the nominal *paterfamilias* to determine his daughter's fate, and were accepted as such by the observers, and by the security forces who observed the murder without intervention (Al-Lami et al., 2012).

Thus honor is similar to PPC marriage in terms of the pattern of distribution of presumed rights over the body of a woman to a family collective. Meeker (1976) notes that there is a distinction between those societies where a husband is permitted to kill for honor and those where the responsibility remains with the victim's agnates (see also Tapper 1991, 16). The latter appears to be the case in these scenarios described here (see also Payton 2014). This occurs, insists Meeker, within societies in which endogamy prevails. Cousins, singly and collectively, as presumed potential future spouses, hold a right over a woman's body even before marriage. This right of access feeds into a motivation to control, monitor, and discipline; to assume the attitude of a jealous and custodial husband in advance of marriage. Thus, if a woman is suspected of embarking into a premarital relationship it may be perceived akin to an adulterous act against a *group* of men whose expectations are that she will ultimately be married to one of their number, and a failure of family obligations by her father and brothers.

Through the institution of cousin marriage, a presumptive allocation of rights of access to a woman's body and responsibility for her behavior derive from the moment of her birth onto a collective of related males, which is able both to form a surveillance network and to discipline noncompliance. The normative expectation of cousin marriage creates a basis for the collective and familial control of women by their cousins, aunts, uncles, and other patrilineal relations, whose interest in safeguarding her virtue is not merely deployed in the service of collective family reputation but also in an individuated and possessive interest in her as a potential bride.

I Am Her Shadow

Aveen Ali, 14, was only four years old when she entered into an exchange marriage. "Out of ten girls in my extended family, six other girls and I were married as kids," she said. One of her uncles had fallen in love with a woman and had asked for her hand, but the woman's family had requested a girl in return. Aveen . . . along with three of her cousins was exchanged for her uncle's bride.

"My father and my uncles didn't regard us as human beings. We were sacrificed for their love," she said.

–Mohammad 2007

Jin be jine, literally meaning "a woman for a woman," is a form of marriage in which one girl is directly exchanged for another, which has been long recorded among Kurds in Iraq (Barth 1953; Dzięgel 1982; Hansen 1961; Leach 1940; Taysi 2009). It is also recorded in the first written history of the Kurdish peoples, the *Sharafnâma* (Bitlîsî 1597/2005, 21, verse 43). Direct-exchange marriage is described by Kurds in Turkey as *berdel*; by Afghans as *badal* (Kargar 2011), *makhtiar* (Tapper 1981), or *alish* (Tapper 1991, 149); and by Pakistanis as *watta-satta* (Jacoby and Mansuri 2007).

Marriage by direct exchange is rare on a global scale (Schlegel and Eloui 1988, 294). It is primarily associated with societies characterized by a horticultural means of production, lower levels of economic complexity, and little accumulation of property (296). Such marriages are often considered the lowest-status form of legitimate marriage (Dzięgel 1982, 258; Ertem and Kocturk 2008; Fricke et al. 1986, 494; Jacoby and Mansuri 2007).

Jin be jine allows cash-poor communities and families to build exogamous alliances without raising bride-price. They create a quadrangular relationship that links the destinies of four persons and duplicates the connection between the respective patrilines. The categories of exogamy and endogamy effectively become unified. A project to register the prevalence of *jin be jine* marriage within the KRI in support of a campaign by Kurdish MP Sara Faqe, which resulted in 5% of the female population of the Pshdar region coming forward to declare their marriages as being conducted by exchange (Mohammad 2007). The response to Faqe's project suggests a wider prevalence in practice, where many of those married in this fashion were likely to be unaware of the initiative, unable or unwilling to come forward, or nonsupportive of her abolitionist stance. In Turkey, Ilkkaracan (2001) also found that one in twenty of her sample population in the Kurdish-dominated region was married via *berdel*. Kudat et al. (2000) found 17% of marriages of this type in villages on the Şanliurfa-Hurran plains of northeastern Turkey. In the town of Karacadağ, over 95% of marriages are reported to take the form of direct exchange (Esmer 2010).

Direct-exchange forms of marriage may benefit families with several daughters. Abdullah Ahmed, a Kurdish man from Pshdar with one brother and seven sisters, divorced three wives upon reaching maturity and deciding on a love marriage. Each had been contracted to him in exchange for one of his sisters by his father during his childhood (Mohammad 2007). The elder generation may also use exchange forms of marriage to accrue additional wives for themselves rather than their sons, trading their daughters and nieces for wives for themselves (Esmer 2010). For Sorani-speaking Kurds, the term *gewre be biçûk*[9] may also be used to denote *jin be jine* where there is a generational gap (Hassanpour 2001)—where one or more young girls are exchanged for an adult woman. "A visitor would give us one of his daughters for two children," stated Mula Ahmed, an elderly villager from Rania, KRI (Johnstone 2009).

Alike in Dignity

Berdel marriages require an absolute symmetry: from an equal number of attendees from each family to identical gifts of jewelry to the bride or furniture to the marital home (Esmer 2010). Some ceremonies have taken place across a bridge over which brides cross simultaneously from opposite ends (Ersen 2002). Marriages, like many collective ceremonies, function as displays of social status: in direct-exchange ceremonies, displays of social and cultural capital are carefully calibrated to give an appearance of parity. Ersen witnessed a marriage ceremony that almost ended in violent acrimony due to one family's perception that the other had exceeded their allowance of guests. "Balanced [marital] exchanges," says Collier (1988, 103), "establish a dyadic relationship in which the exchangers are equal," (or, at the very least, must *appear* to be equal).

Sahlins (1974) outlines a schema of the political economies of nonstate societies based on spheres of reciprocity: the household stands as a central unit in which members are expected to participate for the benefit of the collective as a whole, where the goods and services are considered to be communal ("generalized reciprocity"); but each degree of removal from the household increases the tension around any form of transaction. The differing nature of the transactions connected with each different form of marriage is related to their relative distance from the household. Cousin marriage, operating at the smallest possible degree of removal from the household is the "safest" form, in being the closest to generalized reciprocity, occasioning little in the way of financial recompense. Outside the village or tribe in-groups, in the zone of "negative reciprocity," transactions and negotiations are likely to be characterized by asymmetry. *Jin be jine*, which tends to take place at the level of the village and tribe, falls in an intermediate position between these two forms, striving for the delicate equilibrium of "balanced reciprocity." Transactions that occur within the village/tribe but outside the direct lineage, for Sahlins, are marked by anxiety, where parity in all dealings must be made explicit, at the risk of producing resentment that could endanger the collective life of the community.

The requirement of absolute reciprocity in direct-exchange marriage demands that both couples divorce in the event of one marital breakdown. Ahmet Börek, a young Kurdish man happily married through *berdel* in Turkey, explains that "the brother is his sister's shadow," and that he would not hesitate to break up his own marriage if his sister's failed. The only alternative available for Ahmet and his wife in this instance would be the potential payment of brideprice, changing the form of the marital transaction.

Marital issues arising in these paired couples can, according to journalist Sebnem Eras, lead to violent tribal and interfamilial clashes (Das 2010). Alinia (2013, 121) recounts the effects of one direct-exchange marriage deal that went sour. The negative impacts of these disproportionately fall on the bride due to the patricentric ordering of Kurdish society. HK was married through direct exchange at 13 years of age; however, "HK's husband's family refused to give their daughter to HK's brother. . . . HK's marriage was dissolved, and she was sent back to her family. Her husband's family kept her baby, who was five months old."

Jacoby and Mansuri (2007) propose that similar exchange marriages in Pakistan operate to reduce the mistreatment of brides, pointing to lower levels of estrangement, violence, and depression in *watta-satta* marriage. They explain *watta-satta* as a suboptimal solution for the widespread nature of domestic violence against women in Pakistan, suggesting that a man may feel restrained from beating his wife if he knows that by so doing his sister may be beaten in reprisal. This "argument from deterrence" neglects the distasteful corollary that implies that a man, upon learning his sister has been beaten, appears to be obliged to reciprocate this violence upon the body of his wife, rather than through a direct intervention to the abuser. So while such relational mirroring may encourage restraint, it also has a clear capacity to lead to escalation, where women may become hostages to proliferating male rivalry expressed through violence enacted on their own bodies. That such a stratagem is, at least according to Jacoby and Mansuri, more effective than otherwise, suggests that men may have closer affective ties to their sisters than to their wives.

The *berdel* commitment between families extends beyond the life of the woman, where a widower may take his widow's sister through sororate, or request that his widow's natal family pays half the bride-price required to replace her (Das 2010). This indicates that maintaining the alliance formed by a direct-exchange marriage is the most crucial aspect for the life of the community. In this sense, if direct exchange forms *do* form a disincentive for spousal violence, this appears more likely to be an epiphenomenon than a motivation for the adoption of the form. The mirroring of the relationship is more likely to express a requirement for marital *permanence* than marital accord.

A related form of child marriage is the phenomenon of badal khueen: "It is very common for a girl to be given away in marriage in payment of blood money. Thus if £90 is owing, the price of the blood of one man, the debt might be paid by the delivery of one girl, three cows and a donkey" (Leach 1940, 56).

Badal khueen, literally meaning blood substitute[10] or *jin be xwên* (woman-for-blood), is the distinct form of exchange marriage mentioned in the *Sharaf-nâma*, where it is described as a means of averting blood feuds and vendetta killings, often brokered by arbitrators attempting to mediate tribal disputes. Women married under *badal khueen* may not divorce and are required to sever any contact with their natal family. Such "compensation" marriages are practiced in current times in Pakistan and Afghanistan under the names of *swara* or *vani*. The young bride—who may well be a child for whom no other arrangement has yet been made—may be mistreated by the family in reprisal for the initial killing of their kinsman (Kargar 2011, 67–83; Minallah 2004). In 2005, Bird interviewed a Kurdish *agha* who was involved in dispute mediation still deploying *badal khueen* as a means of building family reconciliation in the aftermath of murders, and disputes over honor and land, in order to avoid blood feuds. "Sometimes I resolve two or three killings a month, sometimes only one a year. The people come to me, and I try to reconcile their two families, with offers of money, or women, or land" (Bird 2005, 234).

Bird observed that it is the poor, unable to raise blood money, who are most likely to marry off their daughters in such forms of reconciliation.

It Is Better to Live on Bread and Water Than Under an Obligation[11]

Taysi assumes a causal relationship between direct-exchange forms of marriage and honor-based violence (2009, 40). Certainly these frequently co-occur in areas like Sindh in Pakistan, Pshdar in the KRI, northeastern Turkey, and rural Afghanistan. However, there are many other commonalities among the varied societies where direct-exchange marriages occur (Schlegel and Eloui 1988), so other factors should be considered.

Sev'er (2005), for instance, commenting on the premeditated honor killing of Semse, identifies the victim as having been married in a direct-exchange format, observing that if one of the brides in the pairing "is unacceptable—not a virgin, the other family may retroactively insist on bride-price. In such cases, either family may consider killing the woman who spoiled the deal." Concerns about spoiling the deal are very pertinent to the practice. In Guizh, a mountain village in Rania, KRI, a young woman immolated herself[12] rather than enter an exchange marriage that had been arranged for her. Her mother told a reporter from Al Jazeera: "I said to my daughter you will bring us shame if you don't marry. Now I wish I had accepted her decision. We have to stop the mullahs and the villagers from doing this" (Johnstone 2009).

Here the daughter's shame is not related to any sense of sexual misbehavior, but through rendering the family unable to fulfill an obligation. The potential for dishonor, in this sense, lies not "between a woman's legs," in Mernissi's pungent phrase (1985), but between the pages of an unbalanced ledger: in a failure to conform to the political and economic norms of communal reciprocity.

Guizh villagers, galvanized by the tragedy, told Al Jazeera's reporter they sought to reject the custom of *jin be jine*. This required the "renegotiation of contracts" (Johnstone 2009a). Not all Guizh males and families could be expected to show the liberality with which Abdullah Ahmed released his three brides in Pshdar; they might instead demand alternative forms of compensation in terms of cash or goods that the families of their promised brides might be unable to muster. The concern for a status parity and reciprocity, which is intrinsic to direct-exchange forms of marriage, suggests structural tensions between patrilines.

As McDowall (1996) observes, "In Kurdish society, like others dependent upon strong blood ties, a quarrel between two people is almost a contradiction in terms. No relatives of someone in a dispute can easily stand apart since they are required to take their relative's side. Thus all disputes take on a dangerous factional quality" (9).

In such an antagonistic scenario, marked by transient loyalties, cross-familial alliances are necessary for self-defense and internal harmony—but are ultimately fragile in nature. "Our families did not marry them, but we did not fight each other," remarked Yezidi agronomist Akim Saringovitch Farizian in 1996, speaking of neighboring Muslim villages (Meiselas 1997, 35). This suggests that these two distinct categories—the people with whom one intermarries and the people with whom one fights—have a diametrical relationship. Tellingly, the Pashtun Durrani have defined themselves as "one people among whom women are exchanged" (Tapper 1981, 392). While the Yezidi eschew intermarriage with Muslims in order to shore up their internal solidarity and consolidate and protect their minority religious identity, this may leave them vulnerable to attacks from the more populous Muslim Kurds, since there are no marital alliances to bridge the communities and provide routes for mediation.

Exogamous marriage alliances may represent an attempt to recruit the other family as allies, or to neutralize any potential threat they represent, through recruiting them into kinship relations: a maneuver that is made particularly explicit in the practice of *badal khueen*. The delicate concern with status matching during marriage ceremonies bespeaks caution, forming an explicit display that both sides are entering into a mutual alliance in good faith.

However, status matching during marriage negotiations allays the volatile nature of interfamilial relations only to a certain degree. One gold bracelet may have an equal weight to another, but the primary axis of exchange—one woman for another, exchanging one family for another—can never be made on a basis of equilibrium. No two women, men, or families are identical.

Sacks (1982, 224–225) finds there are integral contradictions between the roles of sister and wife in lineage-oriented societies: "[a] wife's subordinate relationship to her husband and his lineage was ideologically in sharp contrast to the sisterly equality in her own." It is in the families' interests to groom the departing bride in the image of her shadow, as Joseph's observations (1999) suggest, as the reflection of the docile reproducer of the patriline that they wish to recruit to their number. This also serves as a method of smoothing the transition from sisterly equality in the natal household to the deference appropriate to a wife and daughter-in-law within the marital household. As a form of symbolic capital as well as a social norm, *namûs* represents an available personal attribute, which, unlike attractiveness, personality, or character, can be rendered into some level of uniformity. This inculcates a strong motivation for a family to police their kinswomen so that they are less likely to occasion challenges to the parallel relationship through any questions over their honor, which would void the alliance and create antagonistic relations.

Unlike endogamous marriage, where the incoming bride largely shares the background of her spouse, direct-exchange marriage locates a newlywed within an alien family and with an unknown spouse, whose norms of behavior and expectations may be different from those of her own household. As a normative standard for wifehood, *namûs* operates to resolve these uncertainties.

Young women are hostages not merely to the relationship of their brother but also to political disputes between patrilines due to their liminal role in both families; either divorcing, or occasioning divorce through a perceived failure to conform to the expectations of marriage (framed through conformity to the expectations of *namûs*) will jettison the social capital gained through the alliances.

The shadow relationship of *jin be jine* links individuals and families to the wider political economy of marriage in a very direct sense; through deploying marriages within a geographically delimited community women become conduits, in Rubin's (1975) sense, of strategic relations between families. This position is pertinent to the family's social standing, but it places them in a position of vulnerability through requiring them to maintain alliances—both through their own marriage and through that of their "shadow."

Bride-Price

My mother . . . was fourteen years old when someone came from my village and told my father about her. . . . My father went to get her and brought some jewels. Her family accepted him, he, of course, paid something, and so she left with him. Still today families make the negotiations and still must pay.

–Kurdish *agha*, interviewed in 1996 (in Meiselas 1997, 36)

Bride-wealth, as referred to in the quote above, tends to occur in societies where corporate unilineal descent groups predominate. It is frequently associated with exogamous marriage. In cousin endogamy, payments are often small or fictive. Direct-exchange marriages, as described above, tend to occur within a framework of village-level endogamy and involve delicate status matching. Both of these forms are, indeed, frequently rationalized as a method of evading more financially demanding marital prestations.

Substantial bride-wealth payments frequently co-occur with exogamy, which involves the displacement of a girl or woman from her agnates. This may also be a chance to display status, since exogamous marriage is considered a prestigious form for wife-takers (Yalçın-Heckman 1991, 236).

While the most common marital prestations occurring within the organization of marriage—bride-wealth and dowry—operate in opposite directions, these are not mirror images of each other. The recipient of the prestation is different in each case. Dowries function as premortem inheritance and can be used as start-up capital for a new household. They can be an act of parental investment by the bride's parents into the household, which supports the well-being of the couple and their future grandchildren. They may also form a method of buying status through hypergamous marriages, where the bride comes from a lower socioeconomic stratum or caste than the groom, ensuring social mobility for her children. This is a method of enabling cross-generational social mobility (Nasrin 2011).

Under Islam, marriages require the payment of *mehr*, considerations that accrue directly to the bride and can be considered as a form of bride-wealth (Bell 1998). The amount of *mehr* is specified on state-issued Iraqi marriage certificates. *Mehr* can be described as a form of indirect dowry or "morning gift," with precedents in Judaic and Zoroastrian practice. In common with the rabbinic *mohar* (Satlow 2001, 214) established by Shimon ben Shathach (ca. 120–40 BCE), *mehr* is often at least partially promissory, serving as a divorce settlement where wives have no claim to their husband's property in the event of male-initiated marital dissolution. This aspect of *mehr* is intended to prevent men from recklessly divorcing their wives and also provides financial support for widowed and divorced women between marriages.[13]

Busby (1994) describes gifts to brides among the Kurds in the mid-1990s:

> The cost to the groom's family is substantial. The amount varies depending on the social and financial status of the families involved. Between poor families the groom's family will be expected to buy a complete set of clothes, including shoes, and perhaps a dresser. They must also provide at least one each of the following items of gold: a bracelet or watch, a ring, a neckchain, a pair of earrings, and a gold coin to be hung from the chain. . . . If the families are wealthy, more gold is required. The number of rings, earrings and bracelets, lengths of chain and number of coins are all stipulated and may cost several thousand dollars. (10–11)

For one recent Kurdish groom, these demands amounted to some $12,700 (Rûdaw 2013). This can be an opportunity for families to make conspicuous displays of wealth. Such gold and jewelry become the possession of the wife, forming a pragmatic method of preserving capital and achieving financial security in an environment where economic services are underdeveloped and the currency has historically been vulnerable to hyperinflation and collapse.

The main focus of this section, however, will relate to marital payments that enrich the patriline, rather than those which are directed to the bride. These payments to the bride's patriline are referred to as *naqd* in Arabic, or *şîrbayî* (milk-price) or *xönbayî* (blood-price) in Kurdish (Hassanpour 2001). This type of payment to the family of a bride will be referred to as bride-price in order to position it as a subcategory of bride-wealth, in contradistinction to *mehr*. As these are frequently simultaneously negotiated, they may in practice be some-what muddied categories.

Either form of dowry is an intergenerational transmission, whereas bride-price is retained within the elder generation. Where dowry or bride-price is nego-tiated by elders, this cements gerontocratic control. For instance, couples who seek to marry can be prevented from doing so if the father of the would-be bride insists on receiving a bride-price beyond the capacities of the prospective groom. Bride-price is common in Africa, yet rare in Eurasia, which has tended toward dowry across its history, particularly in European regions.

I now examine the conditions under which a system of bride-price may develop.

Warfare, Polygyny, and the "Girl Subsidy"

Fortunato's (2011) linguistic phylogenesis of Indo-European languages developing from Ancient Hittite suggests that dowry predates bride-price across Eurasia. She finds that the language of bride-price was a later adoption by collectives speaking languages derived from the Indo-Iranian family (which includes Kurd-ish), and that some of these societies have oscillated between dowry and bride-price up to a maximum of four times. For Fortunato, the key variable associated with bride-price across this deep history is *polygyny*—a proposition that is sup-ported by other scholars (Atkinson and Lee 1984; Ember et al. 2007; Grossbard 1978; Patterson 2012). Fortunato (2015) identifies polygyny as the default marriage system, in that it is the most widely expressed across historical and geographical contexts.

Within the KRI, Barth found a level of 4% polygyny across ninety-four men in four villages in the 1950s (1953, 29). Bois (1966) suggests that polygyny was com-mon before the time of his own investigations of Kurdish regions, especially among tribal leaders making political alliances, but estimated a contemporary level of around 2%, suggesting a low and declining level of polygyny.[14] Middle Eastern patterns of polygyny tend to show a fairly low incidence in contradis-tinction to the high levels found in Africa. This suggests a scenario where polyg-yny is the privilege of a small elite. McDowall (1996, 10) identifies that the larger social networks, and hence greater power, of an *agha* related to a history of polyg-ynous marriage within his lineage, which increased his reach. This was unavail-able to male villagers and tenants, who could be subjected to feudal control over their marital choices.

Patterson's (2012) analysis of the Standard Cross-Cultural Sample also shows a significant relationship between bride-price and slavery, finding that half of all societies with bride-price hold slaves, and the presence of bride-price triples the odds of finding institutional slavery. If slavery, bride-price, and polygyny appear to cluster within societies, this may indicate an exterior determinant.

For several writers, this determinant is warfare (Divale and Harris 1976; Ember et al. 2007; White and Burton 1988).

A cross-cultural correlation of warfare with polygyny and polygyny with bride-price has a certain logic: a polygynous society is one that establishes male/male competition for women, who become the rewards for male assertiveness and financial or military success. This can occur either through the high status of the most aggressive males, easily able to acquire brides within their own community, or through the rape and enslavement of captive women. Competition for in-group women may become intense in this scenario, where the most successful males monopolize the reproductive capacity of the collective (Betzig 2012), with particular crises likely when there are fewer captives available, in times of either peace or defeat. This competition would tend to wreck communal solidarity if expressed through violent contestations between men of the in-group. Monetization of this competition, therefore, can express competition within forms that are less likely to lead to physical injuries and the depletion of the military/defensive strength of the community.

Polygyny thus both stratifies men into those wealthy enough to be able to afford more than one wife and those who have no licit means to achieve reproductive relations. Polygyny may benefit some women, particularly senior wives, who are able to pass on the most arduous aspects of household labor to their subordinate juniors, and the mothers of sons. But for junior wives, mothers of daughters, and the children of polygynous marriages, polygyny has numerous and severe hazards (for a summary, see iMAPP 2011).

Societies where males make war to plunder and to enslave female captives are able to replace all of the physical functions of wives with slaves. The sex ratio is in a constant state of disequilibrium due to warfare; defeat may lead to a high level of male death, and victory to an influx of female captives. Where a surplus of females exists, there is a rationale for polygyny, especially within pro-natalist societies that locate women's value in bearing children. Such warlike orientations may also increase son preference, since physical strength is valued for combat while female reproductive capacities run the risk of being co-opted by the enemy.

As Miller finds in a comparative study of Pakistan and Bangladesh (1984), the existence of bride-price can make an economic case for raising daughters within patrilineal societies with a preference for sons: bride-price may effectively form a subsidy encouraging families to raise daughters despite sons being identified as more likely to increase a family's status and well-being. Thus a societal adaptation to bride-price would appear to be adaptive in increasing the reproductive potential of any warlike, polygynous group. Polygyny intersects with son preference, where one of the most common justifications for taking a second wife is the failure of the first to provide a male heir to continue the patriline.

However, the continuance of bride-price in periods where polygyny is a marginal practice remains to be explained.

Worthy of Her Hire

Cultural understandings of how men acquire wives, by structuring the contexts in which some people work for others, also structure the conversations in which people develop culturally acceptable justifications for appropriating the labors of others.

–Collier 1988 (232–233)

In Goody and Tambiah (1973) and Schlegel and Eloui's (1988) explication of modes of marital transaction, direct-exchange and bride-price marriages are described as occurring where women's labor value is particularly significant. They relate the geographical distribution of bride-price and dowry with the dominant technology of production of their time. According to this theory, in sub-Saharan Africa marriage is arranged by bride-price where women are hoe cultivators; in Eurasia marriages are predominantly arranged by dowry where the gendered division of labor is starker, and plow-based male labor is the main form of subsistence. The marriages of African women require bride-price because they participate in subsistence farming, in this analysis; the marriages of European women require dowries because they do not.

At first glance, the evidence in the Kurdish case would appear to bear the asset-value argument out: Bois (1966) well illustrates the industriousness of rural Kurdish agricultural women of his period, whose domestic labors occupy their entire day, from bread making in the early morning to cooking the final meal of the day late at night. Female pastoralists are similarly tireless. Laizer (1991, 10–11) recounts staying in a pastoral encampment during winter, where the men, unable to graze their animals due to snowfall, sipped sweet tea and chatted all day, while the women of the household cooked, cleaned, milled grain, baked bread, churned butter, milked, and cared for hens, geese, goats, sheep, and other larger animals. Johnson (1940), states that Kurdish women of the time were, in fact, responsible for *all* productive labor among transhumant tribes: men slept all day and spent their nights conducting intertribal raids.

For Johnson, the labor value of women was a primary consideration within marriage: "[T]he beauty of a young girl taken in marriage is a secondary consideration in determining her price. . . . Her value will depend upon her utility—her physical strength for manual labor, and her ability to make carpets, rugs, clothes and other things" (54).

Leyla Zana, a Kurdish politician born in 1961 in Turkey, described women's labor in an interview in 1991: "My father slept from the morning through to the evening when he would wake, eat, and go out to see his friends and chat with them. Meanwhile, my mother spent the whole day working, taking care of the animals. . . . [S]he returned home in the evening to prepare food and take care of her family. . . . He believed she should do everything he wanted, just like a slave" (in Tax 2016, 73).

However, it is not clear that such women can be considered any more industrious than other peasant women in similar environments, with similar modes of subsistence: there is little reason to assume that the Sarakastani pastoralist women in Greece described by Campbell (1964) or the Sicilian agricultural women described by Schneider and Schneider (1976, 90) were any less hard working than the Kurdish women described above. Such an either-or model also fails to fit the evidence for the simultaneous coexistence of bride-price transactions within 75% of the societies practicing dowry/indirect dowry (Nunn 2005). Therefore, to see such a distinction in terms of positioning women as an asset-value has numerous problems.

First, it ignores the possibility that such differences may merely be regional, an argument that has statistical support (Burton 1981). Secondly, it conflates various experiences, and various women, as if they were part of the same "market" with the same internal values. Women, and women's labor, may have different kinds of values attributed to them within different societies. In highly pronatalist societies, women may be expected to produce numerous offspring rather than take a major role in primary production, and therefore their ability to contribute labor is less valuable to their affines than their potential fertility. In societies where women are less valued for fertility (indicated by phenomena such as high levels of infanticide, postpartum taboos on sex, etc.), other characteristics, such as practical skills, appearance, or social status, may become more salient indicators of a woman's potential value to her husband and affines.

Bell comments that "in order for dowry to imply a low valuation of women, it must be the case that their parents have attempted to find the highest positive prices for them—actively seeking brideprice—only to find that the highest prices are negative. However, we know that the payment of dowry does not imply the inability to sell the bride for a prestige price. On the contrary, the giving of dowry becomes a prestige practice, not the unfortunate consequence of having a worthless daughter. Dowry and brideprice are not different points on the same scale; they correspond to entirely different institutions" (1998, 206).

The weakest point in the labor-value position on bride-price, I would argue, is the assumption that remuneration for labor, whether direct or indirect, has any straightforward connection to the value of that labor. As Hartsock (1985) identifies, there is a tendency for scholars to use exchange theories assuming that interactions express voluntary exchanges between equals. This neglects the imbalances of power and authority, overstating the voluntarism of any individual's engagement in political and economic relations within their milieu. Importantly, within gender-complementarian societies, neither marriage, nor the various forms of labor required within a marriage, could be considered voluntary (Jaggar 1983, 117). Due to the gendered division of labor and the taboos on premarital sex and illegitimacy, marriage is an essential rite of passage into adulthood, sexual maturity, and parentage for both men and women. Where the gendered division of labor is intense and fiercely policed, each individual man or woman needs a heterosexual counterpart, whatever his or her contribution to production may be, due to the interdependencies introduced by gendered divisions. An adult man who refuses to perform tasks such as laundry or cleaning because they are perceived as emasculating (see White 1999, 38), has an impetus to marry because otherwise he will remain a source of labor to his mother and sisters; an adult woman who is unable to own or rent her own home due to the community's customs must marry, take to the streets, or remain in her childhood home at the sufferance of her father and brothers.

Such an entwinement of social, familial, and economic interdependences means there is little choice in the matter for the individual. Furthermore, either in the capitalist mode or within the combined unit of production and consumption that is the traditional household, it is problematic to assume that the market delivers an accurate reflection of the value of labor, particularly, one might argue, for the labor value of women. Delphy and Leonard's (1992) identification of the persistent cultural devaluation of domestic and secondary processing labor performed by women and girls suggests that there may be widespread misrecognition of the female contribution to subsistence.

Just Recompense

Several writers have presented bride-price as a form of refund for expended resources: as recompense to the bride-giving family for the resources expended in raising her to marital age (as is suggested in the use of the term şîrbayî, meaning milk-price). This would not explain cases where bride-price is absent, minimal, or fictive, as in the forms found earlier in this chapter. A daughter does not consume less of a household's resources if she is married endogamously. Moreover, a resource-refund argument would suggest that the bride-price of a spinster in midlife should be higher than that of a nubile teenager, a position for which there is little supporting evidence and a great deal to the contrary (Borgerhoff Mulder 1988; Rassam 1980, 174).

Barth suggests that for Kurds (1954, 167) bride-price is a form of compensation for eschewing cousin marriage and the patrilineal solidarity that this produces. Yet cousin marriage is far from an iron rule, particularly among nontribal populations. It is difficult to establish whether patterns of bride-price and cousin marriage intersect in ways that could indicate a specific connection between the two forms of marriage: certainly, bride-price is globally a far wider phenomenon than cousin marriage. Barth's explanation thus appears rather unilinear in positing a direct relationship between two opposing poles of marriage, when marriage practices have been shown to have several varying and flexible configurations. Further, sourcing explanations for the purpose of bride-price in emic accounts can be problematic due to the vested self-interest involved around discussions of marital transactions.

Alternatively, bride-price payments could be considered in terms of paying for the transfer of certain specified "rights" over a relative. This assumes that parents have the right to command and transfer these rights, irrespective of their children's volition. As Moghadam (2004, 171) says, rights over a woman's products, be they rugs or offspring, are considered to belong to their male kin and are theirs to exploit or transfer. Marital rights over women that are accrued through marriage may be arranged in separate "packages" concisely summarized by Caplan (1984, 31), which may, or may not, include the following:

Jus in rem: Rights over her as an object

Jus in personam: Rights over her labor

Jus in uxorem: Right to identify her as his wife

Jus in genetricem: Right to assume paternity of her children

Bride-price was one of the practices compared to slavery in the *UN 1956 Convention on the Abolition of Slavery, the Slave Trade and Institutions and Practices Similar to Slavery*. From Wollstonecraft (2002/1759) and Mill (1869) to Pateman (1988) and Ali (2010), feminists have scrutinized the peculiar nature of the marriage contract through making comparisons between wifehood and indentured servitude and slavery. The practice of bride-price, if seen as payment for a woman's body and the right to exploit her labor and reproductive capacity, seems to concretize these arguments through removing the final distinction between the categories. However, bride-price need not position women as outright chattels since those rights over her labor, body, and children that are transmitted by marriage are not necessarily held in perpetuity by the affinal collective, nor are they transferable beyond it.

A heated anthropological debate in the late 1920s and early 1930s concluded that bride-price cannot be considered the outright purchase of a woman, as even wives in the most unfavorable of conditions differed from slaves in at least one respect: that married women cannot be further alienated from their natal families than they already are. Only the natal family has the authority to marry off a woman, and this right is rarely transferred by marriage.[15] The distinction between wife and slave can be very fine indeed; the difference rests rather less in the rights extended to any individual woman than in the rights that are retained by her natal family. Within Islamic law a clear and important distinction is that women maintain ownership of their own property after marriage and their own legal identities, a right that British women, for instance, did not achieve until the passing of the Married Women's Property Act of 1870.

Muslim women could themselves own slaves, although they could not, Ali (2010) notes, make sexual use of their slaves, a liberty that was reserved for Muslim men, due to Islamic concerns about patrilineal paternity. In a horrifying example of this, within the Islamic State, jihadists deployed religious justifications for the organized trade in the bodies of Yezidi women: according to their English language magazine *Dabiq*, "'One fifth of the slaves were transferred to the Islamic State's authority to be divided as khums,' a tax on war spoils, and the rest were divided among the fighters who participated in the Sinjar operation" (Semple 2014).

While there has been a great deal of resistance from anthropologists against describing marriage by bride-price in terms of commerce, this does not mean such exchanges can be considered merely symbolic or ceremonial. Bride-price can be the subject of negotiation, even delicate haggling. Its social function goes far beyond the symbolic representation of an act of transference. According to Van Bruinessen (2000), Kurdish bride-price payments tend to be high rather than tokenistic or symbolic. Their negotiation involves "considerable, subtle diplomacy" (Barth 1953, 26) in calculating the "actual economic value of a woman" (28). Bride-price may, then, become a crucial source of income: catastrophically, in times of financial crisis, young brides may be effectively sold to elderly men for money or to repay familial debts (Brenneman 2007, 98), or trafficked into prostitution under the guise of marriage (Minwalla and Portman 2007).

Tapper (1981) thus argues that wedding prestations "cannot be treated as a closed system, nor understood apart from other prestations (including intangibles such as prestige and political support) which are also part of marriage arrangements; nor can all these prestations themselves be understood apart from a detailed economic and political structure of the total society" (390).

Borgerhoff Mulder's (1988) longitudinal examination of bride-price payments among the Kipsigis certainly shows that these are inflected by the demands of the local market. Kressel's (1992) examination of bride-price among the Israeli Bedouin suggests that the level of bride-price negotiated relates to the respective social positions of the suitor, the bride, and their families: "A suitor in a clearly superior position to the bride's group, economically and in political strength (e.g. having a large number of agnates) may pay a low brideprice plus his implicit patronage for her kinsmen. In addition, a solitary immigrant to the community who may be impecunious may get a bride as an 'act of mercy' almost for free; he thereupon becomes affiliated with her group or lineage. On the other hand, an agnatic outsider seeking a bride in the group may have to pay a top price" (125).

Kressel's first example shows that low bride-wealth may correspond with a greater transmission of social capital to the wife-givers; the second example suggests the absorption of an individual into the wife-giving patriline as a client, benefiting from his subsequent loyalty and labor; and the third redresses the lower availability of the social capital within a connection with a son-in-law with roots outside the community who may well take his wife and leave the area. The greater the distance from the natal family, generally the higher the price: close agnates pay less than distant agnates; unrelated neighbors pay more than distant nonrelatives, and noncountrymen pay the highest of all (Kressel 1977, 444).

This suggests that bride-price can clearly be seen to be operating alongside, and compensating for, exchanges in social capital and labor rights between families, wherein both the capacities of the bride and groom, and the respective statuses and affordances of their families and connections, are all subject to valuation.

A Payment about the Honor of the Bride

Exogamous ties formed through marriage would be considered weaker than those between persons with preexisting relationships, yet these supposedly weak ties may be the most valuable (Granovetter 1973), since they extend links of social influence beyond existing parameters, creating diffuse and varied channels of interfamilial connectivity. They create *bridging capital*, in American political scientist Robert Putnam's sense (Leonard 2004). The strong ties of cousin endogamy and the village-level endogamy of direct-exchange marriages consolidate preexisting relationships and build in-group loyalties—they do not establish new patterns of knowledge/resource sharing or patronage from which the contracting families can profit.

It may, for instance, be valuable to a transhumant pastoralist grouping to marry off some of their womenfolk into sedentary populations, which would tend to provide kinship-mediated routes of access to those resources unobtainable through pastoral life. This creates a route to influence that is an alternative to the exploitative power relations historically observed between pastoralists and farmers. In terms of social capital then, exogamous marriages may have a range of potential benefits, but since the distance between the parties is the greatest, there are more likely to be inequalities between the transacting parties. In this instance, the negotiation of bride-price and marriage itself takes place under circumstances that Sahlins (1974) would characterize as "negative reciprocity"—transactions take place within an atmosphere of mutual suspicion, where negotiations must be conducted with the utmost delicacy and must take into consideration the value of the alliance to each family—as well as the personal characteristics of the bride herself. Pamporov (2007, 473), commenting on marriage among the Bulgarian Roma, outlines the following determinants of bride-price:

1. The appearance of the bride
2. Her practical skills
3. The reputation of her family
4. The wealth and property status of both families
5. The level of connectivity between the two families

So the elements of bride-price that relate to the bride as an individual are erotic/reproductive potential and capacity for labor. In terms of social capital, status (described as wealth and property) will increase the value of the bargain. The other determinant related to her family is somewhat obscurely described by Pamporov as reputation. A Kalaydje Rom clarifies this: bride-price, he says, is "a payment about the honor of the bride" (Pamporov 2007, 472).

Chastity then, and the family's reputation in enforcing this, may be considered one of the determinants of bride-price. Exogamy means that the prospective affines will tend to have less knowledge of the household order under which the young bride has been socialized and may fear buying a pig in a poke. "Bad girls go out" according to Ertem and Kocturk's (2008) Kurdish respondents, suggesting that a girl who has garnered an unfavorable reputation within her natal area may be married exogamously to a family unaware of this status.

Negotiations around exogamous marriage may therefore be particularly tense, combining mutual suspicion with a desire to maximize the value of the alliance. In such circumstances, the appearance of conformity to the standards of honor becomes a particularly salient quality, which must be protected from the least doubt. This occurs during a negotiation where the status of both families taking part in the transaction are subject to valuation, and where disagreements may be interpreted as status challenges.

A Mark of Regard

Early ethnographers of Kurdish regions tended to state that women found bride-price flattering, as a mark of status and regard (Hansen 1961). Leach (1940, 120) reports that Kurdish men claim to have paid high fictive bride-prices for their cousin-wives in order to flatter their feminine vanity. It might be noted, however, that bride-price as a mark of status is likely to be relational: a woman is unlikely to consider her bride-price flattering if it is markedly lower than that of her peers.

Later research has found that most women express hostility toward the practice. Of Ilkkaracan's (2001) Turkish and Kurdish respondents, 61% reported an exchange of money from their husband's patriline to their own in order to realize marriage; 78.9% of women were opposed to the practice of bride-price; and in open-ended questions, 56.3% described their opposition as being due to the commodifying nature of being married in return for payment. In research specifically examining bride-price (Hague et al. 2011; Kaye et al. 2000), less than 0.5% of Ugandan women supported the institution, giving reasons similar to those advanced by Ilkkaracan's respondents:

- It posits women as property.
- It leads to child marriage within impoverished families.

- A refusal to refund bride-price by the natal family leaves women trapped within their husband's kin-group in the event of marital disharmony or widowhood.

Women in societies who have experienced a transition from other forms of marriage toward bride-price feel their status to be degraded (Lovett 1997). Ilk-karacan's respondents added that men who pay for brides believe they have gained "all rights over their wives' sexuality and fertility," suggesting that the monetization of the transference of rights implied in marriage is perceived as instantiating a higher level of control over them. Collier (1988, 165) suggests that limiting a woman's ability to leave is the main purpose of bride-price—to oblige families to pay a financial penalty if the bride returns home, which would be her first response in the event of marital dissatisfaction.

Just as *mehr* could be, in part, considered to form a kind of financial deposit discouraging a man from pronouncing a summary divorce, bride-price could be seen as a corollary: a deposit ensuring against a family's acceptance of a married woman's return to the natal home in the event of marital dishar-mony. Thus the societal co-occurrence and simultaneous negotiation of bride-price and indirect dowry identified by Nunn (2005) can be related to a single motivation: preserving marital relationships (and the social capital accrued through those relationships) through financially underwriting risky interfa-milial connections, such as those with members of out-groups: "Wife-taking and wife-giving are essentially and emotionally different matters. Wife-givers are assumed to have superiority just on the basis of giving a wife (people say that it is easy for women to marry but difficult for men to get wives). Giving wives to outsiders is acceptable if the wife-takers are of a higher socio-economic status but not so high as to take advantage of the status difference and deny the wife-givers working affinal relations. . . . because of the assumed superior-ity of wife-givers it is harder for them to press for working affinal relations" (Yalçın-Heckman 1991, 239).

Negotiations that take place in this insecure terrain place tensions across both families. A female Rom told Pamporov, "If the woman[16] who wants my daughter pays me, if she pays more expensive, it is clear that she is going to love my daughter much more and to give much more care. And if one day my daughter makes a mistake, she is not going to turn her out of the house, because she will be sorry for the money paid."

Here she casts bride-price as an expression of genuine interest, which will reduce the chances of her daughter facing the potential for abuse in the patri-centric household. However, if the family's reputation is linked to concepts of honor, in terms of being a reliable producer of women well-socialized to their future roles as brides, then the performance of honor is financially incentivized. A payment "about honor" invests the recipient family in verifying honor: if honor is a precondition of a financial transaction then honor can become the crux upon which such a transaction succeeds or fails.

The affinal collective may be considered to have legitimate grounds for complaint if honor is found to be lacking. This facility is open to abuse, as a case from my professional experience suggests. A young Kurdish woman had been married off by her impoverished father in return for bride-price that was agreed to be paid by installments. Her husband soon ceased payments, and her father pressured him to meet his obligations. However, according to her account, her husband had determined to kill her under the guise of honor—through alleging she had been unfaithful—in order to avoid future payments and to argue for a return of monies already expended. Thus a desire to contest or demand the return of bride-price can incentivize the identification of women as dishonorable. This is not to argue that the payments of bride-price inevitably lead to crimes justified by honor. It does, however, indicate that there is an incentivization for the stringent control of sexuality within a marriage market in which this is considered a necessary precondition for participation.

Bride-price within this context can perhaps be most aptly described. in Ben-Yorath's term (1980, 3), as an "approximation of the ex-ante differences in the expected values of the packages being exchanged," which includes the agreed rights over women's bodies and labor; the value of the association to the contracting families in terms of status, social capital, and resource sharing; and the cultural expectations of conformity to the moral standards of the collective.

At the Point of His Sword

The tale of *Siyamand and Khadje*, as interpreted by Kurdish folklorist Nourredine Zaza (1962), describes an elopement in gripping detail: "And so, on Khadje's wedding day, when she was due to be taken on horseback from her father's home to that of her husband, Siyamand attacked the convoy, which was guarded by seven of her beloved's brothers. At the point of his sword, he took her from her guardians, threw her onto the back of his horse, and, with the speed of a hawk, ascended the inaccessible peaks of Mount Sipan"[17] (36).

Such folk traditions identify a very different kind of relationship than the instrumental uses of marriage implied in the preceding sections of this chapter, bringing not only a rare expression of overt challenge to gerontocratic power but also of discriminating female desire. This romance reproduces, in heroic idiom, a minority practice in Kurdish history.

> Romantic love . . . is a prominent feature of adolescence. . . . A youth and maiden may arrange rare meeting in secret, and exchange gifts, embroidered handkerchiefs, flowers, apples or even rings. . . . Most of these affairs . . . are ended by one or other of the parties being engaged to some

other person. Several young men told of their love for girls in adolescence, and how their parents had ultimately betrothed them to youths they hardly knew or did not particularly desire. . . . [C]ouples on the rarest occasions may elope, taking sanctuary with a chieftain who will arrange their marriage. Almost all, however, defer to the wishes of their parents. (Masters 1953, 265)

Redûkewtin (which literally means "taking the road") is a long-recorded tradition in Kurdish regions by which young lovers can evade the strictures of gerontocratic control. Five percent of Ilkkaracan's (2001) Turkish respondents had eloped or requested their lovers to "abduct" them; Yalçın-Heckman (1991) reports on several cases of elopement/abduction in her study of the Hamawand of Hakkari. Elopement provides a space for individuals with strong individual preferences to buck the normative system of marriage arrangement. *Redûkewtin* inverts the generational power basis of the system of marriage arrangement, through presenting parents with a fait accompli, placing the parents in the position of having no options except assent or refusal.

While some families will take steps to regularize an elopement, often involving postmarital exchanges of bride-price, others may respond with an honor killing in response to the challenge to parental power. In 2007, Jihan eloped with Jaleel Mustafa, a former *peshmerga* who had applied for her hand without success, and became his second wife in a polygynous household. Mustafa attempted to resolve the issue with Jihan's family through a payment of $5,000 and through giving his sister to her family under *badal khueen*. The families appeared to be reconciled; however, in 2010, when Jihan was pregnant with her second child, four of Jihan's relatives invaded her home and shot her twenty times, killing her and her unborn baby, to the confusion of her husband, who had believed the matter had been settled (Bahaddin 2010b). This episode may indicate some of the uncertainties of dealing with a collective, which may have conflicting factions and face different levels of community pressure over time.

Nevertheless, for *redûkewtin* to have continued as a tradition, even as a minority practice or one confined to certain communities or tribes, many families must be more receptive to runaway daughters, and kidnapping sons-in-law, than Jihan's family. The fact that this practice has even been celebrated as part of the Kurdish identity suggests that it may not be as disruptive to social mores as it appears.

There may be reasons for a father to prefer a dynamic abductor to a meeker suitor, not least because he can use the fact of the elopement to press for a higher bride-price (Sweetman 1994, 139). A man's ability to conduct a successful abduction can demonstrate several character traits that are valued in communities that place a high status on masculine self-assertion: physical courage, ingenuity, and an assertive and dynamic response to any challenges to his status—including the refusal of his initial marital advances. Theatrics are not essential: men of the Hamawand (Yalçın-Heckman 1991), preferred to organize a low-key kidnapping in collaboration with relatives and friends, displaying a valuable capacity for generating and mobilizing an alliance network, demonstrating leadership skills and social capital that may impress a potential father-in-law.

Since cousins have preferential access to related women, an abductor is likely to originate from outside the primary family grouping, so if his family is reputable, this presents all the benefits of exogamy in increasing the families' influence network, without requiring the lengthy and delicate political work of alliance negotiation. In recognition of this, Hamawand fathers of preeminent patrilines have been known to hire bodyguards for their unmarried daughters to prevent them from eloping with, or being abducted by, lower-status males seeking to accrue status through hypergamous marriage (Yalçın-Heckman 1991).

Within the tribal past, redûkewtin may have implied seeking the protection and prospective membership of another tribe, where that tribe's leaders would weigh the benefits of adding a reproductive couple to their number against the potential for violent reprisals from the couple's tribe of origin. If rejected by their own families, a couple sheltered by a hospitable tribe or community could forfeit any claims on their respective patrimonies and dissolve all their existing social connections in order to found a new patriline. A modern alternative to seeking assistance from another tribe is to seek it from the state. Yet as the case of Kurdistan Aziz demonstrates, the state may not respond effectively: she eloped at 16 and sought protection from the local police force in the capital city of Erbil. They carried out a virginity examination and, finding her hymen to be intact and "no signs of sodomy," rather than organizing protective measures, they restored her to her tribe, where she was killed (Begikhani et al. 2010, 71).

Mixed Dancing and Abduction

Elopement clearly signifies a site of intergenerational conflict. Within the short-lived (1946–1947), Soviet-sponsored, Kurdish "Republic of Mahabad" in northern Iran, the following notice was promulgated repeatedly by the National Council:

THE ELOPEMENT (REDÛKEWTIN) OF GIRLS AND WOMEN IS PROHIBITED

The Kurdistan National Council rules that any man who forcibly elopes a married woman or [a woman who] has not moved into [the husband's home] will be sentenced to death; if a girl is eloped the man must be killed; but if a man asks for a girl's hand in marriage and he is refused and there is no erî barrier[18] [to their marriage] and [the girl] is unmarried and consenting, there is no punishment, otherwise there will be three months to three years of jail. (Mojab 2001, 83)

As Mojab observes, this ruling, issued with the authority of religious approval, conforms to a patriarchal reading of marriage: depriving a man of his wife, or his potential wife (who may, of course, be a child bride promised to him from the cradle), carries a death penalty. Abduction, on the other hand, carries a jail penalty, which could potentially be rather short, as long as a subsequent marriage is arranged. Mojab notes that this was presented as an Islamification of rural practices that had not previously felt the influences of *shari'a*, sardonically remarking that this respect for Islamic principle did not extend to land reforms that would allow women to claim inheritance of land or property in accordance with the Qur'an. Further, there is no attempt to regulate *jin be jine*, which is specifically condemned in *ahadith*[19] but which does not, like *redûkewtin*, disrupt male/familial control over marriage.

In response to this ruling, Mihammad-Amin Manguri, a member of the Republic's military administration, stated that this was in conflict with the tribal practices of the Bilbas confederacy because it did not allow for "freedom of loving, flirtation, falling in love, mixed dancing and abduction." Manguri felt that the ruling made young people "hermits" and forbade the pleasures of love and denied them the social status of *redûkewtin*—which for him proved both the desirability of Kurdish women and the courage of Kurdish men. The principle of freedom of romantic love was, for Manguri, a defining aspect of the Kurdish national character, a level of liberty unmatched by Europeans or their Arab and Persian neighbors. Manguri's objections thus mark a potential starting point for a trend in Kurdish discourse to locate *redûkewtin* as a vivid countertradition against the otherwise rigid control over marriage and sexuality by families (Morgan 2000; Talabany 2000). Manguri, and the Bilbas collective, appear to be willing to abdicate paternal power for the sake of their children's freedom.

A key paradox remains, however: there were no effective barriers to the Bilbas allowing free association and marriages or other forms of partnering without requiring the performative act of abduction. *Redûkewtin*, then, appears to have a symbolic status: through creating a visible challenge to elder control it simultaneously acknowledges it, paying a tribute to the ideal of parental control through the formulation of the act of defiance. Further, the gendered asymmetry of the actors' roles in any elopement or abduction is more likely to support young men's access to women's bodies than female sexual autonomy, despite the mystifying romance in which the practice is cloaked.

Rape and Forced Marriage

Despite the ability of elopement to express women's agency in convincing a chosen suitor to "abduct" her, one may question how much agency a woman can ultimately demonstrate when thrown across the back of a horse or trapped in the back of a moving car by her abductor and his confederates. Neither the

Mahabad ruling nor Manguri's objections pay much attention to the principle of consent to the act of abduction, but only consent to a subsequent regularizing marriage. While *redûkewtin* may have a different term than bride capture (*jin helgirtin*), in practice there may be slippage between the categories.

In keeping with the private/public polarization of gender roles, women's encouragement of their chosen abductor (if it exists) is covert, whereas the male's abduction is a public performance, a blatant expression of dominion over a woman's body in defiance of parental wishes. Not all women may be complicit in their abductions; parents may indeed have refused an initial request for their daughter's hand due to her own preference on the matter. The difficulty in establishing whether a case is one of a predatory abduction of an unwilling woman or a consensual elopement arranged between lovers rests upon the ever-present ambiguities around women's consent, and the prevalent double standard that holds women responsible for sexual shame: women abducted without their consent were considered to have connived in an elopement and were punished (Yalçın-Heckman 1993); whereas women who voluntarily eloped were sometimes described as having been abducted so parents could avoid admitting to having an insubordinate daughter (Yalçın-Heckman 1991).

Marriage by abduction is currently often associated with Kyrgyzstan (Wilensky-Lanford 2003), where only 34% of women from 504 households stated that their abduction was by mutual consent (Kleinbach et al. 2004). This practice appears to be spreading to Kazakhstan (Werner 2009) and Tajikistan (Ahmadova 2011) in a post-Soviet era of retraditionalization; bride capture has also been recorded in Azerbaijan (Kiryashova 2005) and Georgia (Amnesty International 2006; Duarte 2006), among other locations.

Werner (2009) notes that marriage by abduction is represented as "authentically" Kyrgyz, despite the lack of any scholarly support for widespread prevalence before Sovietization. She notes that through abduction, men profit from the honor/shame complex around virginity (323): once abducted, a woman is considered not to be a virgin and is thereby unmarriageable to any other man but her abductor. The family of the abductor may even make a display of a clean sheet in their window if an abducted woman does not bleed upon penetration, as if women should keep themselves "pure" with their own lovers and fiancés against the eventuality that a stranger should choose to abduct and then rape them. A woman who vehemently refuses marriage with her captor is considered unmarriageable thereafter, because it is presumed that she has been raped. She may thus be under pressure to marry from her own family, who otherwise face the prospect of maintaining her in the paternal household indefinitely. "Now you are mine forever . . . you will not be able to refuse me," gloated a Kurdish rapist to his victim (Ali 2009, 37).

Indeed, Article 433 of the 1926 Turkish penal code specifically abrogated any charges against a rapist if he agreed to marry the victim, as does Paragraph 398 of the Iraqi Penal Code (Ahmed 2010, 14). In Turkey, this was not reformed until after 2000 (Ilkkaracan 2007). In 2011, Turkish feminists have had to defend their position against suggestions that the principle be reinstated to Turkish law (Hürriyet 2011). In defense of rapist/victim marriages in Turkey, Doğan Soyaslan, consultant to the justice minister, stated, "No man would like to marry a woman who is not a virgin. Marrying a rapist after rape is a reality of Turkey. The brother and father of the girl who was raped would like her to marry the rapist" (in Ilkkaracan 2004, 258).

Several reports point to women being forced to marry their rapists in Kurdish families with similar justifications relating to honor and virginity (The Scotsman 2005; Zaman 2005), otherwise rape victims may become victims of honor killings (Agence France Presse 2009; Hardi 2011, 60; Kara 2004), making marriage to a rapist a preferable option to many women.

Whether this is an available option depends on the relationship between rapist and victim. For Nigar Rahim, raped and impregnated by her brother, there was no possibility of a regularizing marriage, and she was killed shortly after being "returned" to her family, despite their signatures on a commitment not to harm her (OWFI 2012). Neither was it an available option for women raped or forced into transactional sex by camp guards during the *Anfal* pogroms, leading to women remaining silent about such abuses in order to protect their own and their families' reputations (Hardi 2011, 65). Hence these abuses have been hidden from fuller accounts of the genocide. "How many have been forced to marry, and then killed because they were not virgins?" (74).

Redûkewtin is often described as a traditional form of resistance to parental control; however, a broader understanding suggests that such resistance, in which the male is the primary actor, hinges on the ephemerality of women's consent and the centrality of virginity within traditional culture. So, while the existence of *redûkewtin* indicates that the younger generation is not universally compliant with the expectation of marital arrangement, and that the elder generation does not universally demand that compliance, the practice remains an artefact of the system it appears to subvert. The agency it allows certain women who arrange their own abduction in order to obtain marital choice comes at the cost of making women vulnerable to male sexual violence more generally.

If the power relations of traditional patriarchy are seen in terms of a matrix of age and sex, with most power accruing to senior males and the least to junior females, then abduction functions more in terms of intergenerational conflicts between younger and elder males for the control of female bodies, rather than an assumption of autonomy by women themselves. Elopements, then, may represent individual challenges to patriarchal control, but they are embedded within the values of this system.

Tying the Knots

If we consider a patrilineal community as a fabric of discrete but interlinked families and lineages, the lateral patterns of the exchange of women form the horizontal weft connecting the vertical, patrilineal, warp. Young women form peripheral, partible aspects of the family's identity, whereas men embody its continuity through time. The weft threads are fragile, composed of the lives of individual women, whereas the warp strands are thick, woolly plaits of the intertwined interests and identities of fathers and uncles, sons and brothers.

The points of connection between patrilines are also their points of vulnerability. Political enmities, territorial disputes, resentments, grievances, or any other of the vexatious aspects of village or tribal life test the tensile strength of the fabric, with the potential to sunder patrilines from each other, ripping apart the delicate lateral linkages formed by the exchange of women. Persons suspended between groups tend to be vulnerable to intergroup tensions: perhaps then, it is the marginal, liminal status of women within patrilineal orderings, with their shifting identities, loyalties, and interests, that lead to the Islamic characterization of marriage as unstable and fragile (Charrad 2001, 31).

Of the forms of marriage recounted in this chapter, marriages by bride-price, *jin be jine*, and *badal khueen* are transactional, enacted through explicit negotiation, whereas cousin marriage and *redûkewtin* are transformative—the former enacted through a change in status from cousin to spouse, and the latter theoretically enacted through the severance of existing kinship alliances to found a new patriline, although in practice this often disperses into a transactional form through a process of regularization. Interestingly, each collectively ordered configuration can be based in a different mode of Fiske's (1992) elementary forms of sociality: cousin marriage in communal sharing, direct exchange marriage in balanced reciprocity, and exogamous bride-price marriages in relation to market pricing. Yet the values that women must embody are generated across *all* potential forms of marriage so that a family can be flexible in applying whichever mode of marriage its members find appropriate to their needs by the time she reaches marriageable age.

Cousin marriage involves a transformation of an existing familial relationship rather than a transference, yet the simultaneous operation of transactional forms within the same political economy institute similar values for marriageability on all women; for instance, a man cannot allocate a wife of lesser value to his nephew than he would to a stranger without showing disrespect to his kinfolk and thus endangering the most significant relations on which his status, identity, and livelihood rest.

All of the forms described here have an inbuilt impetus to encourage the collective control of female sexuality and reproduction. They can be summarized as follows:

- *Endogamous cousin marriage:* Each cousin sees himself, or one of his brothers, as a potential spouse of his cousin and as such takes a quasi-husbandly role in delimiting her sexuality; disputes arising between fathers and their brothers have the potential to dissipate the patrimony and must be avoided at all costs.
- *Direct exchange marriage:* Families, and brothers within the marital quadrangle in particular are motivated to guarantee marriageability in order to ensure that the parallel marriages endure.
- *Exogamous marriage with bride-price:* Chastity is surveyed in order to ensure a high bride-price, and to avoid becoming liable to repay the bride-price.
- *Abduction/elopement:* The threat of elopement/abduction, which has the potential to alienate the symbolic capital of a woman from her family, is reduced through the family's limiting her interactions and monitoring her movements.

Each household, family, and lineage is engaged in repeated marriage negotiations on behalf of each junior family member and does so within a context of the marriage negotiations of the other members of their lineage. "I am not the owner of myself. Everything I do, I must think of my sisters," stated a young Kurdish woman (Bird 2005, 175). A girl who loses honor may jeopardize the marriage chances of her siblings and cousins through bringing the family name into disrepute, effectively tarnishing the brand image of the family as producers of well-socialized brides for the marriage market.

Taysi's delineation of risk factors for honor-based violence in the KRI includes women forced into marriage, women whose "shame" was public knowledge, women from tribal backgrounds and married women who had an increased risk of honor crimes (2009, 40). Families who force unwilling women into marriage already display more interest in attaining the various forms of capital dependent on the marriage alliance rather than the well-being of the woman concerned; women whose shame is public knowledge risk the corporate reputation of the family, disallowing more discreet solutions; tribes, having an identity based in kinship alliances and facing conflictual relationships with their rivals have the greatest investment in maintaining solidarity.

It is of course questionable how far such forms of marriage persist: being clearly rooted in agrarian/pastoralist value systems within a region that is rapidly industrializing and reinventing itself as an oil-producing nation, the values surrounding marriage have been subjected to seismic changes—which I address in the next chapter.

5

Modernity

The individual man or woman was expected to view the family group's survival or improvement as being of more importance than individual fulfilment. . . . Today that old system is under severe strain through changed political and economic conditions, the transformation from a rural to an industrial society, war and conflict, and the influence and interference of the West.

—Fernea (1985, 26)

War, Pestilence, Famine, and Death

A middle-aged Kurd living in northern Iraq at the time of writing would have lived through the Iran–Iraq War (1980–1988), the genocidal *Anfal* campaign (1986–1989), a campaign of annihilation including chemical warfare, most notably the devastation of the town of Halabja (1988); the invasion of Kuwait (1990); immiserating UN sanctions (1990–1998); Desert Storm (1991); a populist nationalist uprising, which was swiftly crushed through superior Iraqi military power (1991), exacerbated by an embargo which left the Kurdish population near starvation (Laizer 1996, p. 125); a civil war between the two major Kurdish political parties (1994–1998); and the second Gulf War (2003–2011) and the subsequent rise of the Islamic State in neighboring Syria, which led to conflict and a major humanitarian crisis, with an estimated 1,500,000 refugees and others fleeing their homes to the comparative safety of the Kurdistan Region of Iraq (KRI).

Decades of militarism, conflict, and repression by external states overlie and interact with tribal contestations, which have been a perennial, if declining, aspect of Kurdish life in Iraq. The social effects of militarization include increases in both societal violence and the association of masculinity with aggression (Enloe 1983; Saigol 2008). The Ba'athist imagery of men and women as coequals within the socialist workforce became supplanted by the more visceral symbolism of a male defending the honor of his country (and his women), 'violentization'—socialization into violence—through apprenticeships in military or quasi-military units (Sanborn 2003),[1] the ascension of patriotism as a masculine value occluding affective relationships (Rohde 2006), and through the

83

psychological traumas inflicted on individuals (Lindencrona et al. 2008; Smelser 2004). Luft (2008) aptly describes such reorientations as "disaster masculinities." Such historical trauma may well include the precipitous modernization of the area after the Gulf Wars, which is in itself disruptive of the Kurdish way of life—specifically, in the way that it presents radically different experiences and understandings of social life between generations.

As Bird (2005) remarks, Kurds have "lived with the suffocating weight of often indeterminate dangers their whole lives" (74). A middle-aged Kurdish man may be the veteran of several wars, conflicts, and various other insults to his dignity and survival, in which close alliances with kin will have been vital for his well-being. Under an effective police state, there were obvious reasons for restricting relations to those persons one could trust and maintaining boundaries of kinship, clan, and ethnicity. On the other hand, his teenaged daughter will have lived in relative security and increasing prosperity, and an increased contact with the globalized media, from Korean soap operas to American blockbusters, within an increasingly heterogeneous cultural landscape in an increasingly urbanized, industrial, and consumerist society.

Thus, in the KRI, we find a relatively recent history of the homogeneity, pastoral/agrarian bases of society, and corporate kinship organization of resources that lead to high levels of social control overlaid with a high level of societal trauma, overlaid yet again with intergenerational conflicts.

Boom Generation

The Middle East has an overwhelmingly youthful population, particularly in Iraq, with a birthrate of 4.8 children per adult woman (Assad and Roudi-Fahimi 2007; Roudi 2001). Alinia (2013) states that in the KRI, 36% of the population is under 14; only 4% are over 63, and the median age is just over 20 (13). Across the Middle East, high fertility combined with increasing levels of infant survival have led to a notably youthful population, often restricted to subordinated positions in the family through the inability to find work or marry (Singerman 2007). General Middle Eastern demographic trends also show a substantial increase in the age of first childbirth, where over half of women aged 24 are not yet mothers (Panel on Transitions to Adulthood in Developing Countries 2005, 532), significantly increasing the period between first marriage and first childbirth. Increasing age at marriage will mean that conflicts about marital arrangement are more likely to arise, given that younger girls and women are more tractable to parental pressure than older, and likely more educated, women. The older the parties are at a point of a marriage the less convincing it is to argue that young people are too immature to decide on their own marriages. The more young people have the opportunity to associate with each other in the workplace or within educational establishments, the less willing they are to accept parental marriage arrangement (Ghimire et al. 2006).

The demographic trends toward later age at marriage and later entry into motherhood therefore tend to increase the duration of women's liminal status and thus provide a space for women's self-actualization outside the domestic sphere. This simultaneously increases the duration of a period where the family honor is particularly vulnerable. A prolonged period of unmarried adulthood increases the opportunity of norm transgression—and thus of metanormative sanctions.

Following a wider Middle Eastern trend (Singerman 2007), Iraq has seen a decline in age at first marriage and a higher proportion of women remaining unmarried until 1997, at which point the percentage of married women stabilizes in the youngest group and increases within older cohorts (United Nations 2009). The uptick of early marriage recorded in 2007 may be related to the rise in violence and disorder during to the 2003 U.S. invasion of Iraq, including a massively increased incidence of violence against women, and the subsequent conservative religious orientation of the Iraqi leadership (al-Ali and Pratt 2008; Amowitz et al. 2004; Susskind 2008), leading women and their families to identify early marriage as providing security within a chaotic and hazardous environment.

The Kurdish experience of the Allied occupation of Iraq was very different from that of southern and central Iraq in solidifying Kurdish statehood and ridding them of a national enemy. There was little armed conflict in the region, and no power vacuum after the fall of Saddam Hussein, leading many embattled Iraqi minorities, such as Christians, to seek refuge from the tumultuous southern and central regions of Iraq both during and after combat. Political attitudes in the KRI are markedly secular within the Middle Eastern context, since Kurdish nationalism (*kurdayetî*), has tended toward a predominantly pro-secular, leftist, and ethnicized, even essentialist, character (Natali 2005, 182). It could be assumed then, that while Kurdish regions, being slower to industrialize, have historically recorded younger ages at marriage than southern and central Iraq (Kohli 1977), the broader trend for an increase in age of first marriage would be less likely to be have been attenuated by conflict. An increasing age of first marriage represents a long-term change to the family. Changes in the domestic realm and the sex/gender system are rarely welcome to conservatives, who tend take recourse in the language of tradition and religion and nationalism to justify the patricentric family.

The Modernizing Family

The idea of "modern" family is frequently inflected with associations with the normative nuclear family of western Europe. Seccombe (1992) delineates this as follows: "While in the West [of Europe], neo-locality (in the narrow sense) and the weak-stem family form prevailed; in the East, patrilocality was customary in many regions and strong-stem[2] and joint family forms were prevalent, giving rise to larger compound households with extended co-residence and cooperative production" (153).

He describes the four main characteristics of this form as follows:

1. Nuclear family residence, with weak-stem families as a transitional form
2. Late age at first motherhood, in the late 20s or early 30s, with a high proportion of unmarried persons
3. A low age difference between spouses
4. Many persons spending part of their life cycle attached to other households in service, from adolescence onward

By contrast, Tucker (1993) describes the following four structural features of the stereotypical "Oriental" family:

1. Extended family residence
2. Early marriage for women and hence early motherhood, with marriage effectively compulsory
3. A high age difference between spouses, along with a normative marriage arrangement
4. A fixation on family honor and lineage

Within the proto-proletarianized classes of Europe, the younger generation, including girls, left their own households to take up labor wherever they could find it, setting up their own households as boarders or lodgers, sometimes several years in advance of marriage, while they saved up for the expenses of family life (Pooley and Turnbull 1997). Parental economic interests in the mate choice of their children gradually became more distant. Hartman (2004, 57) argues that this change forms the basis of the development of a distinctively modern gender order. To illustrate her argument, she compares two towns—Montaillou, in the French Pyrenees, with a Mediterranean pattern of marriage and kinship, and Salem, Massachusetts, where gender relations were inflected by the Anglo-Saxon values of its colonists.

In Montaillou, marriages were arranged for girls as young as 6, and were certainly expected by menarche. Cousin marriages were practiced in order to shore up lineage solidarity despite these being considered incestuous under Christian mores. Gender roles were rigid; female infanticide was likely to be a common practice. Spousal abuse was widespread and considered acceptable: women bearing the marks of spousal assaults were plainly visible on the streets of Montaillou. Men's primary concerns were with the reputation of their *ostal* (household); women were concerned with their reputation for virginity and chastity, which was guarded by males of their *ostal*.[3] Nonmarital rape was uncommon, and rape was treated as an offense against the *ostal*, rather than as a crime of violence against the woman herself.

In Salem, on the contrary, marriages were late and self-determined. Public attitudes toward women were respectful, although women working outside the household might encounter nonmarital rape—which was prosecuted as an act of violence against the victim rather than her relatives. While women still identified their role primarily as wives and mothers, they made significant incursions into the male realm as coworkers. Gender roles were more fluid: "It is much harder," finds Hartman (2004), "to detect a consensus in Salem [than in Montaillou] on what men and women considered most basic to manhood and womanhood" (143). For Hartman, the moral panic around witchcraft in Salem was disproportionately femicidal precisely because of these mounting anxieties and ambiguities around gender roles in transition. Similarly, the high level of femicide in Guatemala has been described as a backlash against women moving into wage labor and away from traditional domestic roles (Prieto-Carrón et al. 2007).

The traditional model of the family, attuned to the needs of an agrarian society, becomes supplanted by one that fits those of an industrial economy, which severs family continuities, proletarianizes the peasant class into a mobile workforce, and ultimately institutes the late-marrying, conjugal, nuclear family as the "new normal" (Coontz 2004). Rindfuss et al. (1983) describe such changes in the conceptualization of marriage in Southeast and East Asia as the "quiet sexual revolution," where parental authority over marriage has waned or been abdicated across the whole region (Jones 2003b, 2010; Malhotra 1991; Mitchell 1971; Retherford et al. 2001).

Virginity has become less important as a prerequisite for marriage; therefore it has become a matter of reduced concern to parents in areas where it was previously a point of anxiety (Allendorf and Pandian 2017; González-López 2004). For East Asia, the transformation from collective arrangement to individual choice took the form of a "voluntary abdication" of parental power. Here, Jones (2010, 5) argues, due to preexisting bilateral patterns of descent, there was little reason to retain a system of marriage arrangement in the face of rising ages at marriage, and increases in women's education and employment. Furthermore, due to the success of the "tiger economies" of East Asia, rapid economic development cushioned the transition from one family form to another through associating it with prosperity and the consumer comforts of modernity.

Such broad transformations in family systems are also found in available accounts of the Kurdish region. Writing in 1891, Isabella Bishop describes a classically patriarchal Kurdish household: "[W]e lodged in a Kurdish house, typical of the style of architecture common among the settled tribes. . . . The big house is the patriarchal roof, where the patriarch, his sons, their wives and children, and their animals, dwell together" (Bishop 1891, 89).

Mohammadpur's (2012, 2013) investigation of family life among Kurdish tribal groups in Iran shows a transformation of the family form described by

Bishop. He found the intensely patriarchal structures described by Bishop in the nineteenth century were not so distant a memory. One elderly female participant, who defined her family as "feudal" stated, "I come from a family with 30–40 members. Our household affairs were managed and controlled by my uncle, and we had to respect and obey his orders. Even if he asked us to die, we had to die!" (Mohammadpur et al. 2012, 87).

This memory contrasted with the tribe's experiences of modernization, where, while some deplored the loss of traditional values, interest and pride in lineage, and community solidarities, there were greater indications of autonomous mate choice, neolocality, and female agency. Mir Hosseini (1987, 445) similarly notes the effects of proletarianization on an Iranian rural community, which led to fission among the landless and "compromised the economic viability of herders; and caused partial separation of landed households, which become residentially separate while retaining the joint ownership of family land."

Mohammadpur (2013) lists the effects of urbanization, mass media, and modern health and education upon the traditional family: "[l]oosening traditional patterns of family management, privatization of family life, personalization of marriage, declining kinship roles in arranging marriage, decreasing kinship ties, limiting family size, changing attitudes towards family, and redistribution of power among sexes" (128).

From 1927 to 1977, Iraq underwent a period of transformation from a quasi-feudal, quasi-tribal society to a modernized, urban society, although these changes did not at this time significantly alter the lifestyles of rural women (Ismael and Ismael 2000, 189). From the 1920s, after the British conquest of Mesopotamia, land registry marked the first step in the transition to a market economy. This tended to increase the power of *aghas* and tribal leaders, who registered tribal and collective land under their own names, rendering the peasant class formally landless.

Through the typically British colonial strategy of "indirect rule" during the Mandate, existing kinship-based power structures were co-opted into the imperialist project. Charrad (2001) remarks that, "Often, the objective of the colonizer was to make tribal kin groupings serve as conservative, stabilizing elements of the social order, as political power was monopolized by colonial authority. Among the colonized, the extended kinship unit acquired further value as a refuge from those dimensions of society being transformed by the colonizer" (24).

This was supplemented by the mechanization of agricultural labor increasing the movement of seasonal labor into the growing cities, leading to the proletarianization of former sharecroppers (McDowall 1996, 11). To end the resulting flow of migration to the cities, laws were passed favoring *aghas* and tribal communities (Natali 2005, 30). By 1958, 55% of arable land had been consolidated into the hands of 1% of landowners (41).

As the Iraqi state became increasingly dependent on petroleum exports, there was an increasing will to "Arabize" Kurdish oil resources (Natali 2005, 58). Ba'athist petrolization led to a consumer society, where agriculture declined, and an "oil *rentier*" economy developed. Industrialization both proletarianizes former farmers and pastoralists into wage laborers and replaces artisanal labor with mass production. The industrial and state sectors become predominant employers. Waged labor replaces corporate kinship structures, and human capital (qualifications, technical skills, and so forth) becomes an important mode of advancement. This leads young people to pursue education and labor opportunities outside their communities in order to take their place in the new economy, sometimes outside their country: the geographic continuities between generations become more fragile.

Industrialization and urbanization have been both rapid and recent within the KRI: "Following the implementation of Law No. 90, a special agrarian reform law issued in 1975 for the Kurdish areas, many villages lost their gardens and migrated to the major cities. In 1977, according to Iraqi statistics, 53 percent of the inhabitants of the Governate of Sulaymaniyah lived in rural areas, whereas 47 percent lived in urban areas. In 1987, only ten years later, 28.5 percent lived in rural areas and 71.5 percent in the urban centers. In 1977, 92,000 men and women were counted as working in agriculture but by 1987 this figure had dropped to 29,000" (Fischer-Tahir 2009, 27).

These social changes have inevitable impacts on marriage. Hansen (1961) describes Kurdish marital relations in Iraq at the beginning of the 1960s: "The young woman is thus selected by the women with whom she will have to live and work. . . . From her own home she is well trained in the domestic work that can be expected of her. She has been brought up with the quite natural idea that her most important destiny and greatest happiness is to be allowed to bear children. . . . She is not expected to be her husband's comrade on a spiritual or intellectual level" (181).

However, Hansen also states (180) that young men returning from universities outside the region expressed a preference for an educated wife with whom they could share a conjugal relationship. Abu-Rabia-Queder (2007) describes the romanticized conceptualization of these conjugal relationships, cast against traditional models: "narratives of intimacy and love express modern ideas of individualism, freedom of choice and self-fulfillment. . . . [Women are torn] between the global and the local . . . personal autonomy, freedom and individuality, on the one hand, and the cultural expected feminine self, which is communal, embodied in the collective and the tribal, on the other, [and where] narratives of intimacy and love express modern ideas of individualism, freedom of choice and self-fulfillment" (299).

In the KRI, fifty years after Hansen, Fischer-Tahir (2009) describes an increasingly educated young urban populace taking control over their marital and sexual lives:

> In today's Sulaymaniyah the [traditional forms of] marriage . . . are more common among the older generation and in quarters of the city predominated by families that migrated from the rural areas in the 1970s and 1980s. In the educated middle-class milieus, the paths to marriage are very different. First of all, men and women meet as students in the university. Secondly, they are or were colleagues. Thirdly, men and women meet in the fields of politics, culture and sports. Fourthly, their families are close neighbors or live in the same neighborhood. Fifthly, a man likes his best friend's sister, or a woman is attracted to her best friend's brother, relationships that result in marriage. Finally, a woman and her family look systematically for a male migrant in Western Europe or the United States. . . . Although kinship may play a role in these methods of finding a marriage partner, it remains in the background. (46)

These young people of the educated urban middle classes then, are focusing on isogamous marriages that maintain status in terms of socioeconomic class, rather than the prioritization of lineage and patrimony. Changing attitudes toward marriage can also be shown in a rapid increase in divorce: Alinia (2013, 122) notes that the divorce rate in the KRI increased by 66% in 2010.

Traditional marriages are based on a gendered division of labor in which women are major contributors to the subsistence of the family. Ehrenreich and English (2005) delineate the effects co-occurring with the decline of this form. Within an industrialized, consumer society intimate relations are no longer built on a structure of bilateral economic co-dependency, in which distinctive masculine and feminine skill sets were considered complementary within a household. Modernity can lead to the disempowerment of women who have less to bring to the table of marriage in material terms than their grandmothers, whose carpet looms, cheese presses, and tandoors gather dust. Specifically feminine skill sets may easily become subsumed into consumer culture and mass production (cf. Abu-Rabia-Queder 2007, 301). The nuclear household becomes a unit of consumption rather than production. The patriarchal domestic realm comes to rotate around the activities of the absent member—the breadwinner, bearing his paycheck and demanding his dinner. It becomes romanticized as a retreat from the working world for the wage earner rather than being seen as a busy gynocentric locus of production inhabited by women and children.

Where male power becomes removed from kinship status it may become attached to masculinity itself. So-called sexual revolutions may re-create preexisting gendered roles into newer, but similarly restrictive, phallocentric, and heteronormative forms (Abu-Lughod 1998; Jeffreys 1985): forming a transition from the kinship contract identified by Joseph (2000a) to the sexual contract outlined by Pateman (1988). Nazdar, (in Laizer 1996) a Kurdish woman with a domineering husband, comments on the frustrations of conjugal domesticity in terms that might have been familiar to Freidan (1963) over thirty years earlier:

> A man has absolute freedom to do whatever he chooses, but a woman is expected to stay home awaiting her husband and his friends at any time of the day or night, cooking whenever visitors arrive, bringing tea and refreshments at all hours. She is a servant on duty every hour of the day, every day of the year for the rest of her life. . . . Very few of us seem to break out of such a way of existence. A woman's meaning in life had been predicted as someone who serves her father, her brothers, and later on her husband. (181–182)

For Baffoun (1982, 241), while modernity represents a valuable opportunity to shake off sexual and gender-based repression based in the "ancient superstructure of honor, purity and virginity," which pivots on women's role performance of wifehood, daughterhood, and sisterhood, this becomes replaced by "a cult of money," in which status is increasingly viewed in capitalist terms, rather than through kinship hierarchies. This occurs within a milieu of atomization of migrants from rural areas, and the depletion of those kinship networks, which, although they may have been restrictive of individual liberties, also provided a primary means of protection and support.

While honor-based violence (HBV) has been a recorded feature of Kurdish life since at least the mid-1800s, it is difficult to say whether the current eruption of these crimes into the public consciousness represents an increase in crimes in real terms. Nongovernmental organizations have reported rises (Kurdish Globe 2011). This could be related to greater awareness of a phenomenon previously veiled in obscurity. but it could also be seen in terms of a backlash against rapid social changes impacting on the gender order. Increases in the violent implementation of male dominance suggest that the system of socialization that inculcates the values of honor is no longer an adequate means of control; that the general assent to long-established values is waning in the face of a "crisis of patriarchy" (Kandiyoti 1988).

Zakaria (2012) describes the challenge of individualism to the status quo: "When an individual makes a decision based on the criterion of individual desires everything that is communal is immediately threatened. Failure to punish transgressions means that the community is weak, its edicts and pronouncements are not pressing on those wishing to belong and are, in fact, arbitrary and subject to being flouted."

Zakaria (2012) suggests that increasing levels of honor violence are the result of a younger generation attempting to change the basis of decision making in their societies, to relocate executive power from the collective to the individual.

As Alinia (2013) notes, in the KRI, "Women and men who reject forced marriage and the various kinds of control reject and question not only gender roles in their own families, but also a whole system of knowledge, power and domination that has emerged in the intersecting violence of class, gender, ethnicity, sexuality and generation in a historical context permeated by colonialism, brutal ethnic and national oppression, poverty and mass violence" (162).

If honor is seen as the discourse of a system that is losing relevance to a younger generation, then this leads to an increased likelihood that those who wish to maintain control will make increasing recourse to physical violence—and also make stronger appeals to tradition, culture, and religion in order to shore up normative systems that are collapsing in the face of modernization.

Legal and Religious Background

While the term "honor" is used several times in the Qur'an, none of these usages apparently relate to the control of women's sexuality but tend to be associated with military success. However, the "Affair of the Necklace" indicates that the control of women's sexuality was a communal affair for the first Muslims. Aisha, wife of Muhammad, was left behind by the caravan she was traveling with because she was searching for a lost necklace. She returned to the community at Medina with the assistance of a young man, which led to criticisms of her behavior and calls for Muhammad to take action against her. However, honor in the sense of the control of women can be found in the influential tenth-century writings of Al-Ghazzali (as reprinted in 2002), where a woman's sexual behavior is felt to directly impact on the social status of her husband. In contemporary times, Muslim discourse around honor has become associated with the virulent misogyny of some Islamist preachers (Jafri 2008),[4] arising within an Occidentalist worldview that identifies the West as a threat to traditional family life and a source of cultural contamination, a spectacular manifestation of the modern efflorescence of identity politics since the 1980s (Moghadam 1994, 3). As a part of this process, idealized family roles have been reclaimed by conservatives of all stripes, and in all nations (Moghadam 2004, 140). Shehadeh's (2003) survey of key Islamist thinkers finds a recurring theme that women's "conduct, domesticity and veil are vital for the survival of the Islamic way of life, without which culture, religion and morality will crumble" (234). Central to the Islamist perspective, holding a significant symbolic value to many Muslims is the body of Islamic legal traditions, consisting of Qur'anic scholarship (*fiqh*), a codification of Muhammad's rulings over the first Muslim community, supplemented with interpolations generalized from his recorded sayings, the *ahadith*, which is often referred to as shari'a.[5]

Hélie-Lucas (1994) identifies the preservation of *fiqh*-based personal status laws as the preferential symbol of Muslim identity within Islamist thought, noting the passing of several *fiqh*-inspired delimitations of women's autonomy justified in the name of shari'a, in the Muslim world from the 1980s onward. The Islamic legal tradition treats any form of sexual contact outside legal marriage (or the sexual use of a female slave by her male owner, as was Da'esh's justification for the sexual exploitation of female captives) as a crime (known as *zina*) irrespective of the sex of the transgressor, with 100 lashes specified as a penalty for the unmarried, and stoning to death for the married.[6] Throughout the early twentieth century, the Islamic Revival reinvigorated the reclamation of *fiqh*-based criminal law. Nearly all of those sentenced to stoning, lashes, or prison for sexual offenses have been women (Mir Hosseini 2010, 10–11).

There is a broad consensus in *fiqh* that the evidentiary standards for *zina* punishments are high, demanding four eyewitnesses to actual penetration. While making consensual sexual behavior the business of the state is clearly intrusive on personal liberties, at least this tends to diminish the principles of *patria potestas*, which underpin a family's supposed right to kill a family member they perceive as errant, through instantiating an evidentiary requirement.

The vast majority of violent acts against those accused of sexual transgressions under the rubric of honor are not delivered by the state, however, but within the power structures of the household, by relatives and without any evidentiary standards.

The question as to whether vigilantism is permissible in Islam is a matter of lengthy debate (Cook 2001); certainly there appeared to be no question in the minds of members of zealot gangs and militias in Iraq persecuting homosexuals and women that the directive to "command right and forbid wrong" is a duty of faith rather than the business of the state; nor that some of those who see HBV as a family's duty do so within discourse inflected by their own interpretations of Islam, and with the knowledge of these bloody punishments for infractions of Muslim law.

This should be contextualized, however, with awareness that people tend to justify their acts within common idiom; where religious language carries prestige, it is likely to be adopted for this purpose. Pew data find little correlation between religious observance, support for shari'a, and approval of HBV within Muslim populations (Pew Research Center 2013, 73–89). Moreover, the Kurds are notably pro-secular within a Middle Eastern context, which may have aided the legal reforms that have made the judicial system markedly different from the rest of Iraq. As a federated region, the KRI has the power to enact its own laws according to Article 121 of the Iraqi constitution of 2005. While Iraqi law is technically sovereign across the region, local Kurdish legislation has taken a markedly different direction, as outlined by Begikhani and Faraj (2016).

The first reform of the KRI's law was a decree issued in 2000 to argue against the application of certain articles of the Iraqi Penal Code to disallow "lenient punishment" for crimes perpetrated with the "pretext of purifying shame." Other legal changes include a 2011 law directed at domestic violence, which defines and criminalizes several forms of gender-based violence and calls for the provision of specialist services for survivors, such as specialist courts, police units, rehabilitation facilities, thereby blazing a trail for domestic violence responses in the region and representing the campaigning efforts of Kurdish women's rights activists (Begikhani and Faraj 2016, 142–143). In practice police and legal representatives have often fallen short of the intentions of the 2011 reform, and "virginity tests" remain in use as a means of determining a woman's "guilt" (Begikhani and Faraj 2016, 147).

However, the reforming intent behind these changes may be sidestepped through the use of forms of parallel justice systems known as *solhi*, a form of reconciliatory justice, which may be sought by police, legal professionals, and women's rights activists (Begikhani and Faraj 2016). Further, each of the two governing parties has an internal organization to deal with sensitive crimes—which includes those related to honor, through a council of male elders, presenting yet another alternative to the formal law of the region. These, rather than shari'a courts, may represent the most significant challenge to attaining justice in the region.

However, civil law, and specifically laws around marriage, which has the power to shape and express hegemonic ideals around kinship and gender, may also be implicated in the forms of the family. "Agnatism pervades Islamic law" (Charrad 2001, 42). Within Arabia, the Islamic form of marriage (*nikah*) replaced several diverse forms of marriage, some of which were matricentric, including polyandrous unions and matrilineal residence (Ahmed 1992, 42; Robertson Smith 1990/1885).

The traditional Islamic model, by contrast, is firmly patricentric and patrilineal, modeled on a contract of sale according to ninth century Muslim scholar Muhammad al-Bukhari (70:4834)—"in which a man asked another man for his ward or daughter, paid her her dower and then married her" (cited in Mir Hosseini 2012, 158). *Fiqh* effectively diminished the role of consent, particularly women's consent. According to Ali (2010), for the tenth-century jurists, "Marriage was necessarily consensual. It required an agreement, expressed in terms of offer and acceptance, by the two contracting parties. But these were not necessarily the bride and groom. Guardians and legal proxies abound in the legal sources, especially for brides" (30).

Questions of consent differ between schools (*madahib*) of Islamic jurisprudence; however, all allow for the compulsion of a minor into marriage (Ali 2010, 32). Nor is there complete license for the woman who has reached adulthood—the general concurrence of *fiqh* is that such a woman may not be compelled into marriage, but neither can she marry without the consent of her guardian (*wali*) (Ali 2010, 43). The guardian is identified as her father or paternal grandfather in order that the voice of the patriline is represented in marital arrangements. "In elevating religious law to civil status, Middle Eastern states have given senior men and not women and juniors the right to own property in their persons" (Joseph 2000b, 19).

The comparatively liberal Iraqi Personal Status Law of 1959, while claiming conformity with Islamic tradition, is nowhere near so restrictive as these traditions. This is a result of feminist activism (al-Ali and Pratt 2008): forced marriage is forbidden, with a maximum sentence of three years for those who coerce marriage, and relatives are not permitted to prevent a couple from entering marriage under Article 1. Hence, Islamists have criticized Iraqi law as failing to fulfil shari'a requirements, and have attempted to desecularize family law and place it in the hands of clerics. On March 8, 2014, Iraqi women activists took to the street to protest a proposed law, inspired by the Ja'afari school of Islamic jurisprudence, that would lower girls' marriage age to 9, along with various other legal changes similar to Iranian family law (Al-Salhy 2014). This proposition had been greatly feared by Iraqi feminists (Heinrich Böll Stiftung 2010), who are well aware of the antifeminist effects of clerical influence over family law in neighboring Iran. Indeed, increased levels of coerced and child marriages have been recorded in southern and central Iraq since the invasion, signed off by clerics rather than judges (al-Mansour 2012), signaling a de facto shift in the basis of power from the state to the clerisy.

Love, Sympathy and Mutual Responsibility

Iraqi law was amended by the Kurdistan Regional Government in 2008. Men's ability to contract polygynous marriage was greatly delimited (at least in terms recognized by the state, since it remains possible to conduct religious marriage without formal registration). The rhetoric around marriage shows a turn toward valuing conjugality over reproduction, suggesting an adaptation toward postagrarian understandings of marriage. The Iraqi law of 1959 baldly states that the purpose of marriage is "mutual life and children," whereas the Kurdish amendments (Mufti 2008) redefine this as "love, sympathy and mutual responsibility," in a turn away from a reproductive model to one that is amatonormative.[7] While the same amendments pronounced forced marriages legally void, Article 2 removed the necessity for marrying couples to be present at their weddings, allowing Kurdish women to be married off by proxy. While this may be convenient for members of the Kurdish diaspora who can marry without the trouble and expense of attending a wedding, this may be problematic in obtaining a free expression of consent. Furthermore, the conditions for women's ability to divorce hinge upon the gendered model of sexual relations. Women must prove that their husbands have failed to honor the "patriarchal bargain" model of marriage to achieve divorce through providing proof of a failure to provide financial support or suitable accommodation (Article 5; 10.3); any alimony is suspended if the wife is deemed to have been "disobedient," which includes leaving the family home without husbandly permission; mothers are considered legal guardians only by default if the father is absent or dead in Article 5.3, and unequal patterns of Islamic inheritance are preserved in Article 25.

A women's rights activist related her organization's attempted involvement in the process of development of the reformed code: "We held several meetings with parliament about these things and we managed to convince 40 members of parliament. . . . We made them sign our proposals, but unfortunately the ministry of religious affairs did not accept them. . . . [I]t was stopped because according to them it opposed the Shari'a. Then they organized a committee to discuss our suggestions, and the committee consisted mostly of religious clerics and some legal experts and all of them were men and they were all quite old. . . . The outcome was that our opinion was totally disregarded" (Alinia 2013, 103).

So, while family law in Kurdistan may be more progressive than the superordinate law of Iraq, and while criminal law fully recognizes honor crimes as offenses, these still fall short of fully challenging patriarchal practices that increase men's domestic power over their wives.

Neopatrimonialism and Nationalism

Family is . . . a key political resource in most Middle Eastern and North African countries. This is in part because of the frequent inadequacy of government social service programs, and partly because governments privilege family relations in offering access to government resources. Family provides a person with his or her basic political network: family contacts are usually the place to go if one needs access to a government agency. Political leaders, in turn, want to know of a person's family connections and the support of family members. Politicians and administrators often allocate resources to persons through the head of the family, and favor their own families in the process. This constant emphasis on family in the state arena turns family relationships into powerful political tools. And since family is patriarchal, politics also privileges patriarchy.

–Joseph and Slyomovic 2001, 4–5)

Weber, Durkheim, Tönnies, and Parsons have been among the many thinkers who have envisaged the modern state as eroding the ties of village, lineage, and tribe. As King-Irani (2004, 306) observes, given the harsh climates and economic and political insecurity of the Middle East, and the tendency of Middle Eastern states to serve the interests of narrow elites rather than those of the populace, the flexibility and durability of extended kinship relations have remained valuable for individuals in this region despite modernization.

Even with the advent of modernization and the attendant challenges to the structure of the traditional family, she affirms that kinship relations retain "considerable power to galvanize ideologies, shape perceptions and guide actions in the realm of politics, commerce and administration." Wider kinship ties are not "meaningless vestiges of the past, but . . . social forms that serve a real function" (Charrad 2001, 19).

This combines with the predominant Middle Eastern identification of the family as the basic unit of society, wherein citizens are imagined in terms of subnational collectives—such as kingroups, and tribal, ethnic, and religious groupings—rather than the rights-bearing and bounded individual imagined within liberal thought (Joseph 2000b, 11). As Charrad (2000, 72) identifies, particularistic ties, including those of kinship, may retain considerable political relevance within the nation-state. Sharabi (1992) dubs the persistence of the family forms of classical patriarchy within Middle Eastern modernity as *neopatriarchy*, reflecting the survival of the patricentric family in the face of the potentially centrifugal influences of modernity.

Bureaucratization tends to institutionalize asymmetric patron–client bonds and veil their transactional nature (Beekers and Van Gool 2012, 9): where, for instance, the state becomes a major provider of secure employment, and appointments are mediated through interpersonal linkages, kinship remains a valuable resource for obtaining jobs, government contracts, and access to power brokers. For Sharabi, such an ordering leaves Middle Eastern society in an ambiguous position, hovering between Gemeinschaft and Gesellschaft, due to the requirement to accept personalized hierarchies, and the inducements to identify closely with one's own interest group.

The term "neopatrimonialism," coined by Eisenstadt (1973), was developed in order to explain societal change. If the institutionalization of the hierarchies and interconnections of the patriarchal family is core to patrimonialism, then neopatrimonialism represents a synthesis: the centralization and bureaucratization of patrimonial relationships within a modern state. The concept has been found particularly useful in the analysis of modernizing African states, wherein politics built on relations of kinship and patronage inhabit the institutional realm, operating alongside, within, and through modern bureaucracies.

O'Neil (2007, 3–4) sums up three characteristics of the neopatrimonial state:

1. *Weak separation between the public and private spheres:* including clientèlism, nepotism and corruption
2. *Prioritization of vertical over horizontal ties:* prioritizing kinship, religious identity, and ethnicity over class identities
3. *Personalism:* a high concentration of power in a few individuals

He finds these are likely in artificial postcolonial states, with fragmented social organization. Patrimonial relations become centralized within the state, developing a core/periphery dynamic. Neopatrimonial relations tend to exclude groups with fewer connections to the core state bourgeoisie. This can lead to insecurity for those on the periphery (Beekers and Van Gool 2012, 17).

Hashim (2006, 218–219) describes mainstream Kurdish politics as "intolerant of political pluralism and heavily patrimonial" where "intertribal differences . . . resulted in the creation of a political theme of clientelization and neopatrimonialism, which mirrored . . . the similar system that Saddam operated in the rest of the country," wherein leaders buy loyalty with rank, position, power, and money. Brownlee (2002) notes that in Iraq, Saddam Hussein combined family-centered rule, the recruitment of fellow Tikritis to the Republican Guards, and a complex apparatus of state oppression, including several secret services and a network of informants, that bolstered the regime from internal challenges. Such organization by kinship is found from the bottom of the social ladder to the very top: the Kurdish political scene in Iraq has, until 2013, been divided between a duopoly between the two leading political parties—the PUK (Patriotic Union of Kurdistan) and KDP (Kurdish Democratic Party), with accompanying militias, and associated tribal and regional affiliations. Every male member of the leaders' families held senior positions within the party, within the party's security forces, or with the party's massive economic conglomerates (Nore and Ghani 2009, 109).

There is an authoritarian drift to the Kurdish state, including restrictions on the press (Reporters Without Borders 2010), violent suppression of dissent (Ahmad 2013), the harassment of dissidents (Qadir 2007), and the prolongation of presidential rule without elections (Middle East Online 2013). Such kinship and patronage networks can be sustained not merely because of their ability to shore up autocratic power but also due to their comparative *efficiency* in states lacking a developed formal infrastructure. Any social scientist who has used snowball sampling methods can attest to the ability of personal networks to reach large groups of people quickly, yet would also admit that such a method is inevitably partial. Distributing power through social networks leads to the possibility for the development of an insecure underclass, disconnected from elite networks.

Fukuyama (2001) identifies that social capital networks can lead to entrenched and exclusive interest groups. American-Kurdish writer Helene Sairany (2010) recounts attempting to deal with an inefficient and frustrating bureaucracy in the KRI on her blog, commenting, "God help the poor soul who intends to approach a public office for help without having any sort of *wasta*." *Wasta* is a widely used Arabic term for connections. It is used to deal with state bureaucracies, wherein "kinship, locale, ethnicity, religion, and wealth render some people more privileged than others in obtaining employment, university admission, or treatment under the law" (Hutchings and Weir 2006, 151).

Privilege for some implies disenfranchisement for others, hence an inclination to latch on to powerful networks. "Coping with insecurity means investing in the social relationships with friendship groups, family and community, but also in relationships with those in power who might offer a share of the privileges of neopatrimonial rule," according to Beekers and Van Gool (2012, 19).

Nepotism, cronyism, and corruption make family ties important for social advancement; the lack of a reliable welfare state makes them essential for survival. Such connectivity is deployed in countless individual actions in the life of a family, from gaining preference in making applications for scholarships for one's children, to obtaining travel visas. It also operates at the level of politics. Tax (2016) described how in the Kurdish region, for example, a contract for engineering work would be given to a relative of a political leader who would "subcontract to someone who would subcontract to someone else until eventually the contract would reach a real construction company, by which time half the money would be gone" (99).

Qadir (2007) exposes a wide range of institutionalized corruption,[8] which includes the operation of several parallel legal systems: the formal courts, state security courts dealing with political offenses, military courts with jurisdiction over *peshmerga* militias, and two separate KDP and PUK *komalayati* reconciliation tribunals, with similar organizations existing within tribal units.

One activist stated:

> It is supposed that the courts should work according to the new law, but you see women are killed every day and nothing is done to stop it. In those cases where the perpetrator is punished, it is because he is not rich and/ or does not have a powerful contact. . . . I tell you very clearly that those in power create obstacles to these issues. The political power here in Kurdistan is the same as the political parties. They commit crimes against women by protecting murderers and perpetrators. When the issue goes to court we have problems with the legal system's lack of independence. . . . They can close a very serious case with a phone call. . . . [A] person who is not a member of one of the ruling parties cannot be appointed a judge. (Alinia 2013, 100)

Family businesses also reproduce the corporate family in an industrial and commercial era, where individuals remain dependent on the goodwill of relatives for their survival and preferment. The diffusive nature of Islamic inheritance laws may delimit businesses from expansion beyond family levels (Kuran 2010). Individuals are thus motivated to conform to the wider ideology of familism, which includes a reputation for honorable behavior. Wolf (2001) predicts that the existence of such elites will re-create the restrictions on marriage found in the agrarian kinship license "so as to minimize the outward and downward flow of resources" (172).

Marriage thus remains a means of building advantageous social capital rela-tionships within a neopatrimonial state and an economy structured around family relations. Kurdish journalist Sardasht Osman wrote a satirical poem for the *Kurdistan Post* in 2010 entitled "If only I were Massoud Barzani's[9] son-in-law." This was written prior to Osman's abduction and assassination, which were believed to have been a reprisal for the poem. Osman (2010) enumerates the ben-efits his family would accrue through making such a connection: "For my uncles, I would open [a] few offices and departments and they, along with all my nieces and nephews would become high generals, officers, and commanders." As Osman's satire identifies, families that have little influence can use marriage to procure connections.[10] "If a man does not have relatives, he picks a wife who will give him good connections," as a respondent told Morsy (1990, 112).

So the need for marriages to create social linkages may not be delimited to rural populations with concerns about land use, water rights, seasonal labor, and support during raids and blood feuds, but may also apply to an urban bourgeoi-sie, which needs to build strategic kinship relations to mediate interactions with the state and other sources of political power, or to maintain family-run busi-nesses and other enterprises. As an example from my professional experience, some Kurdish women who had been married to Ba'athist operatives by their fam-ilies were ordered to divorce them in the aftermath of the second Gulf War. Due to the fall of Saddam Hussein and the Ba'ath party, these men had lost their util-ity value to the families concerned, and the women's fathers sought to build more advantageous connections, through arranging remarriages that would hide evidence of former collaboration with the regime. A formerly instrumental rela-tionship became an embarrassing mésalliance; women were told that their con-tinuing relationships with their husbands were now perceived as shameful.

"Incorporations of patriarchal kinship modes of operation, moralities or idi-oms are not perceived as disruptions to the state or family boundaries, but continuous with them" (Joseph 2000b, 27). Joseph reformulates Pateman's (1988) "sexual contract" as a "kinship contract" (Joseph 2000a, 110); effectively Wolf's "kinship license," adapted to the structurations of a modern state. Whereas Shar-abi (1992) had suggested that static family forms impede the state from thor-oughgoing modernization, Joseph identifies that the modernizing nation-state, and other political actors,[11] are themselves imbricated in directing kinship and marriage according to political ends.

These political ends include the "desires of Kurdish leaders not to upset their more socially conservative constituency and undermine their political influence in the region," (al-Ali and Pratt 2008, 104). The Kurdish women's movement, and other dissenters to the systemic subordination of women, are therefore frequently pitted against religious and tribal leaders, who have often received the indul-gence of the state, tribes, and Kurdish nationalist leadership and been co-opted by British and American representatives (Alinia 2013, 22). Donor agencies that provided support during the *Anfal* crisis, for instance, tended to deal with established routes of power (Natali 2010, 46), tending to further consolidate patriarchal structures rather than effect positive social changes.

Carrying "Culture"

The very basic rhetorical and organizational principles of the nation are tropes for and expressions of gendered power. They familiarly include rhetorical notions of, and socio-political organization based on, a homo-social community of heterosexual men (who protect women, children and land from foreign threat); the primary identification and allegiance of individual (male) citizens who congregate in the public sphere to rally, lobby, and legislate for the continued (often near-fictive) sequestering of a private sphere where women, children, sexuality and family reside; the genesis of the nation state as the (masculine) principle that brings regulatory order to the undisciplined and excessive (feminized) masses.

–Layoun (2001, 14–15)

King (2008b) valuably conceptualizes *namûs* as a *boundary* that expresses patrilineal sovereignty. Women's bodies, dress, and activities are particularly prone to becoming hostage to ideals of nationhood and identity (Yuval-Davis 1993), especially in time of war when these concepts are particularly charged. Women are burdened with the impossible task of simultaneously representing cultural authenticity and modernity, demarcating cultural boundaries between groups, and carrying the reputation of the patriline alongside their ethnic, class, and religious identities, all within an increasingly diverse and mobile society.

This may be particularly the case where identities are threatened, through the dynamics of assimilation, repression, and resistance. As an example, the Arabization policies of the 1980s encouraged Arab men to marry Kurdish women through providing hefty financial inducements (Cobbett 1989, 132), effectively attempting to undermine Kurdish cultural identity through taking advantage of the partible nature of women's identities within patrilineal systems. King (2008b) cites an interview with a legal professional in 1998, who noted that after the Kurdish Uprising of 1991, the *peshmerga* carried out killings of women on a daily basis, justified by accusations of fraternization with Arab men: "There was a "black list" of the women who had had sexual relations with Ba'ath party men. Some were prostitutes, some operated out of fear of the government of Iraq, some were poor, their husbands were off fighting in the war—there were many reasons. The peshmerga decided to kill one per day. This was their own decision. The law does not support it because they were not killing their own relatives" (335).

This wave of vigilantism, which was apparently directed solely at Kurdish women, was eventually quashed, and the power of life and death restored to the patriline. However, it demonstrates that women are being treated as emblems of national and subnational identity, wherein sexual contact across ethnic (and other) lines is perceived as challenging not just male/familial sovereignty but the nation itself. Within the nationalist struggle, *namûs* becomes nationalized.

As a final example of reputation management in relation to the definition of ethnocultural and in-group boundaries, Thornhill (1997, 82–92) describes a visit to Qushtapa. In 1983, between five and eight thousand men of the Barzani tribe, forced into collective townships in that area, were rounded up and "disappeared" by Ba'athist troops. This left thousands of widows and children without male support, bearing extreme poverty along with the pride of their tribal identity. Thornhill interviewed a mother, who, in the absence of male kin, took upon herself the role of clearing family shame, through killing her 23-year-old daughter (a mother of two) who had been raped by an unknown man while working in the fields. The interview exposes complicated rationalizations for the act: the honor of the nation, of her disappeared kinsmen, of Islam, and of the Barzani tribe.[12]

King (2008b, 335) asks, "If established states invoke the family when building their identities, how much more must a vulnerable, 'illegitimate' state do so?" As she observes (2008a, 215–216), returnees to the KRI from Western diaspora nations make a point of denigrating Western family structures and attitudes toward sexuality in order to display their Kurdish identities as uncorrupted by contact with different attitudes.

Collective and ritualized violence, according to Tilly (2003), is a result of boundary activation, wherein "[v]iolence generally increases and becomes more salient in situations of rising uncertainty across the boundary. It increases because people respond to threats against weighty social arrangements they have built on such boundaries—arrangements such as exploitation by others, property rights, in-group marriage and power over local government" (76).

As Snyder (2000) notes, such factional boundaries become sharpened during transitions toward democracy, which encourage the identification of individual interests with political collectives that are often socioeconomic, ethnic, or religious in nature.

Women's bodies are not just resources but are seen as boundaries between identity groups: controlling women's bodies is a means of claiming cultural exclusivity and asserting the group's identity. This is particularly the case where patrilineal ideology categorizes children according to the identity of their father and subsumes them into his group. Pluralism, particularly where subnational groups are identified as mediators of political power, adds complexity to patrilineal orderings.

Patrilineal loyalties are cross-cut with many alternate identities, each of which draws boundaries around its exclusivity. These are tensions that are particularly pointed within urbanizing settings, where members of particularistic identity groups find themselves thrown together with members of other groups, and where there is an increased potential for relationships to form across established boundaries of identity. These relationships can challenge exclusive identities and the principles of patrilineal sovereignty over women's sexual and reproductive capacities.

Abu-Lughod (1990, 48–49), for instance, found that for Bedouin women, sedentarization led to a far more onerous regime of surveillance on them. Older women lamented the lack of freedom for their daughters, who complained of boredom due to seclusion. Men more frequently leveled accusations of immorality against young wives and adolescent girls. This, says Abu-Lughod, relates to a heightened male anxiety around the custodianship of women within communities that have a greater potential for boundary traversal.

Kurdish women's activism is extremely vibrant. Historically, Kurdish societies have been less resistant to women assuming political power than their Persian and Arab neighbors (Van Bruinessen 2001). As Alinia (2013, 49) states, women's rights activism is well established in the KRI, after being occluded for decades by the Kurdish struggle for identity and self-government, which has been generative to feminist women's own consciousness of the potential for political action. In the KRI, 41% of civil servants are women (Mahmoud 2012) along with 37% of Kurdish members of parliament in 2011 (The Kurdish Globe 2011).[13] Kurdish women participate in feminist debates at a global level; they produce academic journals, run shelters, and participate across all levels of society and have developed a highly distinctive feminist movement and philosophy.

While Kurdish women are making strides toward equality, gender-based violence and female suicide are increasingly identified as the most significant issues confronting Kurdish women. Mitra and Singh (2007) dub this pattern the Kerala Paradox: where male power is no longer firmly vested in the political and economic realm, they argue, physical dominance becomes a method of last resort for maintaining normative male supremacy. Where male dominance in the private and public spheres becomes discrepant, women's accomplishments in the public realm may be paralleled by a rise in private violence committed by those men who are anxious to retain the expected privileges of control.

If women's bodies are less frequently being circulated under a "kinship license" based on agrarian practice in which control of marriage and reputation is deployed to legitimize the distribution of resources and labor, then they are increasingly deployed as emblems of identity. Marriage may remain a means of accessing and maintaining social capital networks, even as the political landscape changes.

The next chapter discusses original data on marriage in the Kurdistan region to explore the process of marriage—and honor—in transition.

6

Quantitative Analysis

To establish how the violence within family dynamics described in the foregoing pages could be applied to a society undergoing modernization and to explore how structures of marriage might impact honor-based violence (HBV), I explored contemporary attitudes and kinship structures using quantitative methods.

Method

I developed an online survey into marriage, family forms, and attitudes toward marriage, honor, and gender roles, initially in English. With the assistance of the Kurdish IT Group and volunteers from the Kurdish community, the open-source LimeSurvey program was adapted to display Kurdish script (which, like other Middle Eastern languages, is read from right to left, whereas most software assumes that text runs from left to right). The team translated my compilation of the necessary phrases for the front-end user interface into Kurdish. I installed this software, configured it with the newly developed Kurdish language pack, and hosted this on my own personal web domain. It was beta tested by five Kurdish volunteers, and the questions were adjusted according to their comments. All the questions and available multiple-choice responses were then translated into the Sorani dialect of Kurdish by a Kurdish academic specializing in Kurdish linguistics. He worked with the more commonly used scripted orthography of the language, which resembles Farsi and Arabic. This was then publicized through Kurdish universities and the *Awene* newspaper, on a Kurdish-language job site, and with the generous help of my personal networks and through the social networking sites Facebook and Twitter (using the popular hashtag *#Twitterkurds*) with short invitations to participate written in Sorani Kurdish (in both script and Latin forms).

Internet surveys are a cost-effective means of reaching a large population and may be particularly useful in countries that lack postal systems, although their tendency to reflect the opinions of those wealthy enough to own personal computers, or those who have access to computers through an institution, is a clear limitation for representative sampling. Much of this distribution was through academic networks, which means that the working class is greatly underrepresented, making up less than 8% of students in the Kurdistan Region of Iraq (KRI), according to Aziz (2011). There was a high rate of failure to complete, which I believe could relate to the unfamiliarity of respondents to the online survey format, since I fielded emails and other personal communications from respondents who needed clarifications around the nature of online surveys. Also, given the delicate nature of research into family life, no questions within the survey were coded as essential, meaning that respondents could, and frequently did, skip questions that they did not wish to answer. In combination this led to almost half of the data being incomplete across all fields.

The intent of the survey was to capture family relations and patterns of marriage as well as attitudes. Respondents were asked to indicate not only practices in relation to their own marriage, where appropriate, but also to those of their siblings, in order to extend the reach of the data—both numerically, and in the hope of gaining greater variation within the sample.

Due to a fair sample size (426 responses), and the design of the survey, which gathered a great deal of data efficiently,[1] the data gathered were sufficient to address the following key questions:

1. What are the structures of marriage and kinship within the sample?
   a. How many marriages within the sample were arranged, and who was involved in their arrangement?
   b. How common are the "traditional" forms of marriage—i.e., those between cousins, direct exchange, and elopements—and what are their characteristics?
   c. What can be determined from the differing levels of consent to marriage arrangement?

2. Do these familial structures correlate with an individual's likelihood to approve of HBV?
3. Are there common factors within families in which HBV has been experienced?

These questions will be addressed through successive univariate, bivariate, and multivariate analyses of the sample.

TABLE 6.1

Sample description

Sex	Age	Background	Marital status
Female: 109 (33.7%)	15–29: 60 (59%) 30–39: 21 (20.1%) 40–54: 20 (19.6%) 55+: 1 (1%)	City: 83 (80%) Town: 10 (9.6%) Collective settlement: 7 (6.7%) Village: 2 (1.9%) Other: 2 (1.9%)	Single: 55 (50.5%) Married: 30 (27.5%) In relationship: 7 (6.4%) Divorced: 10 (9.2%) Engaged: 5 (4.6%) Widowed: 2 (1.8%)
Male: 214 (66.3%)	15–29: 102 (50.5%) 30–39: 81 (40%) 40–54: 16 (7.9%) 55+: 3 (1.5%)	City: 117 (55.2%) Town: 57 (27%) Collective settlement: 17 (8%) Village: 18 (8.5%) Other: 3 (1.4%)	Single: 96 (45.5%) Married: 94 (44%) In relationship: 15 (7%) Divorced: 4 (1.9%) Engaged: 5 (2.3%)

Sample Description and Variables

In questions relating to age and background, there were around 5% missing data across both sexes. The sample's skew toward young, urban males may be considered typical of the demographics of internet users in the Middle East (Malin 2010). Women within the sample were predominantly from urban backgrounds ($\chi^2 = 16.8$, 1 degree of freedom (df), p = < 0.001), using a recoded variable in which towns, collective settlements,[2] and villages were combined into a single *nonurban* category.

SIBLINGS. The respondents had an average of around eight siblings (n = 323, $\mu = 8.06$, standard deviation (s.d.) = 2.81). While the survey only had the capacity to record 10 siblings of either gender, only two responses strained at that threshold, since two respondents had 10 (or possibly more than 10) sisters. The sample of siblings had a fairly even split by sex, with 323 sisters to 325 brothers, and a fairly even distribution across the family. Questions asked about marriage format, levels of consent, levels of approval, and postmarital residence; some questions related to the respondent's own experience; some to those of the respondent's siblings.

These were followed with a bank of attitudinal questions. Of these attitudinal questions, two were particularly pertinent to the aims of the study: one asked for the respondent's *attitude* toward HBV, and one asked if there had been any *experience* of HBV within the family. These were the main dependent variables that I have analyzed in this chapter.

The following sections will each focus initially on data around family structure and marriage forms, and then follow with analysis of the key dependent variables, using increasingly complex analytical strategies.

Univariate Analyses

Univariate analyses look at single variables in isolation. They are used to gain information about the data and the sample. This section provides the first level of data analysis, basic information about the responses to the questions that were asked, and a broad view of the raw data.

Marriage and Family

The first round of univariate analyses outlined marriage practices and family forms within the sample.

RESPONDENT-ONLY QUESTIONS. **Bride-price and remarriage.** Questions solely asked of respondents revealed that there were no instances of bride-price within the sample. This question was not asked of respondents regarding the marriages of their siblings, since it was likely to be unknown to the respondent. Of 83 responses to the question regarding marital prestations, 41 (49%) reported no gifts or money being exchanged in order to realize their marriage, and 34 (41%) stated that the only gifts or contributions were for the couple themselves; 6 (7%) reported reciprocal exchanges between families; and the remainder (1%) were unaware if there had been any exchange of marital prestations. This means that there was no evidence of bride-price as it has been described in this book, so this category was not available for further analysis. This may suggest that the tradition is becoming outmoded for this group of respondents, who are likely to be middle class and express their status through their education and employment rather than their ability to muster cash or jewelry, or that respondents were reluctant to identify bride-price occurring within their marital arrangements because it has negative associations within this population. Of all respondents, only 5 (1%) had married more than once, and in all cases their first marriage ended with divorce, suggesting a very low rate of divorce and remarriage.

ARRANGEMENT AND CONSENT. It was important to gather information on levels of consent to marriage, a subject on which there are few data. Respondents were asked to indicate the levels of consent involved in each marriage—that is, both their own, and those of their siblings—with four given options:

1. **Forced:** I/my brother/my sister was forced to marry against my/his/her will.
2. **Fully arranged:** The marriage was entirely arranged by the family.

3. **Mediated:** The marriage was arranged jointly by me/my brother/my sister and the family working together.
4. **Free choice:** I/my brother/my sister married entirely by my/his/her own choice.

Combined data from both respondents and siblings—totaling 781 marriages—showed that the largest set of marriages within this sample (i.e., respondents and their siblings) were described as freely chosen; only a very small minority were described as forced. However, a slight majority of marriages were not free choice but involved some degree of intervention, with 16% described as fully arranged and 32% as mediated.

Age at marriage arrangement. Forty-three (11%) of the 405 forced, semiarranged, and fully arranged marriages within the sample were arranged when the spouses were minors, of whom 22 were male and 21 were female. This does not necessarily mean that these parties were actually married as minors; the marriage is likely to have been arranged at some point before adulthood but may well have been conducted later on in the life of the individual. These were reported by 18 respondents, representing just over 4% of the sample as a whole, suggesting that a very small minority of families repeatedly arrange marriage for children under 18.

FORMAT OF MARRIAGE. Over 80% (n=599) of marriages within the sample were exogamous, whereas 16% (n=108) of marriages were between cousins, and 5% (n=34) took the direct exchange format. No incidents of elopement or abduction were recorded, so this category is unavailable for analysis. Given that direct-exchange marriages were primarily associated with nonurban respondents ($\chi^2=4$, 1 df, p=0.042), and that the sample is predominantly urban in origin, this hints at a higher prevalence for Kurds living in rural areas. Cousin marriage was also reported, but at a lower level than has been recorded in southern and central Iraq (Al-Ani 2010); again, this is likely to be higher across the general population of the KRI than within this sample, who, being predominantly middle class, are more likely to identify class-based isogamy than endogamy as a productive strategy to maintain status.

POSTMARITAL RESIDENCE. While Kurdish families have been described as patrilineal and patricentric (King 2008b; King and Stone 2010), at least in official terms, it is unclear whether the predominant household pattern is nuclear. A survey of 148 Kurdish women in Istanbul revealed that over 68% had lived with their mother-in-law, particularly in the early years of marriage (Karahan 1995). It should be noted that even the existence of a predominance of nuclear families does not preclude the extended family as the "ideal" form, since nuclear families may become extended later in the household life cycle and may be influenced by demographic factors. Aziz's (2011, 111) survey of university students in the KRI found that nearly 60% were living in households of five to seven members, and around 24% were larger, suggesting that the extended family remains a common ordering of the household. Certainly, the family remains overwhelmingly male dominated, with fathers making all important decisions in 80% of households (115).

It may also be simplistic to view marital residence simply on the basis of the location of the household. If a couple split away from a patrilocal extended family household only to relocate next door, or on the same street, or in a separate apartment within the husband's father's house—the influence of the extended family may prevail even if the wife is now able to command her own private domestic realm. In such a circumstance, the new household may no longer be technically considered virilocal or patrilocal but should be considered patrifocal. I asked respondents to indicate where they, and their siblings, lived after marriage: whether with their spouse's family, near to their spouse's family, near their own family, with their own family, or in a new household that was not close to either family. Patrilocality means that postmarital residence was in the house of the father (for the husband), or the father-in-law (for the wife). Patrifocality indicates that although postmarital residence was not with the father/father-in-law, the marital residence was close to the agnatic household; matrifocality and matrilocality describe the converse situation—residence with or proximate to the bride's mother.

Of 769 marriages of respondents and their siblings, matricentric family forms are the least popular, with a combined value of 15% (7% matrifocal, 8% matrilocal) with patrilocality remarkably strong within the sample at 61% (40% patrilocal, 21% patrilocal); leaving 24% living neolocally. It should be noted that the question asked where the couple lived immediately after the wedding, and for many of these, either patrilocality or matrilocality may have been a temporary arrangement while the couple was locating neolocal accommodation.

The attitudinal questions provide an insight into respondents' views about these different locations for starting their married life. A majority (76% of respondents) strongly agreed that it was preferable for a couple to start their married life in their own home. From cross-tabulation, it can be seen that some 55% of married respondents are, or were, living in family arrangements that they personally considered suboptimal ($\chi^2 = 4$, 5 df, p = 0.535). There may be a strong trend toward traditional patricentric families across the sample, but this does not necessarily seem to be the arrangement that individuals identify as the best. This implies a potential source of intergenerational conflict.

Persons involved in marriage arrangement. I asked respondents to identify the actors who were involved for each forced, arranged, and mediated form of marriage. The survey allowed respondents to select as many options as

TABLE 6.2

Responses to key dependent variables

Prompt	Agree strongly	Agree	No opinion	Disagree	Disagree strongly	Total
Disputes about *namûs* have led to violence in my own family	10.9% (n=21)	17.3% (n=33)	13.6% (n=26)	25% (n=44)	35% (n=67)	100% (n=191)
Violence may sometimes be justified if a person has brought shame to their family	5.6% (n=12)	20.7% (n=44)	12.7% (n=27)	24.9% (n=53)	36.2% (n=77)	100% (n=213)

appropriate, in recognition of the fact that marriage arrangement is often a collaborative affair. There were 134 responses, and while the largest group of 60 respondents (45%) identified a single marriage arranger operating in the family, 12 (9%) identified more than five.

Attitudes

The sample showed strongly negative attitudes toward marriage arrangement and toward traditional forms of marriage in particular. There was a general, if somewhat inconsistent, support for power sharing in relationships and an approval for women's work outside the home within the sample. However, virginity remained a salient aspect of women's role for almost all respondents.

Around a quarter of the sample expressed some level of approval of HBV. A similar amount reported experiences of HBV within their own families, which rose to a third if noncommittal responses were disregarded. Interestingly, questions around the topic of honor raised the most uncertainty. Questions relating to whether HBV had occurred in the respondent's own family and whether a failure to restore honor would lead to social exclusion had disproportionate nonresponses, either as no answer at all (representing 14% of the responses to the question as to whether HBV had occurred in the respondent's own family, compared to 5% for most others), or a noncommittal neutral response.

Bivariate Analyses

Bivariate analyses are used to establish whether, and to what extent, two variables are related. This section identifies and explains significant differences according to sex, to levels of consent to marriage, and attitudes toward and experiences with HBV.

Marriage and Family

Bivariate analysis allowed for a more complex analysis of the structures of marriage in the family, with a particular focus on exploring consent.

MARRIAGE CONSENT VARIABLE. Given that familial influence over marriage is an important aspect of individual freedoms and at the core of the "exchange of women" model identified as foundational to the concept of honor, I created a variable designed to indicate the levels of consent to marriage that were most typical for each family. For the creation of this variable, forced and fully arranged marriages were recoded as 1, demarcating low consent, given Alinia's (2013, 109) observation that some Kurdish women in fully arranged marriages appeared to assume that parents had an absolute right to arrange marriage, which they could not challenge. This makes discrimination between these two forms difficult. Marriages that were arranged in collaboration were recoded as 2, representing mediated consent, and free choice marriages were coded as 3. These were totaled for all respondents and their siblings and then divided by the total number of all marriages reported by each respondent, creating a variable with values between 1 and 3, to give a sense of the general level of family involvement in the marriages of the respondent and the respondent's siblings. Due to the diffuse nature of the data on marriage occurring across the categories of siblings and respondents, combined scores were developed for marriages involving men (i.e., respondents' brothers and male respondents), and marriages involving women (i.e., respondents' sisters and female respondents.)

Autonomy in Marriage. A dependent t-test was conducted using versions of the marriage consent variable that were separated by sex. This used a matched pair analysis to compare levels of autonomy in marriage for male respondents and respondents' brothers against female respondents and respondents' sisters.

This indicated that women were significantly more likely to have had a greater level of family intervention in their marriage than men, where the mean locates most female marriages more closely to the model of mediated consent than it does for males.

For males, the higher mean indicates a significantly greater likelihood of being permitted to make a free choice. The higher the consent level within arranged forms of marriage, the more likely it was that it coexisted with free choice marriage within the family: for example, just 7.8% of families in which a marriage had been forced on one sibling allowed another a free hand in their marital choices ($\chi^2 = 4.8$, 1 df, p = 0.029).

This can be compared with 26.3% of families, in which marriage arranged without consultation co-occurred with free marriage ($\chi^2 = 17.5$, 1 df, p = <0.000), and 49.7% in which marriages were arranged through collaboration ($\chi^2 = 26.2$, 1 df, p = <0.000). It appears then, that levels of consent to marriage may not be

TABLE 6.3

Dependent t-test of marital autonomy by sex

Marriage Consent	$\bar{X}^2$	N	sd	Error	Sig
Female	2.11	144	0.65	0.054	cor= 0.232 p=0.005
Male	2.32	144	0.60	0.050	

identical across siblings, but they are grouped, with each individual family displaying greater or lesser tendencies toward allowing autonomy or maintaining control over the marriages of young people.

Autonomy and Attitudes. Comparison of attitudinal data with the family-wide marital autonomy variables proved to show interesting correlations using analysis of variance (ANOVA). Findings indicated that individuals from families that tended toward greater intervention in the marriages of *female* relatives were more likely to believe that virginity was essential for women, to believe that women's roles were as housewives and mothers, and to support the institution of bride-price, among other patriarchal attitudes. Low marital autonomy, then, appears to correlate with traditional gender roles, and this suggests that there is a linkage between adherence to the expectations of traditional femininity and marriage arrangement.

There was a near-significant correlation (p = 0.057) with the belief that violence could be acceptable against a person who had caused shame to the family and lower levels of marital autonomy, suggesting there may also be a connection between families that exert control over women's marital choices and the approval of HBV.

One significant finding was that respondents from families in which the marriages of *men and boys* had higher levels of intervention were more likely to agree that young people were under pressure to marry from their families, whereas there was no such finding in relation to the female marital autonomy scale. This suggests that lower levels of male autonomy in marriage are more likely to be resented as a parental infringement on individual liberties, whereas lower levels of female autonomy are more likely to be accepted as an aspect of the status quo.

More than 85% of forced marriages took place in families in which the parents were responsible for marriage arrangement (χ^2 = 66, 1 df, p =<0.001), whereas for fully arranged marriages, this was less than 50%, suggesting that parental involvement in marriage is associated with lower levels of consent.

This was tested using ANOVAs on a filtered dataset, from which free choice marriages were temporarily removed from the analysis in order to

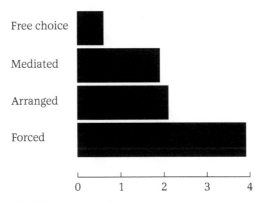

FIGURE 6.1 Mean of marriage arrangers in the family by marriage consent level

provide a fair comparison of arrangers. Whereas parental involvement in marriage arrangement significantly impacted on the marriage consent variable for male respondents and respondents' brothers—reducing it from 2.25 to 2.2 ($F = 2.04, df = 16, p = 0.014$), there was little impact on the marriage consent variable for female respondents and respondents' sisters, which remained largely unchanged ($F = 1.1, df = 14, p = 0.378$). It appears then, that for males, closer kinship relationships between the arrangee and arranger correlate with decreased personal autonomy for the arrangee.

The data were then tested to see if the number of marriage arrangers operating within a family influenced marital autonomy.

A comparison of the means of the numbers of marriage arrangers across the family as a whole is shown in figure 6.1. This gives the impression that the greater the number of individuals who were involved in marriage arrangement within that family, the higher the likelihood of marriages within that family being forced.

ANOVAs indicated that all relationships between marriage type and the number of arrangers were highly significant, for forced marriage ($f = 14.4, df = 11, p = <0.001$), fully arranged marriage ($f = 11.1, df = 11, p = <0.001$), mediated marriage ($f = 29.7, df = 11, p = <0.001$), and free choice marriage ($f = 3.2, df = 11, p = <0.001$). The fully arranged and mediated forms are very close in value. It should be noted that each mediated marriage could be considered to involve an additional marriage arranger—this being the arrangee/spouse him-/herself.

The count of marriage arrangers across a family also has a highly significant correlation, correlating with a lower value within the marriage autonomy variable ($f = 5.3, df = 23, p = <0.001$).

So both parental involvement in marriage arrangement and a higher number of arrangers may be correlated with lower levels of individual autonomy in

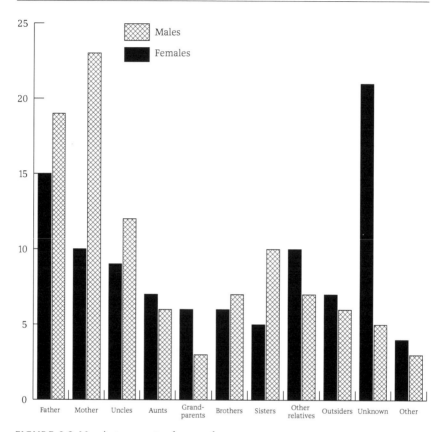

FIGURE 6.2 Marriage arrangers by sex of arrangee

marriage. The more collaborative marriage arrangement is within the family, the more it appears to exclude the arrangee, suggesting these are families in which the interests of the collective are considered to outweigh those of the individual, hence the more persons who are invested within marriage arrangements in a family, the more likely it is that a family member will be coerced into marriage.

Marriage Arrangers and Sex. Figure 6.2 shows the identity of marriage arrangers by the sex of the arrangee. For each category, percentages have been derived to compensate for the unequal numbers of female and male respondents within the survey.[3]

Most strikingly, respondents were significantly likely to say that they did not know who had arranged their sisters' marriages ($\chi^2 = 25$, I df, p = <0.001). Since there was no significant difference between male and female respondents responding that they did not know who arranged their sisters' marriages ($\chi^2 = 2$, 5 df, p = 0.571), it seems likely that generally, marriage arrangements for women are more discreet, and thus they are less likely to be discussed within the family.

Mothers were significantly more likely to arrange marriages for sons rather than daughters (χ^2 = 10, 1 df, p = 0.001); sisters were nearly significantly more likely to arrange marriage for their brothers than for their sisters (χ^2 = 3, 1 df, p = 0.06).

It was found that where mothers arranged marriages for their sons, 80% of these marriages occurred within families with patricentric orderings (χ^2 = 12, 1 df, p = <0.001), meaning that the bride the mother had selected would reside with, or close to, her own residence, suggesting that the dynamics of household politics described in this book, where a mother-in-law wishes to influence the choice of her daughter-in-law, may still apply within some households. To some degree, there may be similar dynamics with sisters who expect to remain in the paternal household, but it may also be the case that sisters are likely to socialize with women of the appropriate age to make suitable matches for their brothers.

Women were more likely to have involved an "other relative" (χ^2 = 4, 1 df, p = 0.04) This may reflect a greater tendency for women to use the extended family for marital networking, possibly because they may be less likely to be involved in workplace and other friendship networks. It could also be related to the fact that women appear to be under a higher expectation to have arranged marriages than men are, and that therefore they may be more motivated to find persons within the family to validate their choices. It could also reflect a recognition that due to androcentric orderings of the family, and the difficulties of divorce for women, marriage may be perceived as more of a risk by women, and therefore they prefer to consult more widely and take advice from trusted relatives before making a decision. It is interesting to observe that "other relatives," such as cousins, nieces, nephews, and so forth, and friends, are more likely to be from the same generation as the arrangee than the family roles provided in the survey, which would suggest a greater attunement to contemporary values around marriage than the parental generation.

Birth Order. Birth order has some effects on marriage autonomy for brothers, but not for sisters, as shown in figure 6.3. For respondents' sisters, the proportion of marriage by free choice remained under 40% regardless of their position in the birth order for the first four siblings.[4] However, respondents' brothers were increasingly likely to have been able to make their own choices the later they came in the birth order, with 16 (80%) of brothers who came fourth in the birth order taking a free-choice marriage. While the eldest brother of the family seemed to be under the same constraints as the eldest sister, younger brothers were accorded increasingly more autonomy than their elders, while younger sisters were not.

For males, this appears to correlate with a declining requirement for traditional forms of marriage, with both cousin marriage and direct-exchange marriages ("traditional" forms) being much more common for males earlier in the birth order.

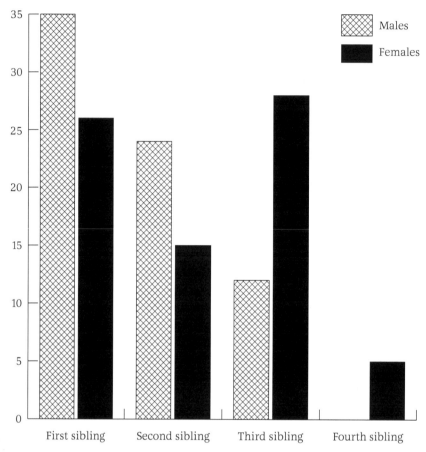

FIGURE 6.3 Sex, birth order, and percentage of traditional marriage forms

There appears to be a clear strategy to marriage arrangement for males: lower levels of free choice for elder brothers indicate responsibilities to build social capital through marriages that build obligations within groups, which pressures weigh less on younger brothers, who are able to assume greater latitude in their choices. On the other hand, women's marriage arrangement has little relationship to birth order. This suggests that while eldest sons have a heightened responsibility to enter strategic marriages, for daughters, this responsibility remains constant throughout the life of the family.

MARRIAGE FORMATS. Direct-exchange forms of marriage were significantly associated with a nonurban background ($\chi^2 = 4.0$, 1 df, p = 0.042), whereas exogamous marriage was nearly significantly associated with an urban environment

($\chi^2 = 3.5$, 1 df, p = 0.052), with no clear pattern behind the occurrence of cousin marriage.

Cousin and direct-exchange forms of marriage revealed themselves to be largely separate phenomena, with only four families having conducted both forms, whereas the crossover between cousin or direct-exchange marriages with exogamy was much larger. This suggests that different microcultures have developed largely separate strategies around marriage; as suggested earlier, direct-exchange marriage may be more likely to be associated with an agricultural, nontribal lifestyle in villages, whereas cousin marriage may be a more effective strategy for people influenced by pastoral/tribal modes of life.

Marriages by direct exchange or cousin marriage were strongly and significantly found in families in which arranged marriages were practiced ($\chi^2 = 82.5$, 1 df, p = <0.001). Few people then, choose marriage with their cousins or by direct exchange on their own initiative. There was also a strikingly high prevalence of marriages arranged while the arrangee was a minor within traditional forms of marriage. Of the marriages arranged before the arrangee reached the age of 18, 66.7% were with a cousin, or in a direct exchange form, against just 15.9% of those married as adults, marking a strongly significant difference ($\chi^2 = 30$, 1 df, p = <0.001).

Early marriage arrangement appears to have a strong correlation with endogamous forms of marriage: the types of marriages that serve to solidify reciprocal relationships within patrilincs and between local families may be the outcome of long-term, multigenerational relationships in which reciprocal marriages may be considered an aspect of maintaining long-term alliances, potentially even before the spouses-to-be are born.

Attitudes and Experiences

VARIABLES. The responses to the key prompts were used to create binary variables, which will be referred to as HBV Experience and HBV Approval, where over a quarter in each category were positive results (by combining "strongly agree" and "agree"), which rose nearly to a third when neutral and missing responses were removed.

There were no significant findings in relation to the correlation of approval of HBV, nor of whether or not HBV had been experienced within their families. However, it is important not to treat these variables as paired: whether or not a person approves of HBV is a directly accessible personal opinion. Whether or not HBV has been experienced within a family is a fact that may or may not be known, and a positive response may describe varying situations. Given that Kurdish families are large, and that modernization has been rapid, it is very likely that respondents have branches of the family in very different conditions,

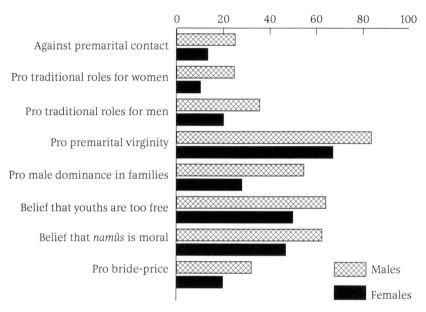

FIGURE 6.4 Attitudes by sex

and with very different attitudes, from their own: for instance, an urban professional reporting an experience of HBV could be recalling the fate of a great-aunt passed down through family legend. These variables should not, therefore, be treated as equivalent; it should be understood that there is likely to be far lesser potential for representativeness and reliability intrinsic to the variable that relates to the experience of HBV within a family in comparison with the individual's own approval of HBV.

ATTITUDES. Each bar in figure 6.4 shows the percentage agreeing/strongly agreeing with each proposition, with neutral and missing responses discarded. Women were less likely to agree that couples should not have relationships before marriage (χ^2=4.2, df=1, p=0.029); they were less likely to agree that women's primary roles were as housewives and mothers (χ^2=6.8, df=1, p=0.006), that women should be virgins before marriage (χ^2=7.4, df=1, p=0.006), that men should be breadwinners (χ^2=5.6, df=1, p=0.013), that husbands should take charge of their family (χ^2=13.6, df=1, p= <0.0001), and that young people had too much freedom (χ^2=3.4, df=1, p=0.046), that *namûs* is the basis of a moral society (χ^2=4.1, df=1, p=0.032), and that bride-price is a mark of respect (χ^2=3.3, df=1, p=0.048).

Approval of HBV. There were several marked differences between those who approved of HBV and the rest of the sample, where HBV approval appeared as part of a constellation of conservative and gender-complementarian attitudes. HBV approvers were comparatively more likely than nonapprovers to believe that "honor" meant controlling women, that premarital contact was immoral, that women and men should act according to traditional gender roles, that virginity was important, and that arranged marriages were superior.

The understanding of honor as relating to the control of women in Kurdish society was cross-tabulated against the paired variable, in which the respondent was given the option to express personal dissent. A majority (75.3%) of those who agreed that honor connoted the control of women in Kurdish society also agreed with the statement that honor should not have that meaning. For this group, the subject of honor is very distinct from the unquestioned acceptance identified among HBV perpetrators by Alinia (2013, 63). This suggests a normative system in transition, undergoing generational change.

Experience of HBV. Respondents who reported experiencing HBV were more likely than those who had not to have an urban background. In terms of attitudes, they were more likely to consider arranged marriage superior to other forms, to relate a loss of honor to experiencing social exclusion, to see marriage as a business arrangement, to describe honor as the control of women, to see *jin be jine* as problematic, and to identify that persons arranging marriages may be self-interested.

The most significant findings were that respondents from families where HBV had been recorded were more likely to agree that parents arranged marriage in their own self-interest ($\chi^2 = 8.6$, df = 1, p = 0.006); that families who failed to restore honor faced exclusion within their own communities ($\chi^2 = 5.5$, df = 1, p = 0.006); that marriage is a business arrangement between two families ($\chi^2 = 8$, df = 1, p = 0.009), and that young people faced pressure around marriage ($\chi^2 = 5$, df = 1, p = 0.021). They were also significantly more likely to report a nonurban background ($\chi^2 = 5$, df = 1, p = 0.02).

In combination, these differences present a view of marriage that is related to the exegesis in this book: marriage is a business arrangement where the benefits accrue to the family rather than the arrangee, in which arrangees are under pressure from their parents within a wider atmosphere of community pressure to conform to the dictates of honor. They were also more likely to disagree that direct-exchange marriage forms were a source of social problems ($\chi^2 = 7.8$, df = 1, p = 0.012). This might be related to the fact that as nonurban dwellers, they were less likely to have negative preconceptions around a form of marriage that has been stigmatized as a rural practice.

However, differences in the attitudes and demographics of those who had experienced HBV in their families and those who had not were not as numerous as those between HBV approvers and nonapprovers. It is also notable that there was little intersection between those who approved of HBV and those who reported experiencing it within their families ($\chi^2 = 0.2$, df = 1, p = 0.522).[5] It is

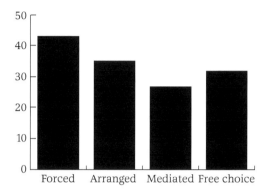

FIGURE 6.5 Percentage of respondents reporting honor-based violence within their families against the range of expressions of consent to marriage

possible that the relationship between individual approval and the experience of HBV within the family may be comparatively weak. There may be a need to look beyond the phallocentric attitudes displayed by HBV approvers and situate the actual occurrence of such crimes within a wider context.

Structurally, there were interesting findings particular to the experiences of HBV shown in figure 6.5.

HBV was most likely to be experienced within families that did not feature the consultative mediated consent method of marriage arrangement ($\chi^2 = 3.3, df = 1, p = 0.049$). This finding suggests that this form, which requires the highest levels of concord between parents and children, is the least likely to instigate conflicts between generations that erupt into violence.[6] This gives weight to the position that HBV is related to intergenerational struggles around marriage choice and autonomy.

Multivariate Analyses

Multivariate analyses help to uncover relationships between several variables and thus help to provide a more nuanced account of the factors related to attitudes and experiences of HBV. These two dependent variables were examined using the technique of binary logistic regression. Each dependent variable was coded as a binary then analyzed using an iterative process to develop the most robust model through a process of elimination, including full cross-checks for multicollinearity. In each case, the model that was developed for one dependent variable was tested against the other to contrast the predictive strength of each model across both conditions.

Measures

DEPENDENT VARIABLES. The same variables were used in this phase of analysis as in the bivariate phase; that is, responses to the questions around approval and experience of HBV were collapsed (1 = Agree and Strongly Agree, 0 = Disagree and Strongly Disagree) to create a dichotomous variable, suitable for use in a logistic regression equation. Missing data and noncommittal responses were recoded leaving the HBV approval variable with 186 responses and the HBV experience variable with 165.

INDEPENDENT VARIABLES. Attitudes were measured using 5-point Likert scales; however, it was necessary to recode these in order to ameliorate the effects of missing data and to make the findings more easily interpretable. First, all nonresponses and neutral responses were recoded to 0. Then the remaining responses were recoded on a scale of 1 to 4 (where 1 means the respondent agrees strongly, 2 that the respondent agrees, and so forth) to allow them to be used as scale variables. Thus a positive coefficient in the model may be interpreted as increasing the likelihood of either approving of HBV or belonging to a family in which HBV has been experienced.

Approval of HBV

BINARY LOGISTIC REGRESSION. There were 186 cases included in this regression, in which 56 individuals had expressed a personal acceptance for violence, justified using the language of honor.

Findings located HBV as an aspect of a patriarchal model of gender relations, with a particular emphasis on virginity: beliefs that women should be virgins before marriage more than doubled the likelihood of approving of HBV. An interesting and unexpected finding was that approval of bride-price was, after attitudes toward female virginity, one of the most important aspects in the model. This, then, tends to support the feminist positions against bride-price noted earlier in this book.

According to the Nagelkerke R^2 value, over 50% of the approval for HBV can be linked with a constellation of attitudes toward women, gender, and family roles that could be considered phallocentric. This is a very robust finding for the social sciences, showing strong interrelations between attitude toward virginity, male dominance, male custodianship of women, and the acceptability of bride-price.

The model proved very weak for predicting the HBV experience variable, however, with only one of the attitudinal variables retaining significance in the model, several reversals, and a very poor R^2 value, which explained less than 8% of the variance in the model. Two of the five variables have negative effects, whereas they are positive in the model for HBV approval. While those who

TABLE 6.4

Binary logistic regression for dependent variables, focusing on HBV approval

Variables	Approval of HBV			Experience of HBV		
	Sig	Impact[a]	ExpB	Sig	Impact	ExpB
Women should be virgins before marriage	**0.001**	**140%**	**2.4**	0.627	0%	1
Bride-price is a mark of respect for a bride and her family	**0.001**	**90%**	**1.9**	0.356	–20%	0.8*
In our society, honor comes from controlling all the women in a family	**0.003**	**70%**	**1.7**	**0.037**	**30%**	**1.3**
A husband should take charge of his family	**0.027**	**60%**	**1.6**	0.861	0%	1*
Husbands and wives should share their responsibilities without either of them taking overall control	**0.001**	**–50%**	**0.5***	0.120	–30%	0.7*
Nagelkerke R²		**0.52**		**0.08**		

* Negative effects: e.g., persons approving of HBV tended to *disagree* with the principle of power sharing in marriage.

[a] This was calculated using the formula [percent = (1 – (SUM(ExpB)/1))* – 1]. See Long (1997, 228). It indicates the impact of each independent variable within the model in percentage terms.

approve of HBV tend support the institution of bride-price and male dominance within the family, those who have reported experiences of HBV tend to take the opposite position.

The fact that it is possible to create an extremely robust model for predicting the HBV approval that is of little use in predicting HBV experience shows a marked discrepancy. This strongly suggests that the attitudes which support HBV and the circumstances that give rise to it may be distinct.

Experience of HBV

I carried out a similar process for attitudinal and other factors that could be predictive of the experience of HBV. This model had a sample size of 165, where 54 had given positive reports of HBV in the family.

The attitudes found among those who had knowledge of HBV within their families had a very different quality from those that predicted approval shown

TABLE 6.5

**Binary logistic regression for dependent variables,
focusing upon HBV experience**

Variables	Experience of HBV			Approval of HBV		
	Sig	Impact	ExpB	Sig	Impact	ExpB
Parents know best and don't need to consult before arranging marriages	**0.038**	**70%**	**1.7**	**0.012**	**90%**	**1.9**
Cousin marriages cause problems	**0.025**	**40%**	**1.4**	0.557	10%	1.1
In our society, honor comes from controlling all the women in a family	**0.048**	**30%**	**1.3**	**<0.001**	**90%**	**1.9**
Couples should not have any relationship before marriage	**0.014**	**–40%**	**0.6**	0.46	–10%	0.9
Nonurban background	**0.023**	**–60%**	**0.4**	0.65	–50%	0.5
Nagelkerke R²		**0.22**		**0.24**		

in the earlier section: rather than the patriarchal attitudes toward gender roles, which were predominant in the model that predicted approval of HBV, these tended instead to refer to the issues of marriage and family structure, where an acceptance of parental authority to arrange marriages is the strongest indicator of experiencing HBV within the family. The constellation of values here is less related to a gendered view of conjugal relations found in this sample, but more related to broader power relations within the family.

It is noteworthy that this model, although the strongest for predicting HBV experience within the available data, was actually better at predicting HBV approval than its actual purpose, despite the fact that most variables were not significant within the model when applied to HBV approval. Those variables that were significant against *both* dependent variables (i.e., respect for parental marriage arrangement, and the belief that honor is located in the control of women), tend to support the position that there may be interactions between the principle of marriage arrangement and the location of *namûs* as a form of symbolic capital, based in the control of women.

In part, the failure of the same models to provide similar responses across both dependent variables may be related to the distancing effect that increases the potential for unexplained measurement errors in the HBV experience variable. Another aspect might be that attitudes are actually rather poor predictors of HBV experience—that, rather than attitudes, there may be *structural* aspects in play.

The attitudes that provided the best fit to HBV experience—negative experiences of cousin marriage, the acceptance of low consent forms of marriage, and the restrictions on male/female socialization—might be more indicative of dynamics around marriage as it relates to the wider household/patriline, rather than within the conjugal realm.

The patterns of marriage among the urban middle class who formed this sample, in which free choice was predominant, were very different from their suburban and rural contemporaries. In order to assess whether families in which marriages were arranged had different formations from those in which marriages were not arranged, I performed a binary logistic regression on a filtered dataset that included only data where the respondents had reported one of the three forms of arranged marriage occurring within their family, thereby reducing the sample size to 184 respondents.

This allowed for the comparison of the different forms of marriage, such as a comparison between cousin marriage and direct-exchange marriage. If the dataset had not been filtered, the presence of freely chosen marriages would tend to confound the comparison of one form of marriage with another. Within families where marriages were arranged, those that featured cousin marriage were the most likely to have reported incidences of HBV ($\chi^2 = 4.2$, 1 df, p = 0.035), whereas there was no such correlation in cases of direct exchange ($\chi^2 = 0.5$, 1 df, p = 0.364) or exogamous marriage ($\chi^2 = 1$, 1 df, p = 0.227).

Due to the requirement for casewise deletion for logistic regression, many cases were excluded, resulting in n = 88. Therefore this model was not able to accept many factors due to the statistical rule of thumb that requires 30 cases per independent variable. Indeed, few factors proved to be significant within the model.

Cousin marriage appears to be a clear risk factor for HBV experience, where the existence of cousin marriage within a family in which marriage is arranged creates a 2.5-fold increase in the likelihood of HBV being experienced within that family—more than doubling the chances of violence being reported within the family. Direct-exchange marriage showed no significant relationship with experiences of HBV, although it should be recalled that families which had used direct-exchange marriage strategies were a very small subset of the population as a whole.

To gain more insight into the relationship between HBV experience, cousin marriage, and consent, I prepared a multilayered cross-tabulation that demonstrated a significant intersection between low consent to marriage, cousin marriage, and the experience of HBV.

Clearly, the mere fact of cousin marriage is not to be understood as causal on a simple level, given its broad and cross-cultural appearance. It could be

TABLE 6.6

**Binary logistic regression for HBV dependent variables,
within families that arrange marriage**

Variables	Experience of HBV			Approval of HBV		
	Sig	Impact	ExpB	Sig	Impact	ExpB
Cousin marriage within the family	**0.041**	**150%**	**2.5**	0.362	50%	1.5
Nonurban background	**0.031**	**−60%**	**0.4**	0.192	−40%	0.6
Nagelkerke R²		*0.11*		*0.03*		

TABLE 6.7

**Multilayered cross-tabulation—HBV experience,
marriage consent level, and cousin marriage**

	Experience of HBV			
	No	Yes	Total	P-Value[a]
High consent				
Other marriage	63 (81%)	31 (89%)	94 (83%)	0.136
Cousin marriage	15 (19%)	4 (11%)	19 (17%)	
Total	78 (100%)	35 (100%)	113 (100%)	
Low consent				
Other marriage	24 (73%)	8 (42%)	32 (62%)	**0.03**
Cousin marriage	9 (27%)	11 (58%)	20 (38%)	
Total	33 (100%)	19 (100%)	52 (100%)	

[a] Probability calculated using Fisher's exact test due to small cell sizes.

posited as being indicative of the strong tendencies toward agnation found in families that feature strategic cousin marriage, which includes a wish to maintain property within the family and to consolidate ties of loyalty and filiation. Patrilateral parallel cousin marriage is the most agnatic form of marriage: by its very nature, it insists on the retention of women within the patriline.

There appears, then, to be a strong association between HBV as agnatically perpetrated violence and the agnatic structure of the family as shown through cousin marriage. This provides one indication for the peculiar contrast found between the approval for HBV and reported experiences: approval of HBV may be an aspect of values related to gender roles, whereas the experience of HBV is linked more closely with particular organizations of the family.

Summary

This section will briefly summarize and contextualize the findings of the quantitative research.

- By a small margin, more marriages within the sample were arranged than freely chosen. A wide range of individuals participate in marriage arrangement.
- Cousin marriage and direct-exchange marriages are rare within this sample and have characteristic profiles.
- There are wide differences between families in attitudes toward marital consent and arrangement, with tendencies for certain families to adopt low consent forms, whereas others tend toward higher consent forms.
- Older siblings are more likely to experience low consent forms of marriage than younger ones.
- Families remain patricentric, despite the wishes of a younger generation.
- Approval of HBV is correlated with patriarchal gender roles, particularly around virginity.
- Experience of HBV is correlated with acceptance of parental authority and is less firmly rooted in attitudes other than approval; it may tend to have more structural than attitudinal elements, which requires further exploration.

Both experience and approval are important aspects of the phenomenon: while experience of HBV has the greatest potential to model risk or posit causal explanations of how HBV arises, the understanding of HBV approval is important for understanding the social acceptability of violence.

Whether or not a person approves of HBV may influence her or his approval of perpetrators, support for violence-reduction programs and legislation on violence, and so forth. Given that I earlier identified community pressures as a distinctive feature of HBV, and that 43.3% of respondents generally, and 66.7% of those in families in which HBV had been reported, agreed that families who did not clear honor were excluded from society, the attitudes of the general public are an important element to be considered in campaigning against the continuation of this form of violence.

However, it is clear that there are marked differences between attitudes toward HBV and the structural situations in which it occurs, with cousin marriage emerging as a particularly strong predictor. The experience of HBV is more closely related to aspects of family life, marriage, and parental control. The approval of HBV, however, co-occurs with a broad spectrum of patriarchal attitudes, such as the requirement for virginity and the maintenance of traditional gendered divisions of labor. This requires further research into the experience of HBV, which could involve taking a sample with more direct experiences of HBV. With this kind of sample, the analysis would be less hampered by the intrinsic distance of an experience of HBV within the wider family, and the respondents' own attitudes and situation, which could be contrasted with the data discussed here to establish if these structural differences would appear more stark with a variable that was able to more directly capture experiences of HBV. Further research might also explore bride-price in more detail given that respect for the principle of bride-price almost doubled the likelihood of approval for HBV. The absence of reported bride-price payments in the sample means that any relationships between these phenomena cannot be explored. Another avenue would be research into patterns of kinship change and violence within the family across Eurasia, where it may be interesting to use longitudinal data to discern patterns of change that lead to the cessation or decline of agnatically perpetrated violence.

Theoretical Implications

It is a core contention of this work that the differing kinship and marriage structures of central Eurasia have led to this particular form of violence, but these kinship and marriage structures are currently subjected to enormous restructurations, particularly among the young, urban, middle-class individuals that made up this sample. If the culture of honor can be considered to originate in the attitudes and gender ideologies generated under the "kinship license," which is becoming a less significant means of organizing society than in previous eras, then it could be argued that namûs, as a form of symbolic capital, may also be undergoing a contemporaneous change in connotation. While the definition of HBV used in this work was developed through empirical research involving a case-file study of those who had experienced such crimes (Payton 2014), it is unlikely that this definition will remain stable through a period of social, political, and economic change.

As the opinions of supporters of HBV show, the concept of namûs still serves as a mark of female compliance with patriarchal norms, but increasingly reflects a compliance to a more individuated understanding of marital and kinship relations that have arisen in a postagrarian economy.

Namûs appears to be developing into a representation of subordinacy to the husband's will within an individualized gender order, rather than to the will of the patriline in a collectivized gender order. The conceptualization of namûs may thus be losing its mooring in conformity to the power structures of the classically patriarchal agnatic family, to become reattributed to conformity to male dominance within conjugal families. In this process it would lose much of the behavioral differences between HBV and the far more globally common patterns of intimate partner violence. This may mark the distinction, identified by Tapper (1991) and Meeker (1976), between societies in which the discourse of honor permits/demands *agnatic* violence, and those in which it permits *spousal* violence (referred to respectively as Model A and B by Tapper (1991, 16–17)). Meeker identifies that Model A is to be associated with societies with high levels of cousin marriage. The tendency of modernization may not, then, work toward the erosion of the restrictions of *namûs*, but the redirection of women's custodianship toward a husband rather than an agnatic collective.

Sirman (2004) tracks a similar change in household organization in Turkey, a society that, with some exceptions, has not been primarily ordered by kinship since the Ottoman Empire. Under both the Ottoman and Turkish nation-states, Sirman suggests, kinship relations of dependency and interdependency, control and dominance, withered and were supplanted by androcentric households, based on women's supposedly voluntary submission to an individual man. Gendered inequalities that are individuated and conjugal eclipsed those that were based in collectivity and patrilineal kinship over the process of modernization.

What we may be seeing then, within this sample of young, educated, and urban people, who could be considered to have the greatest stake in modernity and its values, is a process of transition from one form of understanding honor to another—moving the cultural directive for male dominance/female submission from being an aspect of the patriline's reputation to that of the partner.

7

The End of Honor

Strategies for eradicating [violence against women] must be based on the recognition that it is rooted in a universal patriarchal gender regime, comprised of alternative patriarchies that may complement or contradict one another at any point in history. Therefore, in the final analysis, eliminating . . . honor crimes . . . requires ending patriarchy. This is not going to happen tomorrow but what . . . is happening is the lessening of the patriarchal nature of societies as patriarchal privileges are challenged, weakened and ruptured.

–Ertürk (2009, 67)

[I]t is quite illusory to believe that symbolic violence can be overcome with the weapons of consciousness and will alone. . . . This is seen, in particular, in the case of relations built on kinship and all relations built on that model, in which these durable inclinations of the socialized body are expressed and experienced in the logic of feeling . . . and duty, which are often merged in the experience of respect or devotion and may live on long after the disappearance of their social conditions of production.

–Bourdieu (2006, 341)

The delineation of honor in this book situates it as resulting from a normative/metanormative system developed within particular ecological niches, particular structurations of kinship, and particular understandings of women's roles. There is, then, no single "culture of honor," but distinctive beliefs and practices that have been interactively generated according to similar logics, in order to address similar environmental and political challenges.

To consider honor-based violence (HBV) merely in cultural terms discounts the heterogeneity within each society wherein it occurs. Phenomena like early marriage, low consent forms of marriage, direct-exchange and cousin marriage are more likely to relate to particular, and in some cases distinct, microcultures than to be a facet of some abstract and homogeneous "Kurdish culture." While this study was limited in its sample, it is telling that those surveyed—the urban, educated middle class, who would be considered the most likely to have embraced modernity—provided such strong, if complex, indications of the understanding of *namûs* as being closely interrelated with ideas about marriage and the control of women. It is notable that patrilateral parallel cousin marriage, the form most indicative of strongly agnatic principles of kinship structure, had the strongest association with experiences of HBV, which survivors have emically defined in terms of agnatic perpetration (Payton 2014).

A purely cultural approach ignores the potential for a deeper etiology, based on the materiality of a system of social organization that operates through filiation and marriage. "Honor," then, in the sense of the agnatic custodianship of female reputation, refers to those qualities considered to be valuable, even essential, to the interactions of patricentric communities that are politically and economically organized by kinship, and in which women's marriages become inter-/intrafamilial transactions in social capital. This occurs within the structures of classical patriarchy, understood as a kinship relationship built on inequalities of age and sex and the male exploitation of female reproductive capacities.

Female sexuality is subjected to surveillance and violent correction because it is identified as a point of collective vulnerability. This is a consistent epiphenomenon of patrilineal family structures that aim to maintain and improve their security and status through strategic marriage. These are aspects of a family form that has developed according to the needs of agrarian and pastoral societies in antiquity. They are particularly visible in societies beset by conflicts and that face difficulties in achieving subsistence, such as the intrinsic ecological, economic, social, and political vulnerabilities of the lives of pastoralists and agriculturalists, but which are also manifest in times of social strife and upheaval. Aspects of culture and religion that have originated under the same conditions may underwrite, but sometimes challenge, the values of these systems of power. This reflects a common and co-constitutive point of origin.

In current times, while the anxieties around patrilineal identity and property may be thought to be decreasing in an era of proletarianization and modernization, kinship remains a significant means of access to power. It also informs national and subnational identity groups' self-conceptions. The control of women's behavior, therefore, remains salient due to vested interests in the control of filiation.

The conceptualization of HBV I have presented also indicates productive routes for further exploration, including the interrelation of exclusive identities, such as tribal, ethnic, and religious affiliations, and the control of female sexuality as representing the "borders" of these subgroups, as described by King (2008b); changing patterns and understandings of marriage and gender in societies undergoing industrialization; differences in modes of survival in relation to attitudes toward female autonomy; and, perhaps most interestingly, whether the theorization developed in this book holds out in considerations of other regions and groupings within Eurasia and across history.

My first personal encounters with individuals who had experienced the constructs of honor over a decade ago challenged my preconceptions, and this book represents an attempt to make sense of this. The problem that I identified as the most challenging when I first confronted the system of honor was that of its cost to individuals. It appeared to me that the various pressures of the honor system caused insecurity and anxiety in young women, who lived with an awkward consciousness of the need to maintain appearances. I have also encountered some of their male counterparts who were often ambivalent about the power they held over female relatives, and by the weight of their responsibilities to uphold the public reputation of the family.

As a system it felt too onerous in its demands, both on men and on women, to be accounted for through conformity to shared norms alone. This feeling has provided the incentive for me to seek a satisfactory explanation for honor. Rather than seeing individuals as being caught in a dichotomy between tradition and modernity, I sought to situate these tensions within a materialist analysis. At the outset of this book, I deployed Harris's (2001) terminology of infrastructure, structure, and superstructure in order to conceptualize my approach to describing the etiology of HBV. I now return to this terminology in a gesture toward avenues for reducing violence against women and increasing female autonomy and well-being.

At the level of infrastructure, the agrarian ways of life that initially supported patrilineal orderings of society and rigid control over resources and labor through filiation are in decline, due to the economic transformation of the region into an industrialized society in which the state is a major employer, and where a younger generation predominantly has very different attitudes toward marriage and sexuality than those of their parents. Modernity is not a panacea, however. Boserup (1970) has, most notably, flagged many problems with the assumption that modernity's effects on women are necessarily benign. This assumption is particularly problematic in economies based on the exploitation of mineral resources. As Haghighat (2013) points out, the capital-intensive, petrochemical-based industrialization of the Gulf States has had minimal effects on women's employment or status, but instead has increased the employment (and in many cases, exploitation) of migrant laborers. Meanwhile, women's roles remain domestic and restricted by the dictates of honor. Positive change for women and girls cannot be achieved through an inert reliance on historical processes.

Begikhani and Faraj (2016) propose practical measures on the level of policy and law, including the development of specific courts to deal with domestic violence, further legal reforms, and challenging parallel legal systems that undermine the region's commitment to ending violence against women. These moves will both increase the opportunity cost of perpetration and provide support to survivors. Further, they will push through cultural change from the political levels to the communities and families. Broader cultural change involves a reexamination of the concept of honor itself.

Reclaiming Honor

This research follows Taysi (2009) in showing a middle ground of respondents who identify honor in terms of the control of women, and as a widely shared societal principle—but as one that they differentiate from their own views. A 34-year-old civil servant from Sulaymaniyah City, for instance, provides a delicate criticism of the local conception of honor: "There is no unanimous definition to honor; it changes from one culture to another. For example, in a closed society like mine it is directly and merely related to women and sexuality, but maybe in another culture honesty is considered honor" (Taysi 2009, 20).

Individuals may, then, be rather less committed to honor as individuals than they believe themselves to be as a collective. However, given that honor—in all its forms—is a method of creating systems of accountability, this can lead to an overconformity to misperceived norms bred from pluralistic ignorance (Miller and Prentice 1994). This could create a phenomenon of conservative lag; a particularly significant factor in the management of public identities. This is an especially relevant consideration given that HBV has been identified as a response to community pressures. Just as feminists have identified that rapists benefit from a "rape culture" that normalizes male sexual aggression, perpetrators of HBV may benefit from an "honor culture" that normalizes male/agnatic "disciplinary" violence. Confronting honor culture—and indeed rape culture—requires challenging structural violence.

In this sense, awareness raising around women's human rights and the public condemnation of violence against women, such as is demonstrated by Kurdish women's organizations like *Zhiyan* (Bahaddin 2012), can lead to questioning of how deeply rooted such attitudes are and thereby provoke vital shifts in thinking. This is also demonstrated by the positive legal changes taking place, as described by Begikhani and Faraj (2016), indicating a top-down method of steering cultural change. Encouraging influential secular and progressive clerical voices to unite in the condemnation of violence against women should work toward a paradigm shift as to what, exactly, "honorable behavior" connotes.

Such an approach is in tune with Appiah's (2010) suggestion for a discursive shift around honor that would render honor crimes themselves a source of shame rather than redemption, flipping the current discourse to one that locates high social status in *enabling*, rather than restricting, the autonomy of female relatives. Appiah is correct to identify that it is neither practicable nor necessarily desirable to challenge the broader concept of honor as one of the ethical foundations of human interaction. However, the issues underpinning HBV are not merely semantic: HBV is structured by its basis in inequitable sex/age relations within the family, the "exchange of women" dynamic, and in prejudiced beliefs around women and the enforcement of femininity upon them.

To effectively create new connotations around honor that are not based on exploitative relations, there would be a need for several institutions with diverse interests and views around honor to find a common definition and strategy. This includes a need to avoid mixed messages, ranging from laws that posit honor as mitigatory in many states, inconsistent sentencing of perpetrators, and victim blaming—an almost universal facet of violence against women in all its forms. As Begikhani and Faraj (2016) note, courts may still treat a victim's virginity as evidential, which tends to underscore the hymenization of honor mentioned previously.

However, the idea that it is possible to change the consensus around what "honor" connotes assumes that there is a singular honor culture, rather than a plurality of subnational groupings—tribes, ethnic groups, religious groups, communities—each with interests embedded in particular kinds of reputation management. While education has shown to have positive impacts on young people's opinions on honor in Western settings (Cihangar 2013), this may not be a universal finding. The Jordanian women's movement was one of the first to address honor killings and has tirelessly campaigned for legal and social reform, with strong support from the royal family (Husseini 2009): however, research showed that 46.1% of Jordanian boys and 22.1% of Jordanian girls continue to consider this form of violence justifiable (Eisner and Ghuneim 2013). Recent research in Kuwait (Gengler et al. 2018) indicates that, if anything, younger people are more supportive of honor crimes than their seniors.

A discursive approach clearly has a basis in the tendency for discussions of HBV to take on cultural or scriptural determinist ideations, which I outlined in my introduction, in order that culture may be changed in ways that are more positive to women. Certainly, the questioning of public attitudes toward violence against women is a positive development, but as a sole basis for action it fails to address a materialist dimension—the potential strategic and self-interested aspects in maintaining the patterns of kinship and gender that provide the situations in which honor-based violence occur. As Mojab observes (2004b, 3), attempts to change mentalities are the reduction of a sociological phenomenon into a problem of psychology, representing attempts to correct "a 'wrong,' uninformed, uneducated, or deviationist male attitude." This depoliticizes patriarchy as a system of exploitation, enacting the common maneuver of blaming the individual for societal ills.

The Kurdistan Region of Iraq (KRI) has seen a remarkable attenuation in female genital mutilation (FGM), predominantly in the form of clitoridectomy, since the release of the documentary *A Handful of Ash* and the criminalization of FGM in the KRI in 2011 (Khalil 2013), showing that attitudes toward violence against women can indeed change rapidly due to debates within the public sphere, even without complete political support—Masoud Barzani refused to sign the 2011 law banning FGM, which passed without his signature (Tax 2016, 102). However, only a comparatively small number of people profited from this practice in material terms: the elderly rural women and traditional midwives who conducted the mutilations of young girls can hardly be considered an influential power bloc.

The ideology of honor, on the other hand, underpins the gender order of the society as a whole and supports familiar structurations of social and cultural capital. This may tend to make it far more resilient in the face of discursive shifts.

A semiotic, superstructural shift that attempts to change the symbolism of *namûs* is hobbled as long this symbolism is generated within, and is valuable to, enduring patriarchal orderings of the family. It should also be noted that the data analyzed in chapter 6 tend to indicate that individuals with positive attitudes toward HBV were to some degree distinct from those individuals whose families had histories of HBV. This suggests that the relationship between the approval of honor crimes and having contact with an act of HBV may be complex.

Ending Patriarchy

When violence against women is framed as a matter of "tradition," a distinction is established between, on the one hand, traditions—which are seen to be native, timeless, and unchanging—and on the other, institutions—which appear as contemporary and timely.

–Koğacıoğlu 2004, p. 120)

Cultural and psychological arguments around violence against women, suggests Koğacıoğlu, may be deployed to divert attention from failures of the state and other actors to address gendered inequalities: to place the offenders as mere followers of culture and tradition, beyond its remit and responsibility. This obscures the ways in which the state has a degree of complicity. This applies to the ideation of a particular family form as normative and superior to others. States that remain imbricated within neopatrimonial modes of organization may be particularly poorly placed to challenge the nature of gender relations within the family, given the various embedded interests in maintaining the status quo, from appeasing conservative constituencies to retaining well-established processes of social advancement and privilege. In order to erode the instrumentalization of marriage and the commodification of women's bodies for collective benefits and in-group identity maintenance, there is a need to reduce inequalities of privilege and power, and to begin a process of "boundary deactivation," toward ending internal segregations of sex, gender, ethnicity, and identity. Rydgren and Sofi (2011) suggest that fostering intercommunity links could bridge troubled relationships between various ethnic groups in Kurdish regions, and this policy could also reduce the risk of violence erupting where young people seek partners from outside their group.

These moves—challenging neopatrimonial rule and building intercommunity linkages—are often accomplished by a healthy civil society, able to take counterhegemonic positions, provide checks on state power, and build alliances across groups. Indeed, a strong women's movement has been cross-culturally found to be the best method of reducing violence against women (Weldon 2002).

A distinctively Kurdish civil society has emerged in the aftermath of the Gulf War (Natali 2005, 64), which has included the ascension of several women's organizations (al-Ali and Pratt 2011; Mohammed 2009). Ideally, civil society organizations scrutinize the operations of the state, stimulate political participation, develop leadership, and articulate minority interests. Hyden (1997) notes, however, that such organizations need to be internally democratic, non-hierarchical, accountable, nonexclusive, and autonomous in order to maximize their impact. Civil society needs to model democracy internally as well as enabling the democratic process externally. The creation of even more cliques, coteries, and cabals tends to proliferate rather than challenge neopatrimonial orders. Neopatrimonial states are particularly likely to retard the development of civil society associations. In neopatrimonial states, Tripp finds (2001) that women's activism may be channeled into "patronage machines"—ancillary women's wings, leagues, and associations tied to the preexisting loci of power, inhibited from providing deep structural criticisms of the state through a need to maintain funding and political support. In the KRI, 43% of the civil society organizations surveyed by the National Democratic Institute (2011) were state funded (8); 57% were partnered by political parties (5), which may be beneficial for their financial security and for a certain level of access to power brokers, but which may also compromise neutrality and tend toward proposing solutions that do not disrupt the status quo.

Hyden states that to maintain the counterhegemonic quality of civil society within neopatrimonial states, organizations may need to be funded externally to the existing structures of power rather than being locked into existing patterns of patronage. This can be a particularly fraught issue when related to funding from Euro-American organizations, given anxieties around Westernization and the potential for funding to be tied to neocolonial and Orientalist agendas and goals, or at best, to suffer from association with Western politics. For women's organizations, the absence of neutral funding sources leads to the fraught choice between a neopatrimonial Scylla and a neocolonial Charybdis.

Alinia (2013) indicates that although the policing of HBV in the KRG has developed considerably over the past decades, there is an apparent tendency to gloss over the collective nature of perpetration. Where prosecution of the per-petrators occurs, it appears to end with the individual who pulled the trigger; other collaborators escape justice. Glazer and Abu Ras (1994) note that of three brothers seemingly responsible for a murder in Israel, only one was imprisoned, with strong indications that he had been selected to "take the fall" for the others and that he had been financially compensated for his sacrifice. Such strategies can provide a partial circumvention of collective responsibility for crimes.

Bourdieu (2006) suggests relations built around kinship may survive long beyond the expiry of their utility value, particularly when they maintain preex-isting hierarchies of power. Familial relationships are ambiguous and loaded with emotion; where "affection and brutality coexist in conflict and unity" (Mojab 2002, 61). Policies toward the family are frequently paradoxical: on the one hand, the family is considered "natural," or at least pre-political, and hence exempt from scrutiny. On the other, the kinds of families that can be formed are often tightly regulated and subject to numerous interventions, which tend to favor an "ideal" family form over others—that is, patriarchal, amatonorma-tive, gender-complementarian, pro-natalist, and heterosexist models. Other for-mations are considered heterodox at best, and at worst, deviant, antisocial, and counter to public morality.

While kinship relations are a perennial human institution, there is no sin-gle natural form of the family. The family has endured *because of*, not despite, its incredible diversity—from the "walking marriages" *of* the Na, in which fatherhood is not a recognized status (Hua 2008), to the multiple *paters* of the Canela (Greene and Crocker 1994). The family is resilient, flexible, and adapt-able, capable of taking on various forms. Concerns about the "breakdown of the family" frequently have more relationship to the disruption of preexisting, male-dominated domestic hierarchies than to any realistic apprehensions about the collapse of the primordial mode of social organization among humans. They reflect the vested interests of the existing structure, and the extent to which its predominance renders other forms of the family unthinkable (Joseph 1996).

One aspect of this is its enmeshment with the lack of respect for the human right of individual consent to marriage under Article 16(b) of the Universal Dec laration of Human Rights. The assumption that parents hold hereditary, alien-able rights over the bodies of their children by default must be challenged robustly. This should not, of course, prohibit parents from becoming involved in the intimate lives of their offspring, nor should youngsters be prevented from accessing parental intervention and advice if they so choose. It does, however, call for an adequate and overt expression of consent and an environment in which the bodily sovereignty of women and young people can be asserted freely. Action against honor crimes and actions to curb forced and early marriages must be considered part of the same project, forming a broader movement toward the recognition of the free expression of consensual adult sexuality as an aspect of bodily sovereignty, fundamental to human rights—and toward a concept of human rights that are borne by the individual rather than embedded within kinship or other subnational groupings.

According to Charrad (2001), "Family law raises questions that are at the intersection of kinship and state" (5). Personal status laws have typically been used to prioritize certain family groupings over others, and the personal status laws of the Middle East have been particularly criticized for shoring up male power within families (Anwar 2009). Tunisia and Morocco show the least support for HBV in the Middle East and North Africa region (Pew Research Center 2013, 190). Could this be related to the fact that they also boast the most "woman-friendly" personal status laws in their interpretation of shari'a (Charrad 2012)? The Moroccan family code, for instance, has been identified as enabling the development of matrifocal, rather than patriarchal, family orderings, according to Mir Hosseini (2000, 160). Yount and Agree (2004) credit Tunisian women's status in family law with increasing their power in the household. The lower support for HBV in the former Soviet bloc in central Eurasia (Pew Research Center 2013, 190) may also reflect the historic Russification of personal status laws around marriage (Kane and Gorbenko 2011).

A family law system that allows for the proliferation of family forms rather than prioritizing a patricentric ideal may thus allow for greater flexibility in family formation so that the patricentric family is merely one option among many, rather than a default against which others are negatively compared.

As Ertürk (2009) has suggested, there are emerging fault lines within the edifice of classical patriarchy that can be ruptured, but these fault lines are deeply embedded in the ordering of society itself, from the most intimate level of the household to the seats of government, emanating across history, from ancient folktales to the expressions of modern law. To change this will require the passion, determination, and courage to transform society itself, and to harness and direct those social transformations that are already in progress. This needs to be tempered with resistance to the globalization of the capitalist family, which may replace the subordination of women and girls by their agnates with the subordination of wives by their husbands. The conjugal household may ultimately be just as deadly to women as the agnatic regime (Landau et al. 1974). Phallocentric conjugality may present a family structure that differs greatly from one that is predicated on agnation, but it is ultimately an "alternative patriarchy," as Ertürk describes it, rather than a solution to male dominance.

Ending HBV and violence against women requires challenges to the typical inequalities of gender and generation within the household forms of classical patriarchy, as well as to all interlocking systems of dominance from the state to the household and beyond—toward a radical reimagining of the family and marriage that supports the autonomy of women and children within families.

ACKNOWLEDGMENTS

In 2005, I volunteered for the Iranian and Kurdish Women's Rights Organisation in the UK. This was where I was introduced to the concept of "honor," as well as the violence perpetrated in its name. Through witnessing how profoundly it affected the lives of the women I encountered there I felt a need to understand how it operated, which has culminated in this book.

The book could not have been completed without the generous help of many people. Primarily, I want to acknowledge the help, encouragement, and support from my PhD supervisors at Cardiff University, Dr. Amanda Robinson and Professor Debbie Epstein, who were warm, dedicated, and patient in dealing with an academic outsider; Dr. Alyson Rees, the support staff at Cardiff University, and the staff at the British Library; and the Economic and Social Research Council, which funded my PhD. Thanks must also be extended to my aunt, Rachael Sweeting, for criticism and support, and to my daughters, Marianne and Eloise Woods, for their patience, maturity, and understanding.

Especial thanks go to Dr. Rashwan Salih for his expertise and attention to detail in the translation of the online survey featured in this research, as well as other assistance in relation to the Kurdish language, and to the Kurd IT group for technical support. Various members of the academic and Kurdish communities have provided generous assistance, resources, and advice, including Professor Jamal Ameen, Ahmad Bayiz, Dr. Zouhair Ghazzal, Dr. Choman Hardi, Dr. Hawkar Ibrahim, Dr. Diane E. King, Jamal Mohsin, Dr. Azad Osman, Dr. Marouf Pirouti, and Dr. Izaddin Rasool. I also wish to thank those people who saw potential in my thesis and guided it toward publication: Dr. Lalaie Amreeriar and Dr. Péter Berta, as well as the staff at Rutgers University Press and the anonymous readers for their encouragement, support, and wisdom.

Profound thanks are extended to Diana Nammi and the staff and volunteers at the Iranian and Kurdish Women's Rights Organisation (UK). I also wish to thank my friend Deeyah Khan for her support and continuing interest in my work, and her inspirational energy and compassion.

NOTES

CHAPTER 1   HONOR

1. This can mean a tribal leader or landowning quasi-feudal "nobleman" (Natali 2005, 143)
2. *Rî şpî* literally means "white beard," demonstrating that age and masculinity are considered signs of authority within Kurdish society.
3. Bird (2005, 12) notes that by the 1800s, Kurdish "high culture" had all but collapsed, due to the decline of the Silk Routes, internal warfare, plague, and imperial suppression. Thus Bayezidi's statement should be historically located in a period of "a chaotic tribal order, with an economy based on raiding," which may have led to increases in the prominence of interpersonal violence underpinning Bayezidi's observations.
4. Dirik (2014) identifies the Kurdistan Region of Iraq as the only Kurdish region to have achieved quasi-statehood, and as "the worst for women" of all the Kurdish regions. She particularly contrasts the progressive gender politics instantiated by Syrian Kurdish nationalists in cantonships carved out during the civil war, which started in 2011, with the masculinist, feudal politics governing Kurds in Iraq.
5. Article III (409) of the Iraqi Penal Code sets a limit of three years' imprisonment for a husband who kills his wife after discovering her *in flagrante delicto*. As in other Arab countries, this formulation for crimes of passion is reinterpreted to include premeditated crimes committed by other relatives of the victim if they are justified by honor (Grégoire-Blaise 2010).
6. This is similar to Charrad's findings in the Maghreb (2001, 63).
7. My notes from attending the first trial in the Mahmod case note that her father Mahmod raised a complaint for harassment with his local police station stating that he had received phone calls and faxes in Kurdish, Arabic, and English due to his daughter's behavior. However, he withdrew the complaint subsequently, and when under oath, denied the complaint had ever been made. Banaz herself referred to a campaign of harassment against her family in a police interview recorded on October 10, 2004.
8. This has been particularly relevant since the Syrian state increased the penalty for honor killings under Article 548 to a minimum of two years in 2009 (IRIN 2009).
9. The authors are describing Doluca, a rural–urban migrant neighborhood in the predominantly Kurdish city of Van in Turkey.
10. Bozarslan (2004, 88) notes that junior males may also be subjected to this kind of street discipline by their elders.
11. For an example of containment attempts see also Glazer and Abu Ras's (1994) meticulous single case study.
12. *Crimes passionnels* are a category under Napoleonic law that is understood in the sense of a crime being committed during a brief period of quasi-insanity due to

heightened emotions. This allows for reduced sentencing without a full insanity plea. The paradigmatic example is a husband who catches his wife in adultery and slays both parties in a fit of rage.

CHAPTER 2   THE PROBLEMS OF EARTHLY EXISTENCE

1. That is, the Maasai of Tanzania and the Tuareg of North Africa, both of which are plains-dwelling societies.
2. By "seclusion" Dube is referring to an expectation of the physical segregation of the sexes in order to protect female honor, which is assumed to be compromised through contact with nonagnatic males.
3. Tellingly Kurds may use *mam* and *kak* (elder brother) as honorific terms to show respect.
4. I am using Charrad's (2001) definition of tribes, "a political entity bound by shared conceptions of patrilineal kinship serving as a basis for solidarity, and oriented to the collective defence of itself as a group" (9).
5. It should be noted that Schneider considers access to women as one of these contested resources, since childbearing is essential for labor, economic security of the elderly, and the continued defense of corporate holdings against aggressors.
6. It is also delimited by challenges from within the kinship group. Relationships between brothers are closer to being egalitarian, with only birth order serving as a hierarchy, and hence are often contested. More brothers increase the number of potential antagonists as well as allies.
7. It is in this sense that Cohen and Nisbett (1996) relate the higher levels of violence recorded in the southern United States to an American version of honor culture. They point out that the emergence of southern honor-based codes, based on self-reliance and self-assertion, arose within frontier communities of sharecroppers, prospectors, and ranchers that were both territorially vulnerable and lacking in social order. Certainly, Cohen and Nisbett's description of honor has been shown to correlate with heightened levels of interpersonal violence (Altheimer 2012).
8. *Muhur* or *mahr* is an Islamic requirement for marriage, which could most accurately be described as an indirect dowry. However, the context of al-Dulaymi's statement suggests that she is referring to a prestation which I will refer to as bride-price.
9. Bourdieu (1977) defines symbolic capital as the "prestige and renown attached to a family or a name," and as the "most valuable form of accumulation" in societies based on collective labor (179).
10. Taysi's actual term is "prostitution"; however, among Kurds this term often does not have the Western definition of commercial sex but a more general sense of promiscuity or sexual misconduct. As this appears a more likely interpretation of her respondents' statements, I have rephrased it.
11. Hayek describes exchange relations as *catallactic*. The Greek-derived term means "to exchange" but also "to admit in the community" and "to make friends"—a term that thus encompasses transactions related to social capital alongside those related to exchanges of goods and services. As for Polanyi (1957), "the substantive meaning of economic derives from man's dependence for his livelihood upon nature and his fellows" (243). "Catallaxy," for Hayek, describes the spontaneous order brought about by the mutual adjustment and interactions of many individual economies in a market (Espers 2011, 150).
12. It is in this sense that husbands have been observed to deploy threats of dishonoring as part of a campaign of domestic abuse.

CHAPTER 3   THE PATRIARCHAL ORDER

1. Sonuga-Barke and Mistry (2000) find that the mental well-being of elder females far surpasses that of younger women in South Asian extended households; younger women disproportionately report depression and other mental illnesses, and indeed, comparatively high levels of suicide, which suggest that these intergenerational conflicts between women within the household have serious negative effects on the well-being of junior women.

2. This liminal period of adolescence to early adulthood is also notable for a high occurrence of female suicidality in the KRI (Rasool and Payton 2014) and the Middle East in general (Rezaeian 2010)

3. In private conversation, circa 2006.

4. The original question as phrased in the source text was "Is *it* a virgin or a woman." However, the Kurdish language does not have gendered pronouns, so the use of "it" in this sentence may indicate inconsistent translation rather than dehumanization.

5. An identical punishment is prescribed for unmarried women or girls who break their hymenal membrane in chapter 8, verse 369 of the Hindu *Manusmriti* [8:369], a Brahminical legal treatise.

6. This may allow a couple who have preempted marriage, or a nonvirgin bride with an understanding groom, to keep their secret between themselves and evade any repercussions through fakery, using animal blood, or a small cut to an unobtrusive part of the body to pass the familial muster, if such proofs are indeed required.

7. *'Eyb-e* here is Kurdish for "shameful," and is expressed in terms of a reprimand.

CHAPTER 4   MARRIAGE

1. "Taking the road" is the literal Kurdish term for elopement.

2. Collier's discriminations between the three forms of marriage she identifies—bride-service, equal bride-wealth, and unequal bride-wealth—are based on the forms of prestation accompanying each transaction. However, my discriminations focus instead on the identities of the spouses and their bearing on relations within the family and community.

3. The existing literature preponderantly refers to this form of marriage as FBD marriage—in reference to the bride as the *father's brother's daughter.* I have elected to use alternate terminology to evade the implications of focusing on the identity of the bride rather than the extended family structure.

4. Charrad (2001, 44) notes that in the Maghreb, where families used mechanisms to evade the Islamic strictures of inheritance, in around 75% of cases, these benefited sons rather than daughters.

5. Flocks below this optimum level will not herd together and become impossible to control (Lindner 1983, 57).

6. Farmers may find it valuable to renew matrilateral connectivities through successive matrilateral cousin marriages, a strategy known as the *renchaînement d'alliance* (Richard 1993).

7. Indicating the collective and public nature of such killings, news of Zahra's death was celebrated with festivities in which her entire natal village participated (Zoepf 2007)

8. *A Voice from Kurdistan* is a pamphlet in Kurdish prepared by local activists Rega Rauf and Muzaffar Mohammedi, which attempts to list honor killings and suicides across

the Kurdistan Region of Iraq between the years 1991 and 1999. A translation can be viewed at http://joannepayton.me.uk/wp/?page_id=11.

9. Literally, "a big [woman] for a small [girl]."

10. Etymology provided by Dr. Azad Osman, University of Arbil, northern Iraq. Such marriages are known as *fasliyah* in Arabic, and *swari* and *vani* in Urdu.

11. Kurdish proverb quoted from Noel (1920).

12. This is a very common method of suicide in the KRI, and one that is particularly used by women and girls (Rasool and Payton 2014).

13. Women who initiate divorce on their own behalf waive their rights to *mehr* and are obliged to repay any monies received prior to marriage.

14. However, Bird has the impression that polygyny was actually *increasing* in the KRI in the 2000s, due to increasing wealth inequalities in a modernizing nation and demographic imbalances between the sexes caused by the *Anfal* and male emigration (2005 III).

15. This has the possible exception of levirate, where a widow is obliged to remarry within the patriline of her late spouse in order to maintain interfamily relations.

16. The prospective mother-in-law.

17. My translation.

18. I have not been able to locate an English translation of the word *erî*. It is most likely to refer to the Islamic degrees of prohibition in marriage, as stated in the Qur'an [4:22–24].

19. Direct-exchange marriage is forbidden within strong *ahadith*—Sahih Muslim [3295] and Sahih Al-Bukhari [9.90B], using the Arabic term *shighar*.

CHAPTER 5   MODERNITY

1. Hardi (quoted in Neurink 2014) notes how under Saddam Hussein, violence became a spectacle of power and control, including the exposure of children to brutalizing images during the Iran–Iraq war, where propaganda broadcasts showed mutilated Iranian corpses on primetime Iraqi television.

2. The "stem" formation is associated with primogeniture, whereby a single child co-resides with his or her parents in perpetuity, benefiting from an uncontested inheritance and supporting parents in their old age. Those children who are expected to leave a stem family may do so by marriage (in the "strong" formation) or for other reasons, typically for employment (in the "weak" formation.) The stem formation is often seen as a transitional form occurring between the extended and discontinuous nuclear family formations.

3. However, this did not tend to lead to agnatic violence; rather, women took responsibility for managing their own reputations. Women of Montaillou made frequent recourse to litigation to charge gossips with slander, a pattern of female reputation management that can be found across Mediterranean regions and Spanish colonies after the Renaissance (Cavallo and Cerutti 1990; Gotkowitz 2003), as well as public brawling in which women attacked their accusers (Taylor 2004).

4. As an example, on June 26, 2013, the organization *Zhiyan* raised a court case against Mela Mazhar, Imam of the Qadir Bla mosque in Arbil, for describing women's rights activists as prostitutes and "cattle unfit for sacrifice" in an interview with the Kurdish newspaper *Awene*.

5. This discussion follows Mir Hosseini's (2010, 5) rough distinction between the opinions of the medieval jurisprudents—*fiqh*—which form the basis of many Islamic

personal status laws and shari'a in the sense of a moral/religious/devotional ideal, which she argues have been erroneously treated as isomorphic.

6. The sexual crimes of slaves were reckoned separately and were less severe, suggesting, perhaps, that slaves had a diminished ability to avoid sexual contact.

7. "Amatonormativity" is a term used in Brake's (2012) philosophy to describe the privileging of romantic/erotic relationships over other forms.

8. Qadir's exposures of political corruption in Kurdistan led to a thirty-year sentence for defamation (Rubin 2006). This was reduced to eighteen months under pressure from the Austrian government due to Qadir's citizenship status.

9. President of the Iraqi Kurdistan Region from 2005 to 2017.

10. Discussions of Osman's poem (such as in an edition of *Inside Iraq* broadcast on Al Jazeera on June 25, 2010) have fascinating overtones, where some readings present the poem as an affront to the honor of Barzani's daughter and the Barzani collective rather than a critique of the neopatrimonial rule.

11. Belge (2011), for instance, notes that the reliance of the PKK (Kurdistan Workers' Party -a Kurdish far-left militant nationalist organization based in Turkey and Iraq) on local kinship solidarities led to a reluctance to challenge their structures and practices, despite an ideological commitment to women's equality.

12. In 1993, a doctor working in Qushtapa noted that there had been over twenty such honor killings in recent years (Laizer 1996, 167).

13. However, as Hardi notes (in Neurink 2014) women parliamentarians selected under the quota system may have been chosen for their political and tribal loyalties to the existing system rather than their political skills or support for progressive policies.

CHAPTER 6   QUANTITATIVE ANALYSIS

1. The survey design involved a format structured by logical operators that presented different questions depending on whether the respondent was married, for instance, and that looped a set of questions relating to the marriages of siblings appropriate to how many siblings were identified in an earlier question.

2. Starting in 1974, Saddam Hussein bulldozed an unknown number of Kurdish villages in a region spreading from Khanaqin to Sinjar (areas surrounding the border of Iran and Turkey), as part of his Arabization project, intended both to establish a tighter grip on Iraq's natural resources and to eliminate loci of nationalist resistance. This involved the forcible relocation of over a quarter of a million former villagers and tribesmen. Collective settlements were built to accommodate some of these displaced persons.

3. Arrangers were identified as being involved in the marriages of 161 female respondents/respondents' sisters and 299 male respondents/respondents' brothers.

4. Only the first four siblings were analyzed due to the natural decay in sample size, which meant that although there were 197 marriages for first siblings, there were only 19 for the fourth siblings.

5. Given that these two questions received a disproportionate rate of nonresponses, it should also be noted that a significant relationship may be concealed by the reticence of those who did not respond to these questions: of the 36 respondents who did not provide a response on the topic of whether HBV had caused problems within their own family, 24 also did not choose to indicate their attitude toward HBV.

6. One of the findings from research into suicide by self-immolation in the KRI that I conducted with Dr. Izaddin Rasool (2014) was that women in mediated marriages

were less likely than women married by other means to choose self-immolation as a suicide method ($\chi^2 = 6.1$, 2 df, p = 0.047). In our analysis of this phenomenon, we argued that self-immolation as a method of self-harm had developed a symbolic content for women in the Middle East and central Asia and was used to signal frustrations at the patriarchal order.

REFERENCES

Abu Hassan, R., and L. Welchman. 2005. Changing the Rules? Developments on "Crimes of Honour" in Jordan. In *"Honour": Crimes, Paradigms and Violence against Women*, edited by L. Welchman and S. Hossain, 199–209. London: Zed Books.

Abu-Lughod, L. 1990. The Romance of Resistance: Tracing Transformations of Power through Bedouin Women. *American Ethnologist* 17, no. 1:41–55.

Abu-Lughod, L. 1997. The Interpretation of Culture(s) after Television. In *The Fate of "Culture": Geertz and Beyond*, edited by S. Ortner, 110–136. Berkeley: University of California Press.

Abu-Lughod, L. ed. 1998. *Remaking Women: Feminism and Modernity in the Middle East*. Princeton, N.J.: Princeton University Press.

Abu-Odeh, L. 1996. Crimes of Honour and the Construction of Gender in Arab Societies. In *Feminism and Islam: Legal and Literary Perspectives*, edited by M. Yamani, 141–194. Reading, U.K.: Ithaca Press.

Abu-Rabia, A. 2011. Family Honour Killings: Between Custom and State Law. *Open Psychology Journal* 4, no. 1-M4:34–44.

Abu-Rabia-Queder, S. 2007. Coping with "Forbidden Love" and Loveless Marriage: Educated Bedouin Women from the Negev. *Ethnography* 8, no. 3:297–323.

Abu-Zahra, N. M. 1970. "On the Modesty of Women in Arab Muslim Villages": A reply. *American Anthropologist* 72, no. 5:1079–1088.

Afzal, M., et al. 1994. Consanguineous Marriages in Pakistan. *Pakistan Development Review* 33, no. 4 Pt 2:663–674.

Agence France Presse. 2009. Daughter Pregnant by Rape, Killed by Family. *Brisbane Times*, January 13, 2009.

Ahlberg, N. 2007. *"No Five Fingers Are Alike": What Exiled Kurdish Women in Therapy Told Me*. London: Karnac.

Ahmad, R. 2013. The Unusual Uprising in Iraqi Kurdistan: Two Years On. *MR Zine*, February 16, 2013.

Ahmadova, F. 2011. Tajiks Borrow Bride-Theft from Neighbours. Institute for War and Peace Reporting. Accessed November 29, 2011. http://www.iwpr.net/report-news/tajiks -borrow-bride-theft-neighbours.

Ahmed, H. 2010. Iraq. In *Women's Rights in the Middle East and North Africa: Progress and Resistance*, edited by S. Kelly and J. Breslin, 1–35. New York: Rowman and Littlefield.

Ahmed, L. 1992. *Women and Gender in Islam: Historic Roots of a Modern Debate*. New Haven, Conn.: Yale University Press.

Akbayram, S., et al. 2009. The Frequency of Consanguineous Marriage in Eastern Turkey. *Genetic Counselling* 20, no. 3:207–214.

Alakom, R. 2002. *Folklor û jinên kurd*. NEFEL: Stockholm.

al-Ali, N., and N. Pratt. 2008. *What Kind of Liberation?: Women and the Occupation of Iraq.* Berkeley and Los Angeles: University of California Press.

al-Ali, N., and N. Pratt. 2011. Between Nationalism and Women's Rights: The Kurdish Women's Movement in Iraq. *Middle East Journal of Culture and Communication* 4:337–353.

Al-Ani, Z. R. 2010. Association of Consanguinity with Congenital Heart Diseases in a Teaching Hospital in Western Iraq. *Saudi Medical Journal* 31, no. 9:1021–1027.

Al-Ghazzali, A. H. M. 2002. *Al-Ghazzali on Marriage.* Translated by Muhammad Nur Abdus Salam. Chicago: KAZI Publications.

Al-Lami, M., et al. 2012. Mobilisation and Violence in the New Media Ecology: The Du'a Khalil Aswad and Camilia Shehata Cases. *Critical Studies on Terrorism* 5, no. 2:237–256.

al-Mansour, H. J. 2012. *Underage Marriage: They Took My Doll Away and Gave Me a Husband.* Basra: Niqash. Accessed October 9, 2012. http://www.niqash.org/articles/?id=3129.

Ali, K. 2010. *Marriage and Slavery in Early Islam.* Cambridge, Mass.: Harvard University Press.

Ali, L. 2009. *Betrayed.* Sydney: New Holland.

Alinia, M. 2013. *Honor & Violence against Women in Iraqi Kurdistan.* New York: Palgrave Macmillan.

Allendorf, K., and R. K. Pandian. 2016. The Decline of Arranged Marriage? Marital Change and Continuity in India. *Population and Development Review* 42, no. 3:435–464

Allison, C. 2001. *The Yezidi Oral Tradition in Iraqi Kurdistan.* London: Routledge.

Al-Salhy, S. 2014. Iraqi women protest against proposed Islamic law in Iraq. Reuters. Accessed: 10 March 2014. http://www.reuters.com/article/2014/03/08/us-iraq-women-islam-idUSBREA270NR20140308

Altheimer, I. 2012. Cultural Processes and Homicide across Nations. *International Journal of Offender Therapy and Comparative Criminology* 57, no. 7:842–863.

Altunek, N. S. 2006. Bone and Flesh, Seed and Soil: Patriliny by Father's Brother's Daughter Marriage. *Ethnology* 45, no. 1:59–70.

Amnesty International. 2006. *Georgia: Thousands Suffering in Silence—Violence against Women in Georgia.* London: Amnesty International.

Amowitz, L. L., et al. 2004. Human Rights Abuses and Concerns about Women's Health and Human Rights in Southern Iraq. *JAMA—Journal of the American Medical Association* 291, no. 12:1471–1479.

Anwar, Z., ed. 2009. *Wanted: Equality and Justice in the Muslim Family.* Petaling Jaya, Selangor, Malaysia: Musawah.

Appiah, K. A. 2010. *The Honor Code: How Moral Revolutions Happen.* London: W. W. Norton.

Assad, R., and F. Roudi-Fahimi. 2007. *Youth in the Middle East and North Africa: Demographic Opportunity or Challenge?* Washington: Population Reference Bureau.

Atkinson, M. P., and G. R. Lee. 1984. Structural Correlates of Marriage Payments: Antecedents of the Brideprice. *International Journal of Sociology of the Family* 14, no. 1:67–79.

Awwad, A. 2001. Gossip, Scandal, Shame and Honor Killing: A Case for Social Constructionism and Hegemonic Discourse. *Social Thought and Research* 24, no. 1–2:39–52.

Aykan, H., and D. A. Wolf. 2000. Traditionality, Modernity, and Household Composition: Parent–Child Coresidence in Contemporary Turkey. *Research on Aging* 22, no. 4:395–421.

Aziz, M. A. 2011. *The Kurds of Iraq: National Identity in Iraqi Kurdistan.* London: I B Tauris.

Baffoun, A. 1982. Women and Social Change in the Muslim Arab World. *Women's Studies International Forum* 5, no. 2:227–242.

Bahaddin, S. 2010a. The Killers of 21 Kurdish Women Still Not Arrested in Iraqi Kurdistan. Ekurd Daily. Accessed December 13, 2010. https://ekurd.net/mismas/articles/misc2010/12/state4433.htm

Bahaddin, S. 2010b. *Kurdish Pregnant Woman Shot 20 Times in Honour Killing, Iraqi Kurdistan.* Ekurd Daily. Accessed January 3, 2012. http://www.ekurd.net/mismas/articles/misc2010/7/state4015.htm.

Bahaddin, S. 2012. Women's Group Calls for Nationwide Campaign against Honor Killing. Ekurd Daily. Accessed August 13, 2012. https://ekurd.net/mismas/articles/misc2012/8/state6420.htm

Ballard, R. 2011. Honour Killing? Or Just Plain Homicide? In *Cultural Expertise and Litigation: Patterns, Conflicts, Narratives,* edited by L. Holden, 124–147. London: Routledge.

Bano, S. 2010. Tackling "Crimes of Honour": Evaluating the Social and Legal Responses for Combating Forced Marriages in the UK. In *Honour, Violence, Women and Islam,* edited by M. M. Idriss and T. Abbas, 201–218. London: Routledge.

Baron, B. 2006. Women, Honour, and the State: Evidence from Egypt. *Middle Eastern Studies* 42, no. 1:1–20.

Barth, F. 1953. *Principles of Social Organisation in Southern Kurdistan.* Oslo: Brodene Jorgensen.

Barth, F. 1954. *Father's Brother's Daughter Marriage in Kurdistan.* Albuquerque: University of New Mexico.

Bates, R. H. 2010. *Prosperity and Violence: The Political Economy of Development.* New York: W. W. Norton.

Bedell, G. 2004. Death before Dishonour. *Guardian,* November 21, 2004.

Beekers, D., and B. Van Gool. 2012. *From Patronage to Neopatrimonialism: Postcolonial Governance in Sub-Sahara Africa and Beyond.* Leiden, Netherlands: African Studies Centre.

Begikhani, N. 1998. Jinî Kurd û Izlamism. *Gzing* 21:19–23.

Begikhani, N. 2005. Honour-Based Violence among the Kurds: The Case of Iraqi Kurdistan. In *"Honour": Crimes, Paradigms and Violence against Women,* edited by L. Welchman and S. Hossain, 209–230. London: Zed Books.

Begikhani, N., and N. M. Faraj. 2016. Legal Treatment of Honour Crimes: Comparison between Iraqi National and Kurdistan's Region's Laws. *European Journal of Comparative Law and Governance* 3, no. 2:130–152.

Begikhani, N., et al. 2010. *Honour-Based Violence and Honour-Based Killings in Iraqi Kurdistan and in the Kurdish Diaspora in the UK.* Bristol: Centre for Gender and Violence Research.

Begikhani, N., et al. 2018. Theorising Women and War in Kurdistan: A Feminist and Critical Perspective. *Kurdish Studies* 6, no. 1:5–30.

Belge, C. 2011. State Building and the Limits of Legibility: Kinship Networks and Kurdish Resistance in Turkey. *International Journal of Middle Eastern Studies* 43, 1:95–114.

Bell, D. 1998. Wealth Transfers Occasioned by Marriage: A Comparative Reconsideration. In *Kinship, Networks and Exchange,* edited by T. Schweizer and D. R. White, 187–210. Cambridge: Cambridge University Press.

Ben-Yorath, Y. 1980. The F-Connection: Families, Firms and the Organisation of Exchange. *Population Council* 6, no. 1:1–30.

Betzig, L. 2012. Means, Variances, and Ranges in Reproductive Success: Comparative Evidence. *Evolution and Human Behavior* 33, no. 4:309–317.

Bianquis, T. 1996. The Family in Arab Islam. In *A History of the Family Volume 1,* edited by A. Burgière et al., 637. Cambridge: Polity Press.

Bird, C. 2005. *A Thousand Sighs, A Thousand Revolts: Journeys in Kurdistan.* New York: Random House.

Bishop, I. L. B. 1891. *Journeys in Persia and Kurdistan, Including a Summer in the Upper Karun Region and a Visit to the Nestorian Rayahs*. London: John Murray.

Bitlîsî, S. a.-D. (1597) 2005. *The Sharafnâma, or the History of the Kurdish Nation 1597, Book One*. Costa Mesa, Calif.: Mazda Publishers.

Black, D. 1983. Crime as Social Control. *American Sociological Review* 48, no. 1:4–45.

Blank, H. 2007. *Virgin: The Untouched History*. New York: Bloomsbury.

Bois, T. 1966. *The Kurds*. Beirut: Khayats.

Borgerhoff Mulder, M. 1988. Kipsigis Bridewealth Payments. In *Human Reproductive Behaviour*, edited by L. Betzig et al., 65–82. Cambridge: Cambridge University Press.

Boserup, E. 1970. *Woman's Role in Economic Development*. London: Earthscan.

Bourdieu, P. 1965. The Sentiment of Honour in Kabyle Society. In *Honour and Shame: The Values of Mediterranean Society*, edited by J. G. Peristiany, 191–243. Chicago: University of Chicago Press.

Bourdieu, P. 1977. *Outline of a Theory of Practice*. Cambridge: Cambridge University Press.

Bourdieu, P. 2001. *Masculine Domination*. Cambridge: Polity Press.

Bourdieu, P. 2006. Gender and Symbolic Violence. In *Violence in War and Peace: An Anthology*, edited by N. Scheper-Hughes and P. Bourgois, 339–343. Malden: Blackwell.

Bozarslan, H. 2004. *Violence in the Middle East: From Political Struggle to Self-Sacrifice*. Princeton: Markus Wiener Publishers.

Brake, E. 2012. *Minimizing Marriage: Marriage, Modernity and the Law*. New York: Oxford University Press.

Bredström, A. 2003. Gendered Racism and the Production of Cultural Difference: Media Representations and Identity Work among "Immigrant Youth" in Contemporary Sweden. *NORA—Nordic Journal of Feminist and Gender Research* 11, no. 2:78–88.

Brenneman, R. L. 2007. *As Strong as the Mountains: A Kurdish Cultural Journey*. Long Grove, IL: Waveland Press.

Broude, G. J., and S. J. Greene. 1983. Cross-Cultural Codes on Husband Wife Relationships. *Ethnology* 22, 3:263–280.

Brownlee, J. 2002. . . . And Yet They Persist: Explaining Survival and Transition in Neopatriarchal Regimes. *Studies in Comparative International Development* 37, no. 3:35–63.

Burton, M. L., and K. Reitz. 1981. The Plow, Female Contribution to Agricultural Subsistence and Polygyny: A Log Linear Analysis. *Cross-Cultural Research* 16, no. 3–4:275–305.

Burton, M. L., et al. 1996. Regions Based on Social Structure. *Current Anthropology* 37, no. 1:87–123.

Busby, A. 1994. Kurds: A Culture Straddling National Borders. In *Portraits of Culture: Ethnographic Originals*, edited by C. R. Ember et al, 87–91. Englewood Cliffs, N.J.: Prentice Hall.

Buunk, A. P., and A. C. Solano. 2012. Mate Guarding and Parental Influence on Mate Choice. *Personal Relationships* 19, no. 1:103–112.

Buunk, A. P., et al. 2008. Parent–Offspring Conflict in Mate Preferences. *Review of General Psychology* 12, no. 1:47–62.

Caldwell, J. 1982. *Theory of Fertility Decline*. London: Academic Press.

Campbell, J. K. 1964. *Honour, Family and Patronage: A Study of Institutions and Moral Values in a Greek Mountain Community*. Oxford: Oxford University Press.

Caplan, P. 1984. Cognatic Descent, Islamic Law and Women's Property on the East African Coast. In *Women and Property, Women as Property*, edited by R. Herschon, 23–43. London: Croom Helm.

Caulfield, S. 2000. *In Defense of Honor: Sexual Morality, Modernity and Nation in Early Twentieth Century Brazil*. Durham, N.C.: Duke University Press.

Cavalli-Sforza, L. L. 1996. The Spread of Agriculture and Nomadic Pastoralism: Insights from Genetics, Linguistics and Archaeology. In *The Origins and Spread of Agriculture and Pastoralism in Eurasia*, edited by D. R. Harris, 51–70. London: UCL Press.

Cavallo, S., and S. Cerutti. 1990. Female Honor and the Social Control of Reproduction in Piedmont between 1600 and 1800. In *Sex and Gender in Historical Perspective: Selections from Quaderni Storici*, edited by E. Muir et al., 73–109. Baltimore: Johns Hopkins University Press.

Charrad, M. 2000. Becoming a Citizen: Lineage versus Individual in Tunisia and Morocco. In *Gender and Citizenship in the Middle East*, edited by S. Joseph, 70–88. Syracuse, N.Y.: Syracuse University Press.

Charrad, M. 2001. *States and Women's Rights: The Making of Postcolonial Tunisia, Algeria and Morocco*. Berkeley: University of California Press.

Charrad, M. 2012. *Family Law Reforms in the Arab World: Tunisia and Morocco*. New York: United Nations Department of Economic and Social Affairs.

Chesler, P. 2010. Worldwide Trends in Honor Killings. *Middle East Quarterly* 17, no. 2 (Spring):3–11.

Cihangar, S. 2013. Gender Specific Honor Codes and Cultural Change. *Group Processes & Intergroup Relations* 16, no. 3:319–333.

Cobbett, D. 1989. Women in Iraq. In *Saddam's Iraq: Revolution or Reaction*, edited by the Committee against Repression and for Democratic Right in Iraq, 120–37. London. Zed Books.

Cohen, D., and R. E. Nisbett. 1996. *Culture of Honor: The Psychology of Violence in the South*. Boulder, Colo.: Westview Press.

Cohen, O., and R. Savaya. 1997. "Broken Glass": The Divorced Woman in Moslem Arab Society in Israel. *Family Process* 36, no. 3:225–245.

Collier, J. F. 1988. *Marriage and Inequality in Classless Societies*. Stanford, Calif.: Stanford University Press.

Collins, R. 2008. *Violence: A Micro-sociological Theory*. Princeton, N.J.: Princeton University Press.

Cook, M. 2001. *Commanding Right and Forbidding Wrong in Islamic Thought*. Cambridge: Cambridge University Press.

Coomaraswamy, R. 2005. Preface. In *"Honour": Crimes, Paradigms and Violence against Women*, edited by L. Welchman and S. Hossain, S., xi–xiv. London: Zed Books.

Coontz, S. 2004. The World Historical Transformation of Marriage. *Journal of Marriage and the Family* 66, no. 4:974–979.

Cooper, J. S. 2002. Virginity in Ancient Mesopotamia. In *Sex and Gender in the Ancient Near East : Proceedings of the 47th Rencontre Assyriolgique Internationale*, edited by S. Parpola and R. M. Whiting, 91–112. Helsinki: Helsinki University Press.

Copestake, J. 2006. Gays Flee Iraq as Shia Death Squads Find a New Target. *Guardian*, August 6, 2006.

Danish Immigration Service. 2010. *Honour Crimes against Men in Kurdistan Region of Iraq and the Availability of Protection: Report from the Danish Immigration Service's Fact-Ginding Mission to Erbil and Dahuk, KRI*. Copenhagen: Danish Immigration Service.

Daradkeh, T. K., et al. 2006. Psychiatric Morbidity and Its Sociodemographic Correlates among Women in Irbid, Jordan. *Eastern Mediterranean Health Journal* 12(Suppl. 2): S107–S117.

Das, B. 2010. For Better or Worse, "Sister-Swapping" Persists. Women's ENews. Accessed March 12, 2012. http://womensenews.org/story/marriagedivorcemotherhood/100319 /better-or-worse-sister-swapping-persists.

Das, V. 1995. National Honor and Practical Kinship: Unwanted Women and Children. In *Conceiving the New World Order: The Global Politics of Reproduction*, edited by F. D. Ginsburg and R. Rapp, 212–233. Berkeley: University of California Press.

David, B., and B. O. Olatunji. 2011. The Effect of Disgust Conditioning and Disgust Sensitivity on Appraisals of Moral Transgressions. *Personality and Individual Differences* 50, no. 7:1142–1146.

Deccan, M. 2016. Constructing Honour: Making Sense of Honour Crime. Paper presented at the International Criminology Congress. New Delhi, India.

Delphy, C., and D. Leonard. 1992. *Familiar Exploitation: A New Analysis of Marriage in Contemporary Western Societies*. Cambridge: Polity Press.

Denich, B. S. 1974. Sex and Power in the Balkans. In *Woman, Culture and Society*, edited by M. Z. Rosaldo and L. Lamphere, 243–263. Palo Alto, California: Stanford University Press.

Diamond, J. 2007. *Guns, Germs and Steel*. New York: W. W. Norton.

Dirik, D. 2014. Women, Resistance and the Kurdish Question in the 21st Century. London: Department of Politics and International Relations: Westminster University. Accessed March 22, 2014. https://www.youtube.com/watch?list=UU5wrgpJVEUa-vACRJpwOqEg&v=0QFTPZ2YKSY.

Divale, W. T., and M. Harris. 1976. Population, Warfare, and the Male Supremacist Complex. *American Anthropologist* 78, no. 3:521–538.

Donnan, H., and F. Magowan. 2010. *The Anthropology of Sex*. Oxford and New York: Berg.

Douglas, M. 1966. *Purity and Danger: An Analysis of Concepts of Pollution and Taboo*. London: Routledge.

Duarte, M. 2006. *Violence against Women in Georgia: Report Submitted on the Occasion of the 36th Session of the UN Committee on the Elimination of Discrimination against Women*. New York: Georgian Young Lawyers Association; World Organisation against Torture.

Dube, L. 1997. *Women and Kinship: Comparative Perspectives on Gender in South and South-East Asia*. Tokyo: United Nations University Press.

Dunbar, R. 1998. *Grooming, Gossip and the Evolution of Language*. Cambridge, Mass.: Harvard University Press.

Düzkan, A., and F. Kocali. 2000. An Honour Killing: She Fled, Her Throat Was Cut. In *Women and Sexuality in Muslim Societies*, edited by P. Ilkkaracan, 381–387. Istanbul: Women for Women's Human Rights.

Dyson, T., and M. Moore. 1983. On Kinship Structure, Female Autonomy, and Demographic Behavior in India. *Population and Development Review* 9, no. 1:35–60.

Dzięgel, L. 1982. Life Cycle within the Iraqi Kurd Family. *Ethnologia Polona* 8:247–260.

Efrati, N. 2005. Negotiating Rights in Iraq: Women and the Personal Status Law. *Middle East Journal* 59, no. 4:577–595.

Ehrenreich, B., and D. English. 2005. *For Her Own Good: Two Centuries of the Experts' Advice to Women*. New York: Anchor Books.

Eisenstadt, S. N. 1973. *Traditional Patrimonialism and Modern Neopatrimonialism*. Beverley Hills: Sage.

Eisner, M., and L. Ghuneim. 2013. Honor Killing Attitudes amongst Adolescents in Amman, Jordan. *Aggressive Behaviour* 39, no. 5:415–417.

El Saadawi, N. (1977) 1980. *The Hidden Face of Eve: Women in the Arab World*. London: Zed Books.

Elvin, M. 1984. Female Virtue and the State in China. *Past and Present* 104, 1:111–152.

Ember, M., et al. 2007. Comparing Explanations of Polygyny. *Cross-Cultural Research* 41, no. 4:428–440.

Engels, F. (1884) 2010. *The Origin of the Family, Private Property and the State.* Marxists.org. Accessed December 7, 2011. http://www.marxists.org/archive/marx/works/1884/origin -family/.

Enloe, C. H. 1983. *Does Khaki Become You? The Militarisation of Women's Lives.* London: Pluto Press.

Ersen, M. T. 2002. Parallel Brides: For Some Families in Turkey, Matchmaking Is an Intricate Dance. *Natural History* 111, no. 4:72–79.

Ertem, M., and T. Kocturk. 2008. Opinions on Early-Age Marriage and Marriage Customs among Kurdish-Speaking Women in Southeast Turkey. *Journal of Family Planning and Reproductive Health Care* 34, no. 3:147–152.

Ertürk, Y. 2009. Towards a Post-Patriarchal Gender Order: Confronting the Universality and the Particularity of Violence against Women. *Sociologisk Forskinning* 46, no. 4:58–67.

Esmer, T. 2010. Berdel: A Kurdish Tradition Known as Sister Swapping and Parallel Weddings. *Firat News Agency,* May 30, 2010.

Espers, P. 2011. *Markets.* Malden, Mass.: Polity Press.

Esposito, J. L., and N. J. DeLong-Bass. 2007. *Women in Muslim Family Law.* Syracuse, N.Y.: Syracuse University Press.

Faqir, F. 2001. Intrafamily Femicide in Defence of Honour: The Case of Jordan. *Third World Quarterly* 22, no. 1:65–82.

Fernea, E. W. 1985. Part II: The Family. In *Women and the Family in the Middle East: New Voices of Change,* edited by E. W. Fernea, 25–26. Austin: University of Texas Press.

Fieldhouse, D. K. 2006. Britain in Mesopotamia/Iraq 1918–1958. In *Western Imperialism in the Middle East 1914–1958,* edited by D. K. Fieldhouse, 67–117. Oxford: Oxford University Press.

Fischer, M. 1973. Zoroastrian Iran between Myth and Praxis. PhD diss., University of Chicago Library.

Fischer-Tahir, A. 2009. *Brave Men, Pretty Women?: Gender and Symbolic Violence in Iraqi Kurdish Urban Society.* Berlin: Europäisches Zentrum für Kurdische Studien.

Fisher, H. 1992. *Anatomy of Love: A Natural History of Monogamy, Adultery and Divorce.* London: Simon & Schuster.

Fiske, A. P. 1992. The Four Elementary Forms of Sociality: Framework for a Unified Theory of Social Relations. *Psychological Review* 99, no. 4:689–723.

Fitz-Gibbon, K. 2009. "Till Death Do Us Part": Judging the Men Who Kill Their Intimate Partners. In *Australia & New Zealand Critical Criminology Conference 2009,* edited by M. Segrave, 78–88. Melbourne: Monash University.

Food and Agriculture Organization. 2001. *Pastoralism in the New Millennium.* Rome: United Nations.

Fortunato, L. 2011. Reconstructing the History of Marriage Strategies in Indo-European-Speaking Societies: Monogamy and Bridewealth. *Human Biology* 83, no. 1:87–105.

Fortunato, L. 2015. Evolution of Marriage Systems. In *International Encyclopedia of the Social & Behaviorial Sciences,* vol. 14, 2nd ed., edited by J. D. Wright, 611–619. Oxford: Elsevier.

Fricke, T. E., et al. 1986. Rural Punjabi Social Organisation and Marriage Timing Strategies in Pakistan. *Demography* 23, no. 4:489–508.

Friedan, B. 1963. *The Feminine Mystique.* New York: W. W. Norton.

Fukuyama, F. 2001. Social Capital, Civil Society and Development. *Third World Quarterly* 22, no. 1:7–20.

Gangoli, G., et al. 2006. *Forced Marriage and Domestic Violence among South Asian Communities in North East England.* Bristol: School for Policy Studies, University of Bristol.

Gengler, J. J., et al. 2018. Who Supports Honor Based Violence in the Middle East: Findings from a National Survey of Kuwait. *Journal of Interpersonal Violence*. Accessed May 29, 2019. https://journals.sagepub.com/doi/abs/10.1177/0886260518812067?journalCode=jiva

Geopolicity. 2009. *Iraq Education Sector Scoping Survey*. British Virgin Islands: Geopolicity.

Gezer, M. 2008. Honor Killing Perpetrators Welcomed by Society, Study Reveals. *Sunday's Zaman*, July 12, 2008.

Ghazzal, Z. 2015. The Problem of Recipiency in Honor Killings. In *The Crime of Writing: Narrative and Social Order in Criminal Trials in Ba'athist Syria*. Beyrouth: Presses de l'Ifpo. Accessed May 29, 2019. https://books.openedition.org/ifpo/9377.

Ghimire, Dirgha J., et al. 2006. Social Change, Premarital Nonfamily Experience, and Spouse Choice in an Arranged Marriage Society. *American Journal of Sociology* 111, no. 4:1181–1218.

Gill, A. 2006. Patriarchal Violence in the Name of Honour. *International Journal of Criminal Justice Sciences* 1, no. 1:1–12.

Gill, A. 2009. Honor Killings and the Quest for Justice in Black and Minority Ethnic Communities in the United Kingdom. *Criminal Justice Policy Review* 20, no. 4:475–494.

Gill, A., and A. Brah. 2014. Interrogating Cultural Narratives about "Honour"-based Violence. *European Journal of Women's Studies* 21, no. 1:72–86.

Ginat, J. 1981, Sororicide/Filiacide: Homicide for Family Honor. *Current Anthropology* 22, no. 2:141–158.

Glazer, I., and W. Abu Ras. 1994. On Aggression, Human Rights and Hegemonic Discourse: The Case of a Murder for Family Honour in Israel. *Sex Roles* 30, no. 3/4:296–288.

Goddard, V. 1987. Honour and Shame: The Control of Women's Sexuality and Group Identity in Naples. In *The Cultural Construction of Sexuality*, edited by P. Caplan, 166–192. London: Tavistock Publications.

Goffman, E. 1963. *Stigma: Notes on the Management of Spoiled Identity*. London: Penguin.

Goldschmidt, W. 1971. Independence as an Element in Pastoral Social Systems. *Anthropological Quarterly* 44, no. 3:132–142.

González-López, G. 2004. Fathering Latina Sexualities: Mexican Men and the Virginity of Their Daughters. *Journal of Marriage and Family* 66, no. 5:1118–1130.

Goody, J. 1983. *The Development of the Family and Marriage in Europe*. Cambridge: Cambridge University Press.

Goody, J., and S. J. Tambiah. 1973. *Bridewealth and Dowry*. Cambridge: CUP Archive.

Gotkowitz, L. 2003. Trading Insults: Honor, Violence and the Gendered Culture of Commerce in Cochabamba, Bolivia, 1870s–1950s. *Hispanic American Historical Review* 83, no. 1:83–118.

Granovetter, M. S. 1973. The Strength of Weak Ties. *American Journal of Sociology* 7, no. 6:1360–1380.

Greene, M. E., and W. H. Crocker. 1994. Some Demographic Aspects of the Canela Indians of Brazil. *South American Indian Studies* 4:47–62.

Grégoire-Blaise, M. 2010. *Iraqi Women: Lost liberties*. Brussels: Alternatives; Iraqi Democratic Future Network.

Greiff, S. 2010. *No Justice in Justifications: Violence against Women in the Name of Culture, Religion, and Tradition*. London: Women Living Under Muslim Laws.

Grossbard, A. 1978. Towards a Marriage between Economics and Anthropology and a General Theory of Marriage. *American Economic Review* 68, no. 2:33–37.

Gutiérrez, R. A. 1985. Honor Ideology, Marriage Negotiation, and Class-Gender Domination in New Mexico, 1690–1846. *Latin American Perspectives* 12, no. 1:81–104.

Haarr, R. N. 2010. Suicidality among Battered Women in Tajikistan. *Violence Against Women* 16, no. 7:764–788.

Haghighat, E. 2013. Social Status and Change: The Question of Access to Resources and Women's Empowerment in the Middle East and North Africa. *Journal of International Women's Studies* 14, no. 1:273–299.

Hague, G., et al. 2011. Bride-Price and Its Links to Domestic Violence and Poverty in Uganda: A Participatory Action Research Survey. *Women's Studies International Forum* 34:550–551.

Hansen, H. H. 1961. *The Kurdish Woman's Life: Field Research in a Muslim Society, Iraq.* Copenhagen: Nationalmuseet.

Hardi, C. 2011. *Gendered Experiences of Genocide: Anfal Survivors in Kurdistan-Iraq.* London: Ashgate.

Harris, D. R. 1996. The Origins and Spread of Agriculture and Pastoralism in Eurasia: An Overview. In *The Origins and Spread of Agriculture and Pastoralism in Eurasia*, edited by D. R. Harris, 552–575. London: UCL Press.

Harris, M. 1997. *Culture, People, Nature: An Introduction to General Anthropology.* 7th ed. New York: Longman.

Harris, M. 2001. *Cultural Materialism: The Struggle for a Science of Culture.* Walnut Creek, Calif.: Altamira.

Hartman, M. S. 2004. *The Household and the Making of History: A Subversive View of the Western Past.* Cambridge: Cambridge University Press.

Hartsock, N. 1985. *Money, Sex and Power: Towards a Feminist Historical Materialism.* Boston: Northeastern University Press.

Hashim, A. S. 2006. Contending National Identities: The Kurds and the Shi'a Arabs. In *Insurgency and Counter-Insurgency in Iraq*, edited by A. S. Hashim, 214–230. Ithaca, N.Y.: Cornell University Press.

Hassanpour, A. 2001. The (Re)production of Patriarchy in the Kurdish Language. In *Women of a Non-State Nation: The Kurds*, edited by S. Mojab, 228–260. Costa Mesa, Calif.: Mazda Publishing.

Hay, W. R. (1920) 2008. *Two Years in Kurdistan: Experiences of a Political Officer, 1918–1920.* Washington: Westphalia Press.

Head, S. 1974. *The Kurdish Tragedy.* New York Review of Books, July 18, 1974. Accessed May 23, 2019. https://www.nybooks.com/articles/1974/07/18/the-kurdish-tragedy.

Heinrich Böll Stiftung. 2010. Interview with Hanaa' Edward, Secretary General of the Iraqi Alamal Association and Judge Salem Rawdan al-Moussawi: Iraqi Women and the National Personal Status Law. Beirut: Heinrich Böll Stiftung: Middle East. Accessed October 9, 2012. http://www.lb.boell.org/web/52-263.html.

Hélie-Lucas, M.-A. 1994. The Preferential Symbol for Islamic Identity: Women in Muslim Personal Status Laws. In *Identity Politics and Women: Cultural Reassertions and Feminisms in International Perspective*, edited by V. M. Moghadam, 391–401. Boulder, Colo.: Westview Press.

Him, M. S., and A. G. Hoşgör. 2011. Reproductive Practises: Kurdish Women Responding to Patriarchy. *Women's Studies International Forum* 34, no. 4:335–344.

Hirsi Ali, A. 2007. *The Caged Virgin: A Muslim Woman's Cry for Reason.* London: Pocket Books.

Holý, L. 1989. *Kinship, Honour and Solidarity: Cousin Marriage in the Middle East.* Manchester: Manchester University Press.

Home Office, 2017. *Country Policy and Information Note—Iraq: Kurdish "Honour" Crimes.* London: HM Government.

Horne, C. 2004. Collective Benefits, Exchange Interests and Norm Enforcement. *Social Forces* 82, no. 3:1037–1062.

Houston, C. 2008. *Kurdistan: Crafting of National Selves.* Oxford: Berg.

Hoyek, D., et al. 2005. Murders of Women in the Lebanon: "Crimes of Honour" between Reality and Law. In *"Honour": Crimes, Paradigms and Violence against Women,* edited by L. Welchman and S. Hossain, 111–137. London: Zed Books.

Hsieh, A. K., and J. Spence. 1981. Suicide and the Family in Pre-modern Chinese Society. In *Normal and Abnormal Behavior in Chinese Culture,* Vol. 2, edited by A. Kleinman and T.-Y. Lin, 29–47. Springer Netherlands.

Hua, C. 2008. *A Society without Fathers or Husbands: The Na of China.* New York: Zone Books.

Hürriyet. 2011. Family Minister Slams Proposal on Rapists Marrying Victims. *Hürriyet,* August 19, 2011.

Husseini, R. 2009. *Murder in the Name of Honor.* Oxford: Oneworld Publications.

Hutchings, K., and D. Weir. 2006. Guanxi and Wasta: A Comparison. *Thunderbird International Business Review* 48, no. 1:141–156.

Hyden, G. 1997. Civil Society, Social Capital and Development: Dissection of a Complex Discourse. *Studies in Comparative International Development* 32, no. 1:3–31.

Ibn Khaldūn. (1377) 2005. *The Muqaddimah: An Introduction to History.* Princeton, N.J.: Princeton University Press.

Ilkkaracan, P. 2001. Islam and Women's Sexuality: A Research Report from Turkey. In *Good Sex: Feminist Perspectives from the World's Religions,* edited by M. Hunt et al. New Brunswick, N.J.: Rutgers University Press.

Ilkkaracan, P. 2004. How Adultery Almost Derailed Turkey's Aspiration to Join the European Union. In *Sex Politics: Reports from the Front Lines,* edited by R. Parker et al., 247–277. Rio de Janeiro: Sexuality Policy Watch Secretariat.

Ilkkaracan, P. 2007. *Reforming the Penal Code in Turkey: The Campaign for the Reform of the Turkish Penal Code from a Gender Perspective.* Istanbul: Women for Women's Human Rights.

iMAPP. 2011. British Colombia: The Case against Polygamy. *Institute for Marriage and Public Policy* 40, no. 8:1–9.

International Encyclopedia of the Social Sciences. 1968. Pastoralism. Accessed September 28, 2010. http://www.encyclopedia.com/topic/Pastoral_systems.aspx.

International Rescue Committee. 2004. *Assessment on Violence and Women in Azerbaijan: An Overview of Violence in the Lives of Women in IRC's Beneficiary Population.* International Rescue Committee: Azerbaijan Program.

Iraq Women Integrated Social and Health Survey. 2011. *Knowledge, Behavior and Ambitions of Adolescent Girls.* Geneva: United Nations.

Iraq Women Integrated Social and Health Survey. 2012. *Summary Report.* Ministry of Planning Central Statistical Organization.

Iraqi Civil Solidarity Initiative. 2013. In Iraqi Kurdistan, Those Who Murder Women Go Free. Erbil: Kurd Net. Accessed November 6, 2013. http://www.ekurd.net/mismas/articles/misc2013/5/state7084.htm.

IRIN. 2009. Syria: Half Measures on Honour Killings Not Enough—HRW. Dubai: UN Office for the Coordination of Humanitarian Affairs. Accessed February 6, 2016. http://www.irinnews.org/report/85481/syria-half-measures-against-honour-killings-not-enough-hrw.

Ismael, J. S., and S. T. Ismael. 2000. Gender and State in Iraq. In *Gender and Citizenship in the Middle East,* edited by S. Joseph, 185–215. Syracuse: Syracuse University Press.

IWPR–Syria. 2009. Coerced Cousin Marriages Remain Common. Institute for War and Peace Reporting. Accessed November 29, 2011. http://iwpr.net/report-news/coerced-cousin -marriages-remain-common.

Izady, M. R. 1992. *The Kurds: A Concise Handbook*. Philadelphia: Taylor & Francis.

Jacoby, H. G., and G. Mansuri. 2007. *Watta Satta: Bride Exchange and Women's Welfare in Rural Pakistan*. Washington: The World Bank.

Jafri, A. H. 2008. *Honour Killing: Dilemma, Ritual, Understanding*. Karachi, Pakistan: Oxford University Press.

Jaggar, A. M. 1983. *Feminist Politics and Human Nature*. Lanham, Md.: Rowman & Littlefield.

Jallinoja, R. 2011. Obituaries as Family Assemblages. In *Families and Kinship in Contemporary Europe*, edited by R Jallinoja, R. and E D Widmer, E.D, 78–95. Basingstoke: Palgrave Macmillan.

Jeffreys, S. 1985. *The Spinster and Her Enemies: Feminism and Sexuality 1880–1930*. London: Pandora.

Johnson, J. C. A. 1940. The Kurds of Iraq II. *Geographical Magazine* 11:50–59.

Johnstone, N. 2009. Kurdish Villages Reject Marriage Traditions. Al Jazeera. Accessed May 3, 2019. https://www.youtube.com/watch?v=guuDC-_QqMo

Jones, D. 2003a. Kinship and Deep History: Exploring Connections between Cultural Areas, Genes and Language. *American Anthroplogist* 105, no. 3:501–514.

Jones, G. W. 2003b. *The "Flight from Marriage" in South-East and East Asia*. Singapore: Asian Metacentre for Population and Sustainable Development Analysis.

Jones, G. W. 2010. *Changing Marriage Patterns in Asia*. Singapore: Asia Research Institute, National University of Singapore.

Joseph, S. 1996. Patriarchy and Development in the Arab World. *Gender and Development* 4, no. 2:14–19.

Joseph, S. 1999. Brother–Sister Relationships: Connectivity, Love and Power in the Reproduction of Power in Lebanon. In *Intimate Selving in Arab Families: Gender, Self and Identity*, edited by S. Joseph, 113–141. Syracuse, N.Y.: Syracuse University Press.

Joseph, S. 2000a. Civic Myths, Citizenship and Gender in Lebanon. In *Gender and Citizenship in the Middle East*, edited by S. Joseph, 107–137. Syracuse, N.Y.: Syracuse University Press.

Joseph, S. 2000b. Gendering Citizenship in the Middle East. In *Gender and Citizenship in the Middle East*, edited by S. Joseph, 3–33. Syracuse, N.Y.: Syracuse University Press.

Joseph, S., and S. Slyomovic. 2001. Introduction. In *Women and Power in the Middle East*, edited by S. Joseph and S. Slyomovic, 1–23. Philadelphia: University of Pennsylvania Press.

KA-MER. 2005. *Who's to Blame?: Project for the Development of Permanent Methods in the Struggle against Killings Committed under the Guise of "Honor" in Southeast and East Anatolia Regions*. Diyarbakir: KA-MER.

Kağitçibaşi, C. 1989. Family and Socialization in Cross-Cultural Perspective: A Model of Change. *Current Theory and Research in Motivation*, no. 37:135–200.

Kandiyoti, D. 1988. Bargaining with Patriarchy. *Gender and Society* 2, no. 3:274–290.

Kane, D., and K. Gorbenko. 2011. States and Women's Rights in Central Asia. Presented at American Sociological Association Annual Meeting. Caesar's Palace, Las Vegas, August 19, 2011.

Kara, O. 2004. Töre, bu kez Nuran'ı boğarak öldürdü. *Milliyet*, April 28, 2004.

Karahan, F. 1995. Kurdish Women in Turkish Cities. War Resisters' International. Accessed August 19, 2012. http://wri-irg.org/node/3776.

Kargar, Z. 2011. *Dear Zari: Hidden Stories from Women in Afghanistan*. London: Chatto & Windus.

Katz, J. 1988. *Seductions of Crime*. New York: Basic Books.

Kaye, D. K., et al. 2000. Implications of Bride Price on Domestic Violence and Reproductive Health in Wakiso District, Uganda. *African Health Sciences* 5, no. 4:300–303.

Kelly, K. C. 2000. *Performing Virginity and Testing Chastity in the Middle Ages*. London: Routledge.

Khalil, S. 2013. How Kurdistan Ended Female Genital Mutilation. *GulfNews*, October 24, 2013.

Khan, T. S. 2006. *Beyond Honour: A Historical Materialist Explanation of Honour Related Violence*. Karachi, Pakistan: Oxford University Press.

Khuri, F. I. 1970. Parallel Cousin Marriage Reconsidered: A Middle Eastern Practice That Nullifies the Effects of Marriage on the Intensity of Family Relationships. *Man* 5, no. 4:597–618.

King, D. E. 2008a. Back from the "Outside": Returnees and Diasporic Imagining in Iraqi Kurdistan. *International Journal on Multicultural Societies* 10, no. 2:208–222.

King, D. E. 2008b. The Personal Is Patrilinear: Namus as Sovereignty. *Identities* 15, no. 3:317–342.

King, D. E., and L. Stone, L. 2010. Lineal Masculinity: Gendered Memory within Patriliny. *American Ethnologist* 37, no. 2:323–336.

King-Irani, L. 2004. Kinship, Class and Ethnicity. In *Understanding the Contemporary Middle East*, edited by J. Schwedler and D. J. Gerner, 299–335. Boulder, Colo.: Lynne Reiner Publishers.

Kiryashova, S. 2005. Azeri Bride Kidnappers Risk Heavy Sentences. Institute for War and Peace Reporting. Accessed February 29, 2012. http://iwpr.net/report-news/azeri-bride-kidnappers-risk-heavy-sentences.

Kizilhan, J. I., and M. Noll-Hussong. 2017. Individual, Collective, and Transgenerational Traumatization in the Yazidi. *BMC Medicine* 15:198.

Kleinbach, R., et al. 2004. Характеристика и частота умыкания невест в кыргызской деревне: январь 2004г. Philadephia: Philadelphia University. Accessed March 7, 2012. http://faculty.philau.edu/kleinbachr/2004_study1.htm.

Koğacıoğlu, D. 2011. Knowledge, Practice, and Political Community: The Making of the "Custom" in Turkey. *differences: A Journal of Feminist Cultural Studies* 22, no. 1:172–228.

Koğacıoğlu, D. 2004. The Tradition Effect: Framing Honor Crimes in Turkey. *differences: A journal of feminist cultural studies* 15, no. 2:119–151.

Kohli, K. L. 1977. Regional Variations of Fertility in Iraq and Factors Affecting It. *Journal of Biosocial Science* 9, no. 2:175–182.

Korotayev, A. 2000. Parallel-cousin (FBD) Marriage, Islamization, and Arabization. *Ethnology* 39, no. 4:395–407.

Korteweg, A., and G. Yurdakul. 2009. Islam, Gender, and Immigrant Integration: Boundary Drawing in Discourses on Honour Killing in the Netherlands and Germany. *Ethnic and Racial Studies* 32, no. 2:218–238.

Kressel, G., et al. 1981. Sororicide/Filiacide: Homicide for Family Honour [and comments and reply]. *Current Anthropology* 22, no. 2:141–158.

Kressel, G. M. 1977. Bride-Price Reconsidered [and Comments]. *Current Anthropology* 18, no. 3:441–458.

Kressel, G. M. 1992. *Descent through Males: An Anthropological Investigation into the Patterns Underlying Social Hierarchy, Kinship and Marriage amongst the Former Bedouin in the Ramla-Lod Area (Israel)*. Weisbaden: Otto Harrassowitz.

Kreyenbroek, P. G, and K. Omarkhali. 2016. Introduction to Special Issue: Yezidism and Yezidi Studies in the early 21st Century. *Kurdish Studies* 4, no. 2:122–130.

Kudat, A., et al. 2000. *Social Assessment and Agriculture Reform in Central Asia and Turkey.* Washington: World Bank.

Kulczycki, A., and S. Windle. 2011. Honor Killings in the Middle East and North Africa: A Systematic Review of the Literature. *Violence Against Women* 17, no. 11:1442–1464.

Kuran, T. 2010. *The Long Divergence: How Islamic Law Held Back the Middle East.* Princeton, N.J.: Princeton University Press.

Kurdish Globe. 2011. NGO Survey Finds Abuse of Women Rising. *Kurdish Globe*, October 1, 2011.

Kurdish Globe. 2011. Statistics Suggest Women's Role Is "Weak" in Government, Politics and Civil Society. *Kurdish Globe*, October 1, 2011.

Laizer, S. 1991. *Into Kurdistan: Frontiers under Fire.* London: Zed Books.

Laizer, S. 1996. *Martyrs, Traitors and Patriots: Kurdistan after the Gulf War.* London: Zed Books.

Lamphere, L. 1974. Strategies, Cooperation and Conflict among Women in Domestic Groups. In *Women, Culture and Society*, edited by M. Z. Rosaldo and L. Lamphere, 97–113. Palo Alto, Calif.: Stanford University Press.

Landau, S. F., et al. 1974. Homicide Victims and Offenders: An Israeli Study. *Journal of Criminal Law & Criminology* 65, no. 3:390–396.

Lattimer, M. 2007. Freedom Lost. *Guardian*, December 13, 2007.

Layoun, M. N. 2001. *Wedded to the Land? Gender, Boundaries and Nationalism in Crisis.* Durham, N.C.: Duke University Press.

Leach, E. R. 1940. *Social and Economic Organisation of the Rowanduz Kurds.* London: The London School of Economics and Political Science.

Lee, G. R., and L. H. Stone. 1980. Mate-Selection Systems and Criteria: Variation according to Family Structure. *Journal of Marriage and Family* 42, no. 2:319–326.

Leonard, M. 2004. Bonding and Bridging Social Capital: Reflections from Belfast. *Sociology* 38, no. 5:927–944.

Lévi-Strauss, C. (1949) 1969. *The Elementary Structures of Kinship.* Boston: Beacon Press.

Lindencrona, F., et al. 2008. Mental Health of Recently Resettled Refugees from the Middle East in Sweden: The Impact of Pre-resettlement Trauma, Resettlement Stress and Capacity to Handle Stress. *Social Psychiatry and Psychiatric Epidemiology* 43, no. 2:121–131.

Lindisfarne, N. 1994. Variant Masculinities, Variant Virginities: Rethinking "honour and shame." In *Dislocating Masculinity: Various Ethnographies*, edited by A. Cornwall and N. Lindisfarne, 82–96. London: Routledge.

Lindner, R. P. 1983. *Nomads and Ottomans in Medieval Anatolia.* Bloomington: Indiana University Press.

Lipsett-Rivera, S., and L. L. Johnson, eds. 1998. *The Faces of Honor: Sex, Shame, and Violence in Colonial Latin America.* Albuquerque: University of New Mexico Press.

Long, J. S. 1997. *Regression Models for Categorical and Limited Dependent Variables.* Thousand Oaks, Calif.: Sage.

Lovett, M. L. 1997. From Sisters to Wives and "Slaves": Redefining Matriliny and the Lives of Lakeside Tonga Women, 1885–1955. *Critique of Anthropology* 17, no. 2:171–187.

Luft, R. E. 2008. Looking for Common Ground: Relief Work in Post-Katrina New Orleans as an American Parable of Race and Gender Violence. *National Women's Studies Association Journal* 20, no. 3:5–31.

Mahmoud, N. 2012. Steady Rise in Women Civil Servants. *Rudaw*, May 6, 2012.

Malhotra, A. 1991. Gender and Changing Generational Relations: Spouse Choice in Indonesia. *Demography* 28, no. 4:549–570.

Malin, C. 2010. *Middle East & North Africa Facebook Demographics.* Spot On Public Relations. Accessed May 5, 2019. https://www.spotonpr.com/wp-content/uploads/2017/10/FacebookMENA_24May10.pdf.

Mangalakova, T. 2003. *The Kanun in Present-Day Albania, Kosovo and Montenegro.* Sofia: International Centre for Minority Studies and Intercultural Relations.

Manser, M., and M. Brown. 1980. Marriage and Household Decision-Making: A Bargaining Analysis. *International Economic Review* 21, no. 1:31–44.

Markosian, D. 2012. Chechen Women in Mortal Fear as President Backs Islamic Honor Killings. *Washington Times*, Sunday, April 12, 2012.

Marx, K. 1859. *A Contribution to the Critique of Political Economy.* Moscow: Progress Publishers.

Mason, L. A. 2010. Honor Bound: Exploring the Disparity of Treatment of Women in Kurdistan, Iraq. PhD. diss., Boone, N.C.: Appalachian State University.

Masters, W. M. 1953. Rowanduz: A Kurdish Administrative and Mercantile Center. PhD. diss., Ann Arbor: University of Michigan.

Mayblin, M. 2011. Death by Marriage: Power, Pride and Morality in Northeast Brazil. *Journal of the Royal Anthropological Institute* 17, 1:133–153.

McDowall, D. 1996. *The Kurds.* London: Minority Rights Group International.

McElroy, M. B., and M. J. Horney. 1981. Nash-Bargained Decisions: Towards a Generalization of Demand Theory. *International Economic Review* 22, no. 2:333–349.

Meeker, M. 1976. Meaning and Society in the Near East: Examples from the Black Sea Turks and Levantine Arabs. *International Journal of Middle East Studies* 7, no. 2:383–422.

Meillassoux, C. 1981. *Maidens, Meal and Money: Capitalism and the Domestic Economy.* Cambridge: Cambridge University Press.

Meiselas, S. 1997. *Kurdistan: In the Shadow of History.* Chicago: University of Chicago Press.

Mernissi, F. 1982. Virginity and Patriarchy. *Women's Studies International Journal* 5, no. 2:183–191.

Mernissi, F. 1985. *Beyond the Veil.* London: Al-Saqi.

Middle East Online. 2013. Barzani's Desire to Stay in Power Turns Parliament Session into Fistfight. Accessed July 9, 2013. http://www.middle-east-online.com/english/?id=59789.

Mill, J. S. 1869. *The Subjection of Women.* London: Longmans, Green, Reader & Dyer.

Miller, B. D. 1984. Daughter Neglect, Women's Work, and Marriage: Pakistan and Bangladesh Compared. *Medical Anthropology* 8, no. 2:109–126.

Miller, D. T., and D. A. Prentice. 1994. Collective Errors and Errors about the Collective. *Personality and Social Psychology Bulletin* 20, no. 5:541–550.

Minallah, S. 2004. Swara: Bridge over Troubled Water. Ethnomedia. Accessed May 5, 2019. https://vimeo.com/106359743.

Minnesota Advocates for Human Rights. 2000. *Domestic Violence in Uzbekistan.* Minnesota: Minnesota Advocates for Human Rights.

Minwalla, S., and S. Portman. 2007. *Human Trafficking in Iraq: Patterns and Practises in Forced Labor and Sexual Exploitation.* Chicago: Heartland Alliance.

Mir Hosseini, Z. 1987. Impact of Wage Labour on Household Fission in Rural Iran. *Journal of Comparative Family Studies* 18, no. 3:445–461.

Mir Hosseini, Z. 2000. *Marriage on Trial: A Study of Islamic Family Law.* London: I B Tauris.

Mir Hosseini, Z. 2010. *Criminalizing Sexuality: Zina Laws as Violence against Women in a Muslim Context.* London: Women Living Under Muslim Laws.

Mir Hosseini, Z. 2012. Sexuality and Inequality: The Marriage Contract and Muslim Legal Tradition. In *Sexuality in Muslim Contexts: Restrictions and Resistance*, edited by A. Hélie and H. Hoodfar, 124–148. London: Zed Books.

Mitchell, R. E. 1971. Changes in Fertility Rates and Family Size in Response to Changes in Age at Marriage, the Trend away from Arranged Marriages, and Increasing Urbanization. *Population Studies* 25, no. 3:481–489.

Mitra, A., and P. Singh, P. 2007. Human Capital Attainment and Gender Empowerment: The Kerala Paradox. *Social Science Quarterly* 88, no. 5:1227–1242.

Moghadam, V. M. 1994. Introduction: Women and Identity Politics in Theoretical and Comparative Perspective. In *Identity Politics and Women: Cultural Reassertions and Feminisms in International Perspective*, edited by V. M. Moghadam, 3–27. Boulder, Colo.: Westview Press.

Moghadam, V. M. 2004. Patriarchy in Transition: Women and the Changing Family in the Middle East. *Journal of Comparative Family Studies* 35, no. 2:137–162.

Moghissi, H. 1999. *Feminism and Islamic Fundamentalism: The Limits of Postmodern Analysis*. London: Zed Books.

Mohammad, N. 2007. Brides Pay High Price. Institute of War and Peace Reporting. Accessed September 23, 2018. http://iwpr.net/report-news/brides-pay-high-price.

Mohammadpur, A. 2013. Disembedding the Traditional Family: Grounded Theory and the Study of Family Change among Mangor and Gaverk Tribes of Iranian Kurdistan. *Journal of Comparative Family Studies* 44, no. 1:117–132.

Mohammadpur, A., et al. 2012. Family Changes in Iranian Kurdistan: A Mixed Methods Study of Mangor and Gawerk Tribes. *Przegląd Socjologii Jakościowej* 8, no. 3:76–96.

Mohammed, M. A. 2009. *Combating Physical Violence against Women in Iraqi Kurdistan: The Contribution of Local Women's Organization*. Tromsø, Norway: University of Tromsø, Norway.

Mojab, S. 2001. Women and Nationalism in the Kurdish Republic of 1946. In *Women of a Non-State Nation: The Kurds*, edited by S. Mojab, 71–95. Costa Mesa, Calif.: Mazda Publishing.

Mojab, S. 2002. "Honor Killing": Culture, Politics and Theory. *Middle East Women's Studies Review*. Accessed May 28, 2018. https://www.questia.com/library/journal/1G1-97551157/honor-killing-culture-politics-and-theory.

Mojab, S. 2004a. No Safe Haven: Violence against Women in Iraqi Kurdistan. In *Sites of Violence: Gender and Conflict Zones*, edited by W. Giles and J. Hyndman, 108–134. Berkeley: University of California Press.

Mojab, S. 2004b. The Particularity of "Honour" and the Universality of "Killing": From Early Warning Signs to Feminist Pedagogy. In *Violence in the Name of Honour: Theoretical and Political Challenges*, edited by S. Mojab and N. Abdo, 15–38. Istanbul: İstanbul Bilgi University Publishing.

Morgan, D. 2000. *Honour Killings in Iraqi Kurdistan: Seminar Report*. London: Kurdish Women Action Against Honour Killing.

Moritz, M. 2008. A Critical Examination of Honor Cultures and Herding Societies in Africa. *African Studies Review* 51, no. 2:99–117.

Morsy, S. A. 1990. Rural Women, Work and Gender Ideology: A Study in Egyptian Economic Transformation. In *Women in Arab Society: Work Patterns and Gender Relations in Egypt, Jordan and Sudan*, edited by S. Shami, et al., 87–145. Providence: Berg/Unesco.

Moruzzi, N. C. 2013. Gender and the Revolutions: Critique Interrupted. Middle East Research and Information Project. Accessed October 9, 2013. http://www.merip.org/mer/mer268/gender-revolutions.

Mufti, A. 2008. The Act to Amend the Amended Law No. 188 of the Year 1959; Personal Status Law, in Iraq Kurdistan Region. In 15, edited by the Iraqi Kurdistan National Assembly ed. Arbil.

Mustafa, M., and A. Young. 2008. Feudal Narratives: Contemporary Deployments of Kanun in Shala Valley, Northern Albania. *Anthropological Notebooks* 14, no. 2:87–107.

Narayan, U. 1997. *Dis/locating Cultures/Identities, Traditions, and Third World Feminism.* New York: Routledge.

Nasrin, S. 2011. Crime or Custom? Motivations behind Dowry Practice in Rural Bangladesh. *Indian Journal of Gender Studies* 18, no. 1:27–50.

Nasrullah, M., et al. 2009. The Epidemiological Patterns of Honour Killing of Women in Pakistan. *European Journal of Public Health* 19, no. 2:193–197.

Natali, D. 2005. *The Kurds and the State: Evolving National Identity in Iraq, Turkey and Iran.* Syracuse, N.Y.: Syracuse University Press.

Natali, D. 2010. *The Kurdish Quasi-State: Development and Dependency in Post–Gulf War Iraq.* Syracuse, N.Y.: Syracuse University Press.

National Democratic Institute. 2011. *The Voice of Civil Society in Iraq.* Washington: National Democratic Institute for International Affairs.

Nazneen, R. 1998. Violence in Bangladesh. In *Violence against Women: Philosophical Perspectives*, edited by S. G. French, et al., 77–92. Ithaca, N.Y.: Cornell University Press.

Nelson, S. S. 2003. Mother Kills Raped Daughter to Restore "Honor." *Seattle Times*, November 17, 2003.

Neurink, J. 2014. Researcher: Kurdish Women Are Victims of a Legacy of Violence. *Rûdaw*, March 26, 2014.

Noel, E. 1920. The Character of the Kurds as Illustrated by their Proverbs and Popular Sayings. *Bulletin of the School of Oriental Studies* 1, no. 4:79–90.

Nore, A. W. J., and A. B. A. Ghani. 2009. Insurgency, Political Stability and Economic Performance in Post-Saddam Iraq: An Evaluation. *Journal of Politics and Law* 2, no. 4:103–114.

Nunn, N. 2005. A Model Explaining Simultaneous Payments of a Dowry and Bride-Price (preliminary draft). Harvard: Harvard University Department of Economics. Accessed September 26, 2012. http://www.economics.harvard.edu/faculty/nunn/files/dowries.pdf.

Nussbaum, M. C. 1999. "Secret Sewers of Vice": Disgust, Bodies and the Law. In *The Passions of Law*, edited by S. Bandes, 19–62. New York: New York University Press.

Nye, R. A. 1993. *Masculinity and Male Codes of Honor in Modern France.* Berkeley: University of California Press.

O'Neil, T. 2007. *Neopatrimonialism and Public Sector Performance and Reform.* London: Advisory Board for Irish Aid.

Onal, A. 2008. *Honour Killing: Stories of Men Who Killed.* London: Saqi.

Ortner, S. B. 1978. The Virgin and the State. *Feminist Studies* 4, no. 3:19–35.

Osman, S. 2010. I Am in Love with Massoud Barzani's Daughter: A Poem That Kills—translated by Aryan Baban. Vienna: KurdNet. Accessed July 11, 2013. http://www.ekurd.net/mismas/articles/misc2010/5/state3816.htm.

Otten, Cathy. 2017. *With Ash on Their Faces: Yezidi Women and the Islamic State.* New York: OR Books.

Ottenheimer, M. 1986. Complementarity and the Structures of Parallel-Cousin Marriage. *American Anthropologist* 88, no. 4:934–939.

OWFI. 2012. Justice for Nigar Rahim. Accessed July 4, 2013. http://www.equalityiniraq.com/campaigns/154-justice-for-nigar-rahim.

Pamporov, A. 2007. Sold Like a Donkey? Bride-Price among the Bulgarian Roma. *Journal of the Royal Anthropological Institute* 13, no. 2:471–476.

Panel on Transitions to Adulthood in Developing Countries. 2005. *Growing Up Global: The Changing Transitions to Adulthood in Developing Countries.* Washington: The National Academies Press.

Parla, A. 2001. The "Honour" of the State: Virginity Examinations in Turkey. *Feminist Studies* 27, no. 1:65–88.

Pateman, C. 1988. *The Sexual Contract*. Palo Alto, Calif.: Stanford University Press.

Patterson, O. 2012. Trafficking, Gender and Slavery. In *The Legal Understanding of Slavery: From the Historical to the Contemporary*, edited by J. Allain, 343–353. Oxford: Oxford University Press.

Payton, J. 2014. "Honor," Collectivity, and Agnation: Emerging Risk Factors in "Honor"-Based Violence. *Journal of Interpersonal Violence* 29, no. 16. 2863–2883.

Pérez-Molina, I. 2001. Honour and Disgrace: Women and the Law in Early Modern Catalonia. Ph.D. diss., Barcelona, Spain: Univeristy of Barcelona.

Peristiany, J. G., ed. 1966. *Honour and Shame: The Values of Mediterranean Society*. Chicago: University of Chicago Press.

Pervizat, L. 2006. An Interdisciplinary and a Holistic Attempt to Understand the Honor Killings in Turkey. In *Perspectiva Comparativa Sobre "Crimes de Honra" / Family Life: A Comparative Perspective on Crimes of Honour*, edited by M. Corrêa and É. R. Souza, 295–322. Campinas: UNICAMP.

Pew Research Center. 2013. *The World's Muslims: Religion, Politics and Society*. Washington: The Pew Forum on Religion and Public Life.

Pirro, D. 2008. *Franca Viola: With No Shame and No Blame*. The Florentine. Accessed September 23, 2010. http://www.theflorentine.net/lifestyle/2008/04/franca-viola/

Pitt-Rivers, J. 1965. Honour and Social Status. In *Honour and Shame: The Values of Mediterranean Society*, edited by J. G. Peristiany, 19–79. Chicago: University of Chicago Press.

Polanyi, K. 1957. *The Great Transformation: The Political and Economic Origins of Our Time*. Boston: Beacon Press.

Pollit, K. 1999. Whose Culture? In *Is Multiculturalism Bad for Women?* edited by S. M. Okin, 27–31. Princeton: Princeton University Press.

Pooley, C. G., and J. Turnbull. 1997. Leaving Home: The Experience of Migration from the Parental Household in Britain since c 1770. *Journal of Family History* 22, no. 4:390–424.

Pope, N. 2012. *Honor Killings in the Twenty-First Century*. New York: Palgrave Macmillan.

Pratt Ewing, K. 2008. *Stolen Honour: Stigmatising Muslim Men in Berlin*. Palo Alto, Calif.: Stanford University Press.

Prieto-Carrón, M., et al. 2007. No More Killings! Women Respond to Femicides in Central America. *Gender & Development* 15, no. 1:25–40.

Puhar, A. 1993. On Childhood Origins of Violence in Yugoslavia: II, the Zadruga. *Journal of Psychohistory* 21, no. 2:171–197.

Qadir, K. S. 2007. Iraqi Kurdistan's Downward Spiral. *Middle East Quarterly* 14, no. 3:19–26.

Rasool, I. A., and J. L. Payton. 2014. Tongues of Fire: Women's Suicide and Self-Injury by Burns in the Kurdistan Region of Iraq. *Sociological Review* 62, no. 2: 237–254.

Rassam, A. 1980. Women and Domestic Power in Morocco. *International Journal of Middle East Studies* 12, no. 2:171–179.

Reddy, R. 2008. Gender, Culture and the Law: Approaches to "Honour Crimes" in the UK. *Feminist Legal Studies* 16, no. 3:305–321.

Renfrew, C. 1996. Language Families and the Spread of Farming. In *The Origins and Spread of Agriculture and Pastoralism*, edited by D. R. Harris, 70–93. London: UCL Press.

Reporters Without Borders. 2010. *Between Freedom and Abuses: The Media Paradox in Iraqi Kurdistan*. Paris: Reporters without Borders.

Retherford, R. D., et al. 2001. Late Marriage and Less Marriage in Japan. *Population and Development Review* 27, no. 1:65–102.

Rezaeian, M. 2010. Suicide among Young Middle Eastern Females: The Perspective of an Iranian Epidemiologist. *Crisis* 31, no. 1:36–42.

Richard, P. 1993. Étude des renchaînements d'alliance. *Mathématiques et sciences humaines* 124:5–35.

Rindfuss, R., et al. 1983. The Timing of Entry to Motherhood in Asia: A Comparative Perspective. *Population Studies* 37, no. 2:253–272.

Robertson Smith, W. (1885) 1990. *Kinship and Marriage in Early Arabia*. London: Darf Publishers Ltd.

Rohde, A. 2006. Opportunities for Masculinity and Love: Cultural Production in Ba'thist Iraq during the 1980s. In *Islamic Masculinities*, edited by L. Ouzgane, 184–201. London: Zed Books.

Roudi, F. 2001. *Population Trends and Challenges in the Middle East and North Africa*. Washington: Population Reference Bureau.

Rubin, G. 1975. The Traffic in Women: Notes on the "Political Economy" of Sex. In *Towards an Anthropology of Women*, edited by R. Reiter, 157–211. New York: Monthly Review Press.

Rubin, M. 2006. Dissident Watch: Kamal Sayid Qadir. Middle East Forum. Accessed May 1, 2019. https://www.meforum.org/922/dissident-watch-kamal-sayid-qadir

Rûdaw. 2013. Prospective Grooms Eye Lower Gold Prices in Kurdistan. *Rudaw*, May 30, 2013.

Rydgren, J., and D. Sofi. 2011. Interethnic Relations in Northern Iraq: Brokerage, Social Capital and the Potential for Reconciliation. *International Sociology* 26, no. 1:25–49.

Sacks, K. 1982. *Sisters and Wives: The Past and Future of Sexual Equality*. Urbana: University of Illinois Press.

Safilios-Rothschild, C. 1969. "Honour" Crimes in Contemporary Greece. *British Journal of Sociology* 20, no. 2:205–218.

Sahlins, M. 1974. *Stone Age Economics*. London: Tavistock Publications.

Saigol, R. 2008. Militarization, Nation and Gender: Women's Bodies as Arenas of Violent Conflict. In *Deconstructing Sexuality in the Middle East*, edited by P. Ilkkaracan, 165–177. London: Ashgate.

Sairany, H. A. 2010. The Moment I Wished I Never Came Back to Work in Kurdistan. *Colors Make Me Happy*, personal blog. Accessed May 28, 2019. http://helinamin.blogspot.com /2010/10/moment-i-wished-i-never-came-back-to.html.

Sanborn, J. 2003. The Short Course for Murder: How Soldiers and Criminals Learn How to Kill. In *Violent Acts and Violentization: Assessing, Applying and Developing Lonnie Athens' Theories*, edited by L. Athens and J. T. Ulmer, 107–125. Oxford: Elsevier Science.

Sanmartìn, R. 1982. Marriage and Inheritance in a Mediterranean Fishing Community. *Man* 17, no. 4:664–685.

Satlow, M. L. 2001. *Jewish Marriage Law in Antiquity*. Princeton, N.J.: Princeton University Press.

Schlegel, A. 1991. Status, Property and the Value on Virginity. *American Ethnologist* 18, no. 4:719–734.

Schlegel, A. 1995. The Cultural Management of Adolescent Sexuality. In *Sexual Nature, Sexual Culture*, edited by P. R. Abramson and S. D. Pinkerton, 177–195. Chicago: University of Chicago Press.

Schlegel, A., and R. Eloui. 1988. Marriage Transactions: Labour, Property, Status. *American Anthropologist* 90, no. 2:291–309.

Schneider, J. 1971. Of Vigilance and Virgins: Honor, Shame and Access to Resources in Mediterranean Societies. *Ethnology* 10, no. 1:1–24.

Schneider, J., and P. Schneider. 1976. *Culture and Political Economy in Western Sicily*. New York: Academic Press.

Scotsman. 2005. Women "Forced to Marry Rapists or Die." *Scotsman*. Accessed November 22, 2005. https://www.scotsman.com/news/world/women-forced-to-wed-rapists-or-die-1 -1110401.

Seccombe, W. 1992. *A Millenium of Family Change: Feudalism to Capitalism in North-Western Europe*. London: Verso.

Semple, K. 2014. Yazidi Girls Seized by ISIS Speak Out after Escape. *New York Times*, Accessed November 14, 2014. https://www.nytimes.com/2014/11/15/world/middleeast/yazidi-girls -seized-by-isis-speak-out-after-escape.html

Segalen, M. 1986. *Historical Anthropology of the Family*. Cambridge: Cambridge University Press.

Sen, P. 2005. "Crimes of Honour": Value and Meaning. In *Honour: Crimes, Paradigms and Violence against Women*, edited by L. Welchman and S. Hossain, 42–64. London: Zed Books.

Sev'er, A. 2005. In the Name of Fathers: Honour Killings and Some Examples from South-Eastern Turkey. *Atlantis: A Woman's Studies Journal* 31, no. 1:129–145.

Sev'er, A., and G. Yurdakul. 2001. Culture of Honor, Culture of Change: A Feminist Analysis of Honor Killings in Rural Turkey. *Violence Against Women* 7, no. 9:964–998.

Shalhoub-Kevorkian, N. 2004. *Mapping and Analyzing the Landscape of Femicide in Palestinian Society*. Women's Center for Legal Aid and Counselling.

Sharabi, H. 1992. *Neopatriarchy: A Theory of Distorted Change in Arab Society*. Oxford: Oxford University Press.

Shaw, A., and K. Charsley. 2006. Rishtas: Adding Emotion to Strategy in Understanding British Pakistani Transnational Marriages. *Global Networks* 6, no. 4:405–421.

Shehadeh, L. R. 2003. *The Idea of Women in Fundamentalist Islam*. Gainesville: Unversity Press of Florida.

Shiba, H. 2003. Genesis of Chastity-Honour Code in Spain and Its Evolution: A Case Study of Gender Construction. *Anales de la Fundación Joaquín Costa*, no. 20:117–140.

Singerman, D. 2007. *The Economic Imperatives of Marriage: Emerging Practises and Identities among Youth in the Middle East*. Dubai: Wolfensohn Center for Development; Dubai School of Government.

Sır, A. 2005. Perceptions of Honor: A Survey Research. In *Who's to Blame? Project for the Development of Permanent Methods in the Struggle against Killings Committed under the Guise of "Honor" in the Southeast and East Anatolia Regions*, edited by KA-MER, 211–251. Diyarbakir: KA-MER.

Sirman, N. 2004. Kinship, Politics and Love: Honour in Post-colonial Contexts. In *Violence in the Name of Honour: Theoretical and Political Challenges*, edited by S. Mojab and N. Abdo, 39–56. Istanbul: İstanbul Bilgi University Publishing.

Smelser, N. J. 2004. Psychological Trauma and Cultural Trauma. In *Cultural Trauma and Collective Identity*, edited by J. C. Alexander, 31–59. Berkeley: University of California Press.

Snyder, J. 2000. *From Voting to Violence: Democratization and Nationalist Conflict*. New York: W. W. Norton.

Song, S. 2007. *Justice, Gender and the Politics of Multiculturalism*. Cambridge: Cambridge University Press.

Sonuga-Barke, E. J. S., and M. Mistry. 2000. The Effect of Extended Family Living on the Mental Health of Three Generations within Two Asian Communities. *British Journal of Clinical Psychology* 39, no. 2:129–141.

Spaht, K. S. 2002. Lousiana's Covenant Marriage Law: Recapturing the Meaning of Marriage for the Sake of the Children. In *The Law and Economics of Marriage and Divorce*, edited by A. W. Dnes and R. Rowthorn. Cambridge: Cambridge University Press.

Spruyt, B., and M. Elchardus. 2012. Are Anti-Muslim Feelings More Widespread Than Anti-Foreigner Feelings?: Evidence from Two Split-Sample Experiments. *Ethnicities* 12, no. 6:800–820.

Stone, L. 2006. *Kinship and Gender: An Introduction.* Boulder, Colo.: Westview Press.

Stowasser, B. F., and Z. Abul-Magd. 2004. Tahlil Marriage in Shari'a, Legal Codes, and the Contemporary Fatwa Literature. In *Islamic Law and the Challenge of Modernity*, edited by Y. Y. Haddad and B. F. Stowasser, 161–182. Walnut Creek, Calif.: Altamira Press.

Strathern, M. 1990. *The Gender of the Gift: Problems with Women and Problems with Society in Melanesia.* Berkeley: University of California Press.

Susskind, Y. 2008. *Promising Democracy, Imposing Theocracy: Gender-Based Violence and the US War on Iraq.* New York: MADRE.

Sweetman, D. L. 1994. *Kurdish Culture: A Cross-Cultural Guide.* Bonn: Verlag für Kultur and Wissenschaft.

Taher, N. 2012. We Are Not Women, We Are Egyptians. *City* 16, no. 3:369–376.

Talabany, N. 2000. Honour Killing in Iraqi Kurdistan. Kurdish Women Action Against Honour Killing. Accessed February 27, 2011. http://www.kwahk.org/articles.asp?id=27.

Tapper, N. 1981. Direct Exchange and Brideprice: Alternative Forms in a Complex Marriage System. *Man* 16, no. 3:387–407.

Tapper, N. 1991. *Bartered Brides: Gender and Marriage in an Afghan Tribal Society.* Cambridge: Cambridge University Press.

Taylor, S. K. 2004. Women, Honour and Violence in a Castilian Town 1600–1650. *Sixteenth Century Journal* 34, no. 5:1079–1097.

Taysi, T. B. 2009. *Eliminating Violence against Women: Perspectives on Honor-Related Violence in the Iraqi Kurdistan Region, Sulaimaniya Governate.* Sulemaniya: United Nations Assistance Mission in Iraq/ASUDA.

Tax, M. 2016. *A Road Unforeseen: Women Fight the Islamic State.* New York: Bellevue Literary Press.

Theiss, J. 2004. Female Suicide, Subjectivity and the State in Eighteenth-Century China. *Gender & History* 16, no. 3:513–537.

Thornhill, T. 1997. *Sweet Tea with Cardamom: A Journey through Iraqi Kurdistan.* London: Pandora.

Tien, J.-K. 1997. *Male Anxiety and Female Chastity: A Comparative Study of Chinese Ethical Values in Ming-Ching Times* Leiden: Brill Academic Publishing.

Tillion, G. 1966/2007. *My Cousin, My Husband: Clans and Kinship in Mediterranean Societies.* London: Al-Saqi.

Tilly, C. 2003. *The Politics of Collective Violence.* Cambridge: Cambridge University Press.

Torry, W. I. 2001. Social Change, Crime and Culture: The Defence of Provocation. *Crime, Law & Social Change* 36, no. 3:309–325.

Triandis, H. C. 1995. *Individualism and Collectivism.* Boulder, Colo.: Westview Press.

Tripp, A. 2001. Women's Movements and Challenges to Neopatrimonial Rule: Preliminary Observations from Africa. *Development and Change* 32, no. 1:33–54.

Tucker, J. E. 1993. The Arab Family in History: "Otherness" and the Study of the Family. In *Arab Women: New Boundaries, Old Frontiers*, edited by J. E. Tucker, 195–207. Bloomington: Indiana University Press.

Turner, V. W. 1964. Betwixt and Between: The Liminal Period in Rites de Passage. *Proceedings of the American Ethnological Society*, 4–20.

UNICEF. 2004. *Iraq: Standard Tables as of August 17, 2004.* Geneva: UNICEF.

United Nations. 2009. World Marriage Data 2008, edited by the Department of Economic and Social Affairs; Population Division. Geneva: United Nations.

Urban, W. 2016. Small Wars and Their Influence on Nation States: 1500 to the Present. Barnsley, U.K.: Frontline Books.

Van Bruinessen, M. M. 1978. *Agha, State and Sheikh: On the Social and Political Organisation of Kurdistan.* Utrecht, Netherlands: Rijksuniversitat te Utrecht.

Van Bruinessen, M. M. 2000. The Ethnic Identity of the Kurds in Turkey. In *Kurdish Ethno-Nationalism Versus Nation-Building States: Collected Articles*, edited by M. M. van Bruinessen, 15–25. Istanbul: ISIS.

Van Bruinessen, M. M. 2001. From Adela Khyanum to Leyla Zana: Women as Political Leaders in Kurdish History. In *Women of a Non-State Nation: The Kurds*, edited by S. Mojab, 95–113. Costa Mesa, Calif.: Mazda Publishing.

VanEck, C. 2003. *Purified by Blood: Honour Killings amongst Turks in the Netherlands.* Amsterdam: Amsterdam University Press.

Veleanu, C. 2012. La passion et le juridique: le crime passionnel en anglais et dans quelques langues romanes. *Interstudia (Revista Centrului Interdisciplinar de Studiu al Formelor Discursive Contemporane Interstud)* 12:113–121.

Warraich, S. A. 2005. "Honour Killings" and the Law in Pakistan. In *"Honour": Crimes, Paradigms and Violence against Women*, edited by L. Welchman and S. Hossain, 78–111. London: Zed Books.

Warrick, C. 2005. The Vanishing Victim: Criminal Law and Gender in Jordan. *Law & Society Review* 39, no. 2:315–348.

Webster, S. K. 1982. Women, Sex and Marriage in Moroccan Proverbs. *International Journal of Middle East Studies* 14, no. 2:173–184.

Wehbi, S. 2002. "Women with Nothing to Lose": Marriageability and Women's Perceptions of Rape and Consent in Contemporary Beirut. *Women's Studies International Forum* 25, no. 3:287–300.

Weiner, A. B. 1992. *Inalienable Possessions: The Paradox of Keeping-While-Giving.* Berkeley: University of California Press.

Weldon, S. L. 2002. *Protest, Policy and the Problem of Violence against Women: A Cross-National Comparison.* Pittsburgh, Pa.: Pittsburgh University Press.

Werner, C. 2009. Bride Abduction in Post-Soviet Central Asia: Marking a Shift Towards Patriarchy through Local Discourses of Shame and Tradition. *Journal of the Royal Anthropological Institute* 15:314–331.

White, D. R., and M. L. Burton. 1988. Causes of Polygamy: Ecology, Economy, Kinship and Warfare. *American Anthropologist* 90, no. 4:871–887.

White, J. B. 1999. *Money Makes Us Relatives: Women's Labor in Urban Turkey.* Austin: University of Texas Press.

WHO/Iraq. 2006/7. *Republic of Iraq: Iraq Family Health Survey.* Baghdad: World Health Organisation; Republic of Iraq.

Wiesehöfer, J. 2009. The Achaemenid Empire. In *The Dynamics of Ancient Empires: State Power from Assyria to Byzantium*, edited by I. Morris and W. Scheidel, 66–99. Oxford: Oxford University Press.

Wilensky-Lanford, E. 2003. Nationalist Tensions: Tradition and Modernity in Discussions of Kyrgyz Bride-Capture. *Anthropology of East Europe Review* 21, no. 2:81–83.

Wolf, E. R. 1951. The Social Organisation of Mecca and the Origins of Islam. *Southwestern Journal of Anthropology* 7, no. 4:329–356.

Wolf, E. R. 1982. *Europe and the People without History.* Berkeley: University of California Press.

Wolf, E. R. 2001. *Pathways of Power: Building an Anthropology of the Modern World.* Berkeley: University of California Press.

Wolf, M. 1972. *Women and the Family in Rural Taiwan*. Palo Alto, Calif.: Stanford University Press.

Wolf, M. 1974. Chinese Women: New Skills in an Old Context. In *Women, Culture and Society*, edited by M. Z. Rosaldo and L. Lamphere, 157–173. Palo Alto, Calif.: Stanford University Press.

Wolf, R. 2010. Dishonourable Killings: Punishing the Innocent. Filmed in Turkey. Films Media Group, 26 min.

Wollstonecraft, M. (1759) 2002. *A Vindication of the Rights of Women*. The Gutenberg Project. Accessed February 20, 2013. http://www.gutenberg.org/dirs/etext02/vorow10.txt.

Yalçın-Heckman, L. 1991. *Tribe and Kinship among the Kurds*. Bern: Peter Land.

Yalçın-Heckman, L. 1993. Aşirleti Kadın: Goçer ve yari-goçer toplumlarda cinisyet rolleri ve kadin stratejileri. In *1980'ler Türkiye 'sinde Kadin Bakiş Açisindan Kandinlar*, edited by Ş. Tekeli, 247–258. Instanbul: Hetişim Yayinlari.

Yıldız, K., et al. 2008. *A Fact-Finding Mission to Kurdistan, Iraq: Gaps in the Human Rights Infrastructure*. London: Kurdish Human Rights Project.

Yount, K. M., and E. M. Agree. 2004. The Power of Older Women and Men in Egyptian and Tunisian Families. *Journal of Marriage and Family* 66, no. 1:126–146.

Yuval-Davis, N. 1993. Gender and Nation. *Ethnic and Racial Studies* 16, no. 4:621–632.

Zakaria, R. 2012. The Honor Problem. *Dawn*, Accessed March 14, 2012. https://www.dawn.com/news/702500

Zaman, A. 2005. Where Girls Marry Rapists for Honour. *Los Angeles Times*. Accessed May 5, 2019. https://notices.californiatimes.com/gdpr/latimes.com/.

Zaza, N. 1962. *Contes et poèmes Kurdes*. Geneva: Editions Peuples et Création.

Zelder, M. 2002. For Better or For Worse? Is Bargaining in Marriage and Divorce Efficient. In *The Law and Economics of Marriage and Divorce*, edited by A. W. Dnes and R. Rowthorn, 157–170. Cambridge: Cambridge University Press.

Zilhão, J. 1993. The Spread of Agro-pastoral Economies across Mediterranean Europe: A View from the Far West. *Journal of Mediterranean Archaeology* 6:5–23.

Zoepf, K. 2007. A Dishonorable Affair. *New York Times Magazine*, September 23, 2007.

Zuhur, S. 2005. *Gender, Sexuality and the Criminal Laws in the Middle East and North Africa: A Comparative Study*. Istanbul: Women for Women's Human Rights—New Ways.

INDEX

ABOUT THE AUTHORS

JOANNE PAYTON has worked with the UK-based Iranian and Kurdish Women's Rights Organisation (IKWRO) since 2005, focusing on violence against women and harmful traditional practices. She completed a PhD in criminology in 2015. She works with the media company Fuuse, appearing in the Emmy-award-winning film *Banaz: A Love Story*, which explores an "honor" killing.

DEEYAH KHAN is an award-winning documentary film director. Her films explore the social and psychological tensions of modern, multicultural societies. Her debut film explored the "honor" killing of a British-Kurdish woman. It won an Emmy and a Peabody award, and received an RTS nomination. Her next film, *Jihad*, nominated for a Grierson and a Bafta, involved two years interviewing Islamic extremists and convicted terrorists. *White Right: Meeting the Enemy*, a documentary on the growth of white extremism in the United States, was also Bafta-nominated and won an Emmy award for Best International Current Affairs Documentary in 2018.